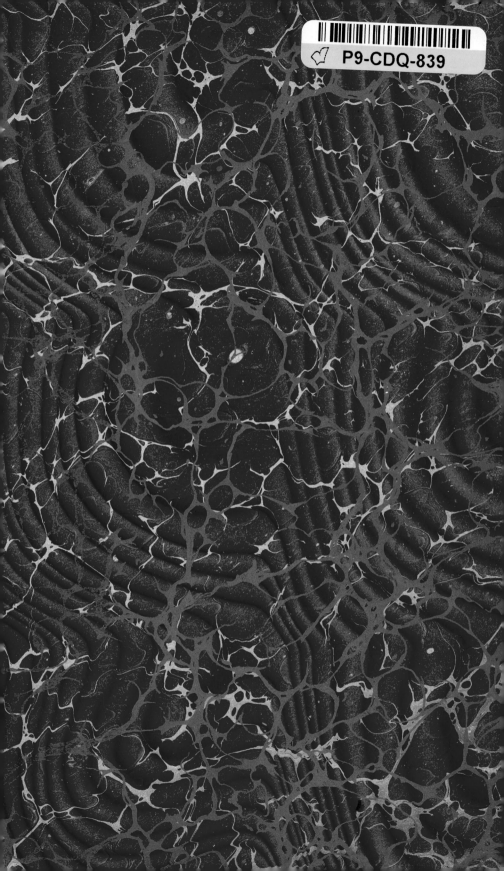

History of Egypt

From 330 B. C. to the Present Time

By S. RAPPOPORT, Doctor of Philosophy, Basel; Member of the Ecole Langues Orientales, Paris; Russian, German, French Orientalist and Philologist

VOL. II

Containing over Twelve Hundred Colored Plates and Illustrations

THE GROLIER SOCIETY
PUBLISHERS △ △ △ LONDON

CONTENTS

CHAPTER I.

EGYPT UNDER THE ROMAN EMPIRE

CHAPTER II.

THE CHRISTIAN PERIOD IN EGYPT

CHAPTER III.

EGYPT DURING THE MUHAMMEDAN PERIOD

LIST OF ILLUSTRATIONS

THE ROMAN, CHRISTIAN, AND ARABIC PERIODS

THE ROMAN ADMINISTRATION IN EGYPT — THE RISE OF CHRISTIANITY — THE ARIAN CONTROVERSY — THE GROWTH OF MONASTICISM — THE DECLINE OF ALEXANDRIA — THE ARAB INVASION AND THE SPREAD OF MUHAMMEDANISM — THE ARAB DYNASTIES.

Augustus remodels the government of Egypt — A new calendar introduced — Egypt surveyed — Dissension between Jews and Greeks at Alexandria — Strabo's visit — The Egyptian religion at Rome — Wise administration of Tiberius — The rise of the Therapeutæ — Lake Mœris destroyed — The origin of Chemistry — The fable of the Phœnix — Christianity introduced — Fiscal reforms under Galba — Vespasian in Egypt — Fall of Jerusalem — The Nile Canal restored — Hadrian's voyage up the Nile — Death of Antinous — Christians and Gnostics — Astrology and Astronomy — Roman roads in Egypt — Commerce and Sports — The Growth of Christianity — Severus visits Egypt — The massacre of the Alexandrians — Ammonius Saccas and the Alexandrian Platonists — The School of Origen — Rise of Controversy — Decline of Commerce — Zenobia in Syria — Growing importance of the Arabs — Revolt and recapture of Alexandria — Persecution of the Christians under Diocletian — Introduction of the Manichean heresy.

Constantine the Great converted — Privileges of the clergy — Dogmatic disputes — Council of Nicœa and the first Nicene Creed — Athanasian and Arian controversies —Founding of Constantinople — Decline of Alexandria — Imperial appointments in the Church — Religious riots — Triumphs of Athanasius — Persecution by Bishop George of Cappadocia — Early mission work — Development of the monastic system — Text of the Bible — The monks and military service — Saracenic encroachments — Theodosius overthrows Paganism — Destruction of the Great Library — Pagan and Christian literature — Story of Hypatia — The Arabs defeat the Romans — The Koptic New Testament — Egypt separated from Rome — The Council of Chalcedon — Paganism restored in Upper Egypt — The Henoticon — The writings of Hierocles — Relations with Persia — Inroads of the Arabs — Justinian's fiscal reforms — Coinage restored — The Persians enter Egypt.

The Life of Muhammed — Amr conquers Egypt — The legend of Omar and the Great Library — The founding of Fostât — The Christians taxed — Muhammedan oppression in Egypt — The Ommayad and Abbasid dynasties — Caliph Harun er-Rashid — Turkish bodyguards — Rise of the Tulunite Dynasty — Office of Prince of Princes — Reign of Muhammed el-Ikshid — War with Byzantium — Fatimite Caliphs — The Ismailians and Mahdism — Reign of Mustanssir — Turkish Rapacity — End of the Fatimite Rule.

ORNAMENT FROM THE MORISTAN OF KILAWUN.

CHAPTER I

EGYPT UNDER THE ROMAN EMPIRE

The Roman dominion on the Nile : Settlement of the Egyptian frontiers : Religious developments : Rebellions.

COIN OF AUGUSTUS.

AUGUSTUS began his reign in Egypt in B. C. 30 by ordering all the statues of Antony, of which there were more than fifty ornamenting the various public buildings of the city, to be broken to pieces; and it is said he had the meanness to receive a bribe of one thousand talents from Archibus, a friend of Cleopatra, that the queen's statues might be left standing. It seems to have been part of his kingcraft to give the offices of greatest trust to men of low birth, who were at the same time well aware that they owed their employments to their seeming want of ambition. Thus the government of Egypt, the greatest and richest of the provinces, was given to Cornelius Gallus.

Before the fall of the republic the senate had given the command of the provinces to members of their own body only; and therefore Augustus, not wishing to alter the law, obtained from the senate for himself all those governments which he meant to give to men of lower rank. By this legal fiction, these equestrian prefects were answerable for their conduct to nobody but the emperor on a petition, and they could not be sued at law before the senate for their misdeeds. But he made an exception in the case of Egypt. While on the one hand in that province he gave to the prefect's edicts the force of law, on the other he allowed him to be cited before the senate, though appointed by himself. The power thus given to the senate they never ventured to use, and the prefect of Egypt was never punished or removed but by the emperor. Under the prefect was the chief justice of the province, who heard himself, or by deputy, all causes except those which were reserved for the decision of the emperor in person. These last were decided by a second judge, or in modern language a chancellor, as they were too numerous and too trifling to be taken to Rome. Under these judges were numerous freedmen of the emperor, and clerks entrusted with affairs of greater and less weight. Of the native magistrates the chief were the keeper of the records, the police judge, the prefect of the night, and the *Exegetes*, or interpreter of the Egyptian law, who was allowed to wear a purple robe like a Roman magistrate. But these Egyptian magistrates were never treated as citizens; they were barbarians, little better than slaves, and only raised to the rank of the emperor's freedmen.

Augustus showed not a little jealousy in the rest of the laws by which his new province was to be governed. While other conquered cities usually had a senate or municipal form of government granted to them, no city in Egypt was allowed that privilege, which, by teaching the citizens the art of governing themselves and the advantages of union, might have made them less at the mercy of their masters. He not only gave the command of the kingdom to a man below the rank of a senator, but ordered that no senator should even be allowed to set foot in Egypt without leave from himself; and centuries later, when the weakness of the country had led the emperors to soften some of the other stern laws of Augustus, this was still strictly enforced.

Among other changes then brought in by the Romans was the use of a fixed year in all civil reckonings. The Egyptians, for all the common purposes of life, called the day of the heliacal rising of the dogstar, about our 18th of July, their new year's day, and the husbandman marked it with religious ceremonies as the time when the Nile began to overflow; while for all civil purposes, and dates of kings' reigns, they used a year of three hundred and sixty-five days, which, of course, had a movable new year's day. But by the orders of Augustus all public deeds were henceforth dated by the new year of three hundred and sixty-five days and a quarter, which was named, after Julius Cæsar, the Julian year. The years from B. C. 24 were made to begin on the 29th of August, the day on which the movable new year's day then happened to fall, and were numbered from the year following the last of Cleopatra, as from the first year of the reign of Augustus. But notwithstanding the many advantages of the Julian year, which was used throughout Europe for sixteen centuries, till its faultiness was pointed out by Pope Gregory XIII., the Egyptian astronomers and mathematicians distrusted it from the first, and chose to stick to their old year, in which there could be no mistake about its length. Thus there were at the same time three years and three new year's days in use in Egypt: one about the 18th of July, used by the common people; one on the 29th of August, used by order of the emperor; and one movable, used by the astronomers.

By the conquest of Egypt, Augustus was also able to extend another of the plans of his late uncle. Julius Cæsar, whose powerful mind found all sciences within its grasp, had ordered a survey to be taken of the whole of the Roman provinces, and the length of all the roads to be measured for the use of the tax-gatherers and of the army; and Augustus was now able to add Egypt to the survey. Polyclitus was employed on this southern portion of the empire; and, after thirty-two years from its beginning by Julius, the measurement of nearly the whole known world was finished and reported to the senate.

At Alexandria Augustus was visited by Herod, who hastened to beg of him those portions of his kingdom which Antony had given to Cleopatra. Augustus received him as a friend; gave him back the territory which Antony had taken from him, and added the province of Samaria and the free cities on the coast. He also gave to him the body of four hundred Gauls, who formed part of the Egyptian army and had been Cleopatra's bodyguard. He thus removed from Alexandria the last re-

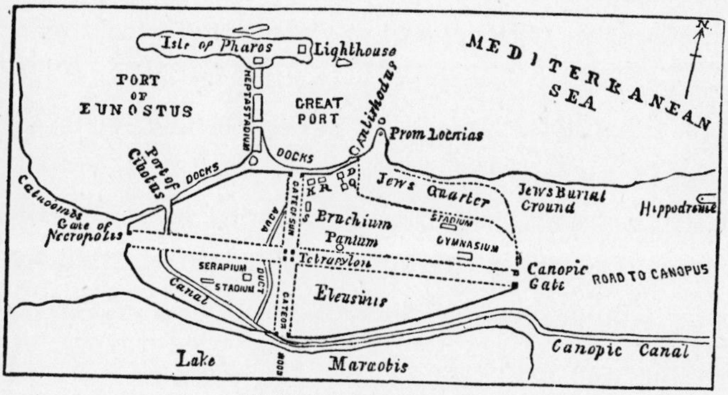

PLAN OF ALEXANDRIA.

mains of the Gallic mercenaries, of whom the Ptolemies had usually had a troop in their service.

Augustus visited the royal burial-place to see the body of Alexander, and devoutly added a golden crown and a garland of flowers to the other ornaments on the sarcophagus of the Macedonian. But he would take no pains to please either the Alexandrians or Egyptians; he despised them both. When asked if he would not like to see the Alexandrian monarchs lying in their mummy-cases in the same tomb, he answered: "No, I came to see the king, not dead men." His contempt for Cleopatra and her father made him forget the great qualities of Ptolemy Soter. So when he was at Memphis he refused to humour the national prejudice of two thousand years' standing by visiting the bull Apis. Of the former conquerors, Cambyses had stabbed the sacred bull, Alexander had sacrificed to it; had Augustus had the violent temper of either, he would have copied Cambyses. The Egyptians always found the treatment of the sacred bull a foretaste of what they were themselves to receive from their sovereigns.

The Greeks of Alexandria, who had for some time past very unwillingly yielded to the Jews the right of citizenship, now urged upon Augustus that it should no longer be granted. Augustus, however, had received great services from the Jews, and at once refused the prayer; and he set up in Alexandria an inscription granting to the Jews the full privileges of Macedonians, which they claimed and had hitherto enjoyed under the Ptolemies. They were allowed their own magistrates and courts of justice, with the free exercise of their own religion; and soon afterwards, when their high priest died, they were allowed as usual to choose his successor. The Greek Jews of Alexandria were indeed very important, both from their numbers and their learning; they spread over Syria and Asia Minor: they had a synagogue in Jerusalem in common with the Jews of Cyrene and Libya; and we find that one of the chief teachers of Christianity after the apostles was Apollos, the Alexandrian, who preached the new religion in Ephesus, in Corinth, and in Crete.

On his return to Rome, Augustus carried with him the whole of the royal treasure; and though perhaps there might have been less gold and silver than usual in the palace of the Ptolemies, still it was so large a sum that when, upon the establishment of peace over all the world, the rate of interest upon loans fell in Rome, and the price of land rose, the change was thought to have been caused by the money from Alexandria. At the same time were carried away the valuable jewels, furniture, and ornaments, which had been handed down from father to son, with the crown of Upper and Lower Egypt. These were drawn in waggons through the streets of Rome in triumph; and with them were shown in chains to the wondering crowd Alexander Helius and Cleopatra Selene, the children of Cleopatra and Antony.

Augustus threatened a severe punishment to the Alexandrians in the building of a new capital. Only four miles from the Canopic or eastern gate of Alexandria he laid out the plan of his new city of Nicopolis, on the spot where he had routed Mark Antony's forces. Here he began several large temples, and removed to them the public sacrifices and the priesthood from the temples of Alexandria. But the work was carried no farther, and soon abandoned; and the only change made by it in Alexandria was that the temple of Serapis and the other temples were for a time deserted.

The rest of the world had long been used to see their finest works of art carried away by their conquerors; and the Egyptians soon learned that, if any of the monuments of which they were so justly proud were to be left to them, it would only be because they were too heavy to be moved by the Roman engineers. Beside many other smaller Egyptian works, two of the large obelisks, which even now ornament Rome, were carried away by Augustus, that of Thûtmosis IV., which stands in the Piazza del Popolo, and that of Psammetichus, on Monte Citorio.

Cornelius Gallus, the prefect of Egypt, seems either to have misunderstood, or soon forgotten, the terms of his appointment. He set up statues of himself in the cities of Egypt, and, copying the kings of the country, he carved his name and deeds upon the pyramids. On this Augustus recalled him, and he killed himself to avoid punishment. The emperor's wish to check the tyranny of the prefects and tax-gatherers was strongly marked in the case of the champion fighting-cock. The Alexandrians bred these birds with great care, and eagerly watched their battles in the theatre. A powerful cock, that had hitherto slain all its rivals and always strutted over the table unconquered, had gained a great name in the city; and this bird, Eros, a tax-gatherer, roasted and ate. Augustus, on hearing of this insult to the people, sent for the man, and, on his owning what he had done, ordered him to be crucified. Three legions and nine cohorts were found force enough to keep this great kingdom in quiet obedience to their new masters; and when Heroopolis revolted, and afterwards when a rebellion broke out in the Thebaid against the Roman tax-gatherers, these risings were easily crushed. The spirit of the nation, both of the Greeks and Egyptians, seems to have been wholly broken; and Petronius, who succeeded Cornelius Gallus, found no difficulty in putting down a rising of the Alexandrians.

The canals, through which the overflowing waters of the Nile were carried to the more distant fields, were, of course, each year more or less blocked up by the same mud which made the fields fruitful; and the clearing of these canals was one of the greatest boons that the monarch could bestow upon the tillers of the soil. This had often been neglected by the less powerful and less prudent kings of Egypt, in whose reigns the husbandman believed that Heaven in its displeasure withheld part of the wished-for overflow; but Petronius employed the leisure of his soldiers on this wise and benevolent work. In order better to understand the rise of the Nile, to fix the amount of the land-tax, and more fairly to regulate the overflow through the canals, the Nilometer on the Island of Elephantine was at this time made.

THE NILOMETER AT ELEPHANTINE.

It was under Ælius Gallus, the third prefect, that Egypt was visited by Strabo, the most careful and judicious of all the ancient travellers. He had come to study mathematics, astronomy, and geography in the museum, under the successors of Euclid, Eratosthenes, and Hipparchus. He accompanied the prefect in a march to

Syênê (Aswan), the border town, and he has left us a valuable account of the state of the country at that time. Alexandria was the chief object that engaged his attention. Its two harbours held more ships than were to be seen in any other port in the world, and its export trade was thought greater than that of all Italy. The docks on each side of the causeway, and the ship canal, from the harbour of Eunostus to the Mareotic Lake, were full of bustle and activity. The palace or citadel on the promontory of Lochias on one side of the great harbour was as striking an object as the lighthouse on the other. The temples and palaces covered a space of ground equal to more than one-fourth part of the city, and the suburbs reached even beyond the Mareotic Lake. Among the chief buildings were the Soma, which held the bodies of Alexander and of the Ptolemies; the court of justice; the museum of philosophy, which had been rebuilt since the burning by Cæsar's soldiers; the exchange, crowded with merchants, the temple of Neptune, and Mark Antony's fortress, called the Timonium, on a point of land which jutted into the harbour; the Cæsarium, or new palace; and the great temple of Serapis, which was on the western side of the city, and was the largest and most ornamented of all these buildings. Farther off was the beautiful gymnasium for wrestlers and boxers, with its porticoes of a stadium in length, where the citizens used to meet in public assembly. From the top of the temple of Pan, which rose like a sugar-loaf in the middle of the city, and was mounted by a winding staircase, the whole of this remarkable capital might be seen spread out before the eye. On the east of the city was the circus, for chariot races, and on the west lay the public gardens and pale green palm-groves, and the Necropolis ornamenting the roadside with tombs for miles along the seashore. Other tombs were in the catacombs underground on the same side of the city. The banks of the Mareotic Lake were fringed with vineyards, which bore the famed wine of the same name, and which formed a pleasant contrast with the burning whiteness of the desert beyond. The canal from the lake to the Nile marked its course through the plain by the greater freshness of the green along its banks. In the distance were the new buildings of Augustus' city of Nicopolis. The arts of Greece and the wealth of Egypt had united to adorn the capital of the Ptolemies. Heliopolis, the ancient seat of Egyptian learning, had never been wholly repaired since its siege by Cambyses, and was then almost a deserted city. Its schools were empty, its teachers silent; but the houses in which Plato and his friend Eudoxus were said to have dwelt and studied were pointed out to the traveller, to warm his love of knowledge and encourage him in the pursuit of virtue. Memphis was the second city in Egypt, while Thebes and Abydos, the former capitals, had fallen to the size and rank of villages. At Memphis Strabo saw the bull-fights in the circus, and was allowed to look at the bull Apis through a window of his stable. At Crocodilopolis he saw the sacred crocodile caught on the banks of the lake and fed with cakes and wine. Ptolemais, which was at first only an encampment of Greek soldiers, had risen under the sovereigns to whom it owed its name to be the largest city in the Thebaid, and scarcely less than Memphis. It was built wholly by the Greeks, and, like Alexandria, it was under Greek laws, while the other cities in Egypt were under Egyptian laws and magistrates. It was situated between Panopolis and Abydos; but, while the temples of Thebes, which were built so many centuries earlier, are still standing in awful grandeur, scarcely a trace of this Greek city can be found in the villages of El Menshieh and Girgeh (Cerkasoros), which now stand on the spot. Strabo and the Roman generals did not forget to visit the broken colossal statue of Amenhôthes, near Thebes, which sent forth its musical sounds every morning, as the sun, rising over the Arabian hills, first shone upon its face; but this inquiring traveller could not make up his mind whether the music came from the statue, or the base, or the people around it. He ended his tour with watching the sunshine at the bottom of the astronomical well at Syênê, which, on the longest day, is exactly under the sun's northern edge, and with admiring the skill of the boatmen who shot down the cataracts in their wicker boats, for the amusement of the Roman generals.

In the earlier periods of Egyptian history Ethiopia was peopled, or, at least, governed, by a race of men, whom, as they spoke the same language and worshipped the same gods as their neighbours of Upper Egypt, we must call the Kopts. But the Arabs, under the name of Troglodytæ, and other tribes, had made an early settlement on the African side of the Red Sea. So numerous were they in Upper Egypt that in the time of Strabo half the population of the city of Koptos were Arabs; they were the camel-drivers and carriers for the Theban merchants in the trade across the desert. Some of the conquests of Ramses had been over that nation in southern Ethiopia, and the Arab power must have further risen after the defeat of the Ethiopians by Euergetes I. Ethiopia in the time of Augustus was held by Arabs; a race who thought peace a state of disgraceful idleness, and war the only employment worthy of men; and who made frequent hasty inroads into Nubia, and sometimes into Egypt. They fought for plunder, not for conquest, and usually retreated as quickly as they came, with such booty as they laid their hands on. To use words which were proverbial while the Nile swarmed with crocodiles, "They did as the dogs do, they drank and ran away;" and the Romans found it necessary to place a body of troops near the cataracts of Syênê to stop their marching northward and laying waste the Thebaid. While the larger part of the Roman legions was withdrawn into Arabia on an unsuccessful quest for treasure, a body of thirty thousand of these men, whom we may call either Arabs, from their blood and language, or Ethiopians, from their country, marched northward into Egypt, and overpowered the three Roman cohorts at Elephantine, Syênê, and Philæ. Badly armed and badly trained, they were led on by the generals of Candace, Queen of Napata, to the fourth cataract. They were, however, easily driven back when Gallus led against them an army of ten thousand men, and drove them to Ethiopian Pselchis, now remaining as the modern village of Dakkeh. There he defeated them again, and took the city by storm. From Pselchis he marched across the Nubian desert two hundred and fifty miles to Premnis, on the northerly bend of the river, and then made himself master of Napata, the capital. A guard was at the moment left in the country to check any future inroads; but the Romans made no attempts to hold it.

Of the state of the Ethiopic

ON THE EDGE OF THE DESERT.

Arabs under Queen Candace we learn but little from this hasty inroad; but some of the tribes must have been very far from the barbarians that, from their ignorance of the arts of war, the Romans judged them to be. Those nearest to the Egyptian frontiers, the Troglodytæ and Blemmyes, were unsettled, wandering, and plundering; but the inhabitants of Meroë were of a more civilised race. The Jews had settled in southern Ethiopia in large numbers, and for a long time; Solomon's trade had made them acquainted with Adule and Auxum; some of them were employed in the highest offices, and must have brought with them the arts of civilised life. A few years later (Acts VIII. 27) we meet with a Jewish eunuch, the treasurer of Queen Candace, travelling with some pomp from Ethiopia to the religious festivals at Jerusalem.

The Egyptian coins of Augustus and his successors are all Greek; the conquest of the country by the Romans made no change in its language. Though the chief part of the population spoke Koptic, it was still a Greek province of the Roman empire; the decrees of the prefects of Alexandria and of the upper provinces were written in Greek; and every Roman traveller, who, like a schoolboy, has scratched his name upon the foot of the musical statue of Amenhôthes, to let the world know the extent of his travels, has helped to prove that the Roman government of the country was carried on in the Greek language. The coins often bear the eagle and thunderbolt on one side, while on the other is the emperor's head, with his name and titles; and, after a few years, they are all dated with the year of the emperor's reign. In the earliest he is styled a Son of God, in imitation of the Egyptian title of Son of the Sun. After Egypt lost its liberty, we no longer find any gold coinage in the country; that metal, with everything else that was most costly, was carried away to pay the Roman tribute. This was chiefly taken in money, except, indeed, the tax on grain, which the Egyptian kings had always received in kind, and which was still gathered in the same way, and each year shipped to Rome, to be distributed among the idle poor of that great city. At this time it amounted to twenty millions of bushels, which was four times what was levied in the reign of Philadelphus. The trade to the east was increasing, but as yet not large. About one hundred and twenty small vessels sailed every year to India from Myos-Hormos, which was now the chief port on the Red Sea.

No change was made in the Egyptian religion by this change of masters; and, though the means of the priests were lessened, they still carried forward the buildings which were in progress, and even began new ones. The small temple of Isis, at Tentyra, behind the great temple of Hâthor, was either built or finished in this reign, and it was dedicated to the goddess, and to the honour of the emperor as Jupiter Liberator, in a Greek inscription on the cornice, in the thirty-first year of the reign, when Publius Octavius was prefect of the province. The large temple at Talmis, in Nubia, was also then built, though not wholly finished; and we find the name of Augustus at Philæ, on some of the additions to the temple of Isis, which had been built in the reign of Philadelphus. In the hieroglyphical inscriptions on these temples, Augustus is called Autocrator Cæsar, and is styled Son of the Sun, King of Upper and Lower Egypt, with the other

A KOPTIC MAIDEN.

titles which had always been given by the priests to the Ptolemies and their own native sovereigns for so many centuries. These claims were evidently unknown in Rome, where the modesty of Augustus was almost proverbial.

The Greeks had at all times been forward in owning the Egyptians as their teachers in religion; and in the dog Cerberus, the judge Minos, the boat of Charon, and the river Styx of their mythology, we see a clear proof that it was in Egypt that the Greeks gained their faint glimpse of the immortality of the soul, a day of judgment, and a future state of rewards and punishments; and, now that Rome was in close intercourse with Egypt, the Romans were equally ready to borrow thence their religious ceremonies. They brought to Rome the Egyptian opinions with the statues of the gods. They ran into the new superstition to avoid the painful uneasiness of believing nothing, and, though the Romans ridiculed their own gods, they believed in those of Egypt. So fashionable was the worship of Isis and Serapis becoming in Italy, that Augustus made a law that no Egyptian ceremonies should enter the city or even the suburbs of Rome. His subjects might copy the luxuries, the follies, and the vices of the Alexandrians, but not the gloomy devotion of the Egyptians. But the spread of opinions was not so checked; even Virgil taught the doctrine of the Egyptian millennium, or the resurrection from the dead when the thousand years were ended; and the cripple asking for alms in the streets of Rome would beg in the name of the holy Osiris.

Egypt felt no change on the death of Augustus. The province was well governed during the whole of the reign of Tiberius, and the Alexandrians completed the beautiful temple to his honour, named the Sebaste, or Cæsar's Temple. It stood by the side of the harbour, and was surrounded with a sacred grove. It was ornamented with porticoes, and fitted up with libraries, paintings, and statues, and was the most lofty building in the city. In front of this temple they set up two ancient obelisks, which had been made by Thûtmosis III. and carved by Ramses II., and which, like the other monuments of the Theban kings, have outlived all the temples and palaces of their Greek and Roman successors. These obelisks are now generally known as "Cleopatra's Needles." One of them, in 1878, was taken to London and set up on the Thames Embankment; the other was soon afterward brought to New York, and is now in Central Park in that city. It is sixty-seven feet high to its sharpened apex, and seven feet, seven inches in diameter at its base. On its face are deeply incised inscriptions in hieroglyphic character, giving the names Thûtmosis III., Ramses II., and Seti II.

The harsh justice with which Tiberius began his reign was at Rome soon changed into a cruel tyranny; but in the provinces it was only felt as a check to the injustice of the prefects. On one occasion, when Æmilius Rectus sent home from Egypt a larger amount of taxes than was usual, he hoped that his zeal would be praised by Tiberius. But the emperor's message to the prefect was as stern as it was humane: "I should wish my sheep to be

FRAGMENTS IN STONE AND WOOD, PAINTED.

sheared, but not to be flayed." On the death of one of the prefects, there was found among his property at Rome a statue of Menelaus, carved in Ethiopian obsidian, which had been used in the religious ceremonies in the temple of Heliopolis, and Tiberius returned it to the priests of that city as its rightful owners. Another proof of the equal justice with which this province was governed was to be seen in the buildings then carried on by the priests in Upper Egypt. We find the name of Tiberius carved in hieroglyphics on additions or repairs made to the temples at Thebes, at Aphroditopolis, at Berenicê, on the Red Sea, at Philæ, and at the Greek city of Parembole, in Nubia. The great portico was at this time added to the temple at Tentyra, with an inscription dedicating it to the goddess in Greek and in hieroglyphics. As a building is often the work of years, while sculpture is only the work of weeks, so the fashion of the former is always far less changing than that of the latter. The sculptures on the walls of this beautiful portico are crowded and graceless; while, on the other hand, the building itself has the same grand simplicity and massive strength that we find in the older temples of Upper Egypt.

We cannot but admire the zeal of the Egyptians by whom this work was then finished. They were treated as slaves by their Greek fellow-countrymen; their houses were ransacked every third year by military authority in search of arms; they could have had no help from their Roman masters, who only drained the province of its wealth; and the temple had perhaps never been heard of by the emperor, who could have been little aware that the most lasting monument of his reign was being raised in the distant province of Egypt. The priests of

TEMPLE AT TENTYRA, ENLARGED BY ROMAN ARCHITECTS.

the other parts of the country sent gifts out of their poverty in aid of this pious work; and among the figures on the walls we see those of forty cities, from Semneh, at the second cataract, to Memphis and Saïs, in the Delta, each presenting an offering to the god of the temple.

In the third year of this reign Germanicus Cæsar, who, much against his will, had been sent into the East as governor, found time to leave his own province, and to snatch a hasty view of the time-honoured buildings of Egypt. Descending the river to Thebes, and, while gazing on the huge remains of the temples, he asked the priests to read to him the hieroglyphical writing on the walls. He was told that it recounted the greatness of the country in the time of King Ramses, when there were seven hundred thousand Egyptians of an age to bear arms; and that with these troops Ramses had conquered the Libyans, Ethiopians, Medes, Persians, Bactrians, Scythians, Syrians, Armenians, Cappadocians, Bithynians, and Lycians. He was also told the tributes laid upon each of those nations; the weight of gold and silver, the number of chariots and horses, the gifts of ivory and scents for the temples, and the quantity of grain which the conquered provinces sent to feed the population of Thebes. After listening to the musical statue of Amenhôthes, Germanicus went on to Elephantine and Syênê; and, on his return, he turned aside to the pyramids and the Lake of Mœris, which regulated the overflow of the Nile on the neighbouring fields. At Memphis, Germanicus consulted the sacred bull Apis as to his future fortune, and met with an unfavourable answer. The manner of consulting Apis was for the visitor to hold out some food in his hand, and the answer was understood to be favourable if the bull turned his head to eat, but unfavourable if he looked another way. When Germanicus accordingly held out a handful of grain, the well-fed animal turned his head sullenly towards the other side of his stall; and on the death of this young prince, which shortly followed, the Egyptians did not forget to praise the bull's foresight. This blameless and seemingly praiseworthy visit of Germanicus did not, however, escape the notice of the jealous Tiberius. He had been guilty of gaining the love of the people by walking about without guards, in a plain Greek dress, and of lowering the price of grain in a famine by opening the public granaries; and Tiberius sternly reproached him with breaking the known law of Augustus, by which no Roman citizen of consular or even of equestrian rank might enter Alexandria without leave from the emperor.

There were at this time about a million of Jews in Egypt. In Alexandria they seem to have been about one-third of the population, as they formed the majority in two wards out of the five into which the city was divided. They lived under their own elders and Sanhedrim, going up at their solemn feasts to worship in their own temple at Onion; but, from their mixing with the Greeks, they had become less strict than their Hebrew brethren in their observance of the traditions. Some few of them, however, held themselves in obedience to the Sanhedrim in Jerusalem, and looked upon the temple of Jerusalem as the only Jewish temple; and these men were in the habit of sending an embassy on the stated solemn feasts of the nation to offer the appointed sacrifices and prayers to Jahveh in the holy city on their behalf. But though the decree by Cæsar, which declared that the Jews were Alexandrian citizens, was engraved on a pillar in the city, yet they were by no means treated as such, either by the government, or by the Greeks, or by the Egyptians. When, during the famine, the public granaries seemed unable to supply the whole city with food, even the humane Germanicus ordered that the Jews, like the Egyptians, should have no share of the gift. They were

ON THE BANKS OF THE NILE.

despised even by the Egyptians themselves, who, to insult them, said that the wicked god Typhon had two sons, Hierosolymus and Judæus, and that from these the Jews were descended.

In the neighbourhood of Alexandria, on a hill near the shores of the Lake Mareotis, was a little colony of Jews, who, joining their own religion with the mystical opinions and gloomy habits of the Egyptians, have left us one of the earliest known examples of the monastic life. They bore the name of Therapeutæ. They had left, says Philo, their worldly wealth to their families or friends; they had forsaken wives, children, brethren, parents, and the society of men, to bury themselves in solitude and pass their lives in the contemplation of the divine essence. Seized by this heavenly love, they were eager to enter upon the next world, as though they were already dead to this. Every one, whether man or woman, lived alone in his cell or monastery, caring for neither food nor raiment, but having his thoughts wholly turned to the Law and the Prophets, or to sacred hymns of their own composing. They had their God always in their thoughts, and even the broken sentences which they uttered in their dreams were treasures of religious wisdom. They prayed every morning at sunrise, and then spent the day in turning over the sacred volumes, and the commentaries, which explained the allegories, or pointed out a secondary meaning as hidden beneath the surface of even the historical books of the Old Testament. At sunset they again prayed, and then tasted their first and only meal. Self-denial indeed was the foundation of all their virtues. Some made only three meals in the week, that their meditations might be more free; while others even attempted to prolong their fast to the sixth day. During six days of the week they saw nobody, not even one another. On the seventh day they met together in the synagogue. Here they sat, each according to his age; the women separated from the men. Each wore a plain, modest robe, which covered the arms and hands, and they sat in silence while one of the elders preached. As they studied the mystic powers of numbers, they thought the number seven was a holy number, and that seven times seven made a great week, and hence they kept the fiftieth day as a solemn festival. On that day they dined together, the men on one side and the women on the other. The rushy papyrus formed the couches; bread was their only meat, water their drink, salt the seasoning, and cresses the delicacy. They would keep no slaves, saying that all men were born equal. Nobody spoke, unless it was to propose a question out of the Old

BEDOUIN TENT IN THE DESERT.

Testament, or to answer the question of another. The feast ended with a hymn of praise.

The ascetic Jews of Palestine, the Essenes on the banks of the Dead Sea, by no means, according to Philo, thus quitted the active duties of life; and it would seem that the Therapeutæ rather borrowed their customs from the country in which they had settled, than from any sects of the Jewish nation. Some classes of the Egyptian priesthood had always held the same views of their religious duties. These Egyptian monks slept on a hard bed of palm branches, with a still harder wooden pillow for the head; they were plain in their dress, slow in walking, spare in diet, and scarcely allowed themselves to smile. They washed thrice a day, and prayed as often; at sunrise, at noon, and at sunset. They often fasted from animal food, and at all times refused many meats as unclean. They passed their lives alone, either in study or wrapped in religious thought. They never met one another but at set times, and were seldom seen by strangers. Thus, leaving to others the pleasures, wealth, and lesser prizes of this life, they received from them in return what most men value higher, namely, honour, fame, and power.

The Romans, like the Greeks, feeling but little partiality in favour of their own gods, were rarely guilty of intolerance against those of others; and would hardly have checked the introduction of a new religion unless it made its followers worse citizens. But in Rome, where every act of its civil or military authorities was accompanied with a religious rite, any slight towards the gods was a slight towards the magistrate; many devout Romans had begun to keep holy the seventh day; and Egypt was now so closely joined to Italy that the Roman senate made a new law against the Egyptian and Jewish superstitions, and, in A. D. 19, banished to Sardinia four thousand men who were found guilty of being Jews.

Egypt had lost with its liberties its gold coinage, and it was now made to feel a further proof of being a conquered country in having its silver much alloyed with copper. But Tiberius, in the tenth year of his reign, altogether stopped the Alexandrian mint, as well as those of the other cities which occasionally coined; and after this year we find no more coins, but the few with the head and name of Augustus Cæsar, which seem hardly to have been meant for money, but to commemorate on some peculiar occasions the emperor's adoption by his step-father. The Nubian gold mines were probably by this time wholly deserted; they had been so far worked out as to be no longer profitable. For fifteen hundred years, ever since Ethiopia was conquered by Thebes, wages and prices had been higher in Egypt than in the neighbouring countries. But this was now no longer the case. Egypt had been getting poorer during the reigns of the latter Ptolemies; and by this time it is probable that both wages and prices were higher in Rome.

It seems to have been usual to change the prefect of Egypt every few years, and the prefect-elect was often sent to Alexandria to wait till his predecessor's term of years had ended. Thus in this reign of twenty-three years Æmilius Rectus was succeeded by Vetrasius Pollio; and on his death Tiberius gave the government to his freedman Iberus. During the last five years Egypt was under the able but stern government of Flaccus Avillius, whose name is carved on the temple of Tentyra with that of the emperor. He was a man who united all those qualities of prudent forethought, with prompt execution and attention to business, which was so necessary in controlling the irritable Alexandrians, who were liable to be fired into rebellion by the smallest spark. Justice was administered fairly; the great were not allowed to tyrannise over the poor, nor the people to meet in tumultuous mobs; and the legions were regularly paid, so that they had no excuse for plundering the Egyptians.

On the death of Tiberius, in A. D. 37, the old quarrel again broke out between Jews and Greeks. The Alexandrians were not slow in learning the feelings of his successor, Caius, or Caligula, towards the Jews, nor in turning against them the new law that the emperor's statue should be honoured in every temple of the empire. They had very unwillingly yielded a half-obedience to the law of Augustus that the Jews should still be allowed the privileges of citizenship; and, as soon as they heard that Caligula was to be worshipped in every temple of the empire, they denounced the Jews as traitors and rebels, who refused so to honour the emperor in their synagogues. It happened, unfortunately, that their countryman, King Agrippa, at this time came to Alexandria. He had full leave from the emperor to touch there, as being the quickest and most certain way of making the voyage from Rome to the seat of his own government. Indeed, the Alexandrian voyage had another merit in the eyes of a Jew; for, whereas wooden water-vessels were declared by the Law to be unclean, an exception was made by their tradition in favour of the larger size of the water-wells in the Alexandrian ships. Agrippa had seen Egypt before, on his way to Rome, and he meant to make no stay there; but, though he landed purposely after dark, and with no pomp or show, he seems to have raised the anger of the prefect Flaccus, who felt jealous at any man of higher rank than himself coming into his province. The Greeks fell into the prefect's humour, and during the stay of Agrippa in Alexandria they lampooned him in songs and ballads, of which the raillery was not of the most delicate kind. They mocked him by leading about the streets a poor idiot dressed up with a paper crown and a reed for a sceptre, in ridicule of his rather doubtful right to the style of royalty.

As these insults towards the emperor's friend passed wholly unchecked by the prefect, the Greeks next assaulted the Jews in the streets and market-place, attacked their houses, rooted up the groves of trees around their synagogues, and tore down the decree by which the privileges of citizenship had been confirmed to them. The Greeks then proceeded to set up by force a statue of the emperor in each Jewish synagogue, as if the new decree had included those places of worship among the temples, and, not finding statues enough, they made use of the statues of the Ptolemies, which they carried away from the gymnasium for that purpose. During the last reign, under the stern government of Tiberius, Flaccus had governed with justice and prudence, but under Caligula he seemed to have lost all judgment in his zeal against the Jews. When the riots in the streets could no longer be overlooked, instead of defending the injured party, he issued a decree in which he styled the Jews foreigners; thus at one word robbing them of their privileges and condemning them unheard. By this the Greeks were hurried forward into further acts of injustice, and the Jews of resistance. But the Jews were the weaker party: they were overpowered, and all driven into one ward, and four hundred of their houses in the other wards were plundered, and the spoil divided as if taken in war. They were stoned, and even burnt in the streets, if they ventured forth to buy food for their families. Flaccus seized and scourged in the theatre thirty-eight of their venerable councillors, and, to show them that they were no longer citizens, the punishment was inflicted by the hands of Egyptian executioners. While the city was in this state of riot, the Greeks gave out that the Jews were concealing arms; and Flaccus, to give them a fresh proof that they had lost the rights of citizenship, ordered that their houses should be forcibly entered and searched by a centurion and a band of soldiers.

During their troubles the Jews had not been allowed to complain to the emperor, or to send an embassy to Rome to make known their grievances. But the Jewish King Agrippa, who was on his way from Rome to his kingdom, forwarded to Caligula the complaints of his countrymen, the Jews, with an account of the rebellious state of Alexandria. The riots, it is true, had been wholly raised by the prefect's zeal in setting up the emperor's statue in the synagogues to be worshipped by the Jews, and in carrying into effect the emperor's decree; but, as he had not been able to keep his province quiet, it was necessary that he should be recalled, and punished for his want of success. To have found it necessary to call out the troops was of course a fault in a governor; but doubly so at a time and in a province where a successful general might so easily become a formidable rebel. Accordingly, a centurion, with a trusty cohort of soldiers, was sent from Rome for the recall of the prefect. On approaching the flat coast of Egypt, they kept the vessel in deep water till sunset, and then entered the harbour of Alexandria in the dark. The centurion, on landing, met with a freedman of the emperor, from whom he learned that the prefect was then at supper, entertaining a large company of friends. The freedman led the cohort quietly into the palace, into the very room where Flaccus was sitting at table; and the first tidings that he heard of his government being disapproved of in Rome was his finding himself a prisoner in his own palace. The friends stood motionless with surprise, the centurion produced the emperor's order for what he was doing, and as no resistance was attempted all passed off quietly; Flaccus was hurried on board the vessel then at anchor in the harbour on the same evening and immediately taken to Rome.

It so happened that on the night that Flaccus was seized, the Jews had met together to celebrate their autumnal feast, the feast of the Tabernacles: not as in former years with joy and pomp, but in fear, in grief, and in prayer. Their chief men were in prison, their nation smarting under its wrongs and in daily fear of fresh cruelties; and it was not without alarm that they heard the noise of soldiers moving to and fro through the city, and the heavy tread of the guards marching by torchlight from the camp to the palace. But their fear was soon turned into joy when they heard that Flaccus, the author of all their wrongs, was already a prisoner on board the vessel in the harbour; and they gave glory to God, not, says Philo, that their enemy was going to be punished, but because their own sufferings were at an end.

The Jews then, having had leave given them by the prefect, sent an embassy to Rome, at the head of which was Philo, the platonic philosopher, who was to lay their grievances before the emperor, and to beg for redress. The Greeks also at the same time sent their embassy, at the head of which was the learned grammarian Apion, who was to accuse the Jews of not worshipping the statue of the emperor, and to argue that they had no right to the same privileges of citizenship with those who boasted of their Macedonian blood. But, as the Jews did not deny the charge that was brought against them, Caligula would hear nothing that they had to say; and Philo withdrew with the remark, "Though the emperor is against us, God will be our friend."

We learn the sad tale of the Jews' suffering under Caligula from the pages of their own historian only. But though Philo may have felt and written as one of the sufferers, his truth is undoubted. He was a man of unblemished character, and the writer of greatest learning and of the greatest note at that time in Alexandria; being also of a great age, he well deserved the honour of being sent on the embassy to Caligula. He was in religion a Jew, in his philosophy a platonist, and by birth an Egyptian: and in his numerous writings we may trace the three sources from which he drew his opinions. He is always devotional and in earnest, full of pure and lofty thoughts, and often eloquent. His fondness for the mystical properties of numbers, and for finding an allegory or secondary meaning in the plainest narrative, seems borrowed from the Egyptians. According to the Eastern proverb every word in a wise book has seventy-two meanings; and this mode of interpretation was called into use by the necessity which the Jews felt of making the Old Testament speak a meaning more agreeable to their modern views of religion. In Philo's speculative theology he seems to have borrowed less from Moses than from the abstractions of Plato, whose shadowy hints he has embodied in a more solid form. He was the first Jewish writer that applied to the Deity the mystical notion of the Egyptians, that everything perfect was of three parts. Philo's writings are valuable as showing the steps by which the philosophy of Greece may be traced from the writings of Plato to those of Justin Martyr and Clemens Alexandrinus. They give us the earliest example of how the mystical interpretation of the Scriptures was formed into a system, by which every text was made to unfold some important philosophic or religious truth to the learned student, at the same time that to the unlearned reader it conveyed only the simple historic fact.

The Hellenistic Jews, while suffering under severe political disabilities, had taken up a high literary position in Alexandria, and had forced their opinions into the notice of the Greeks. The glowing earnestness of their philosophy, now put forward in a platonic dress, and their improved style, approaching even classic elegance, placed their writings on a lofty eminence far above anything which the cold,lifeless grammarians of the museum were then producing. Apion, who went to Rome to plead against Philo, was a native of the Great Oasis, but as he was born of Greek parents, he claimed and received the title and privileges of an Alexandrian, which he denied to the Jews who were born in the city. He had studied under Didymus and Apollonius and Euphranor, and was one of the most laborious of the grammarians and editors of Homer. All his writings are now lost. Some of them were attacks upon the Jews and their religion, calling in question the truth of the Jewish history and the justice of that nation's claim to high antiquity; and to these attacks we owe Josephus' *Answer*, in which several valuable fragments of history are saved by being quoted against the pagans in support of the Old Testament. One of his works was his *Ægyptiaca*, an account of what he thought most curious in Egypt. But his learned trifling is now lost, and nothing remains of it but his account of the meeting between Androclus and the lion, which took place in the amphitheatre at Rome when Apion was there on his embassy. Androclus was a runaway slave, who, when retaken, was brought to Rome to be thrown before an African lion for the amusement of the citizens, and as a punishment for his flight. But the fierce and hungry beast, instead of tearing him to pieces, wagged his tail at him, and licked his feet. It seems that the slave, when he fled from his master, had gained the friendship of the lion in the Libyan desert, first by pulling a thorn out of his foot, and then by living three years with him in a cave; and, when both were brought in chains to Rome, Androclus found a grateful friend in the amphitheatre where he thought to have met with a cruel death.

We may for a moment leave our history, to bid a last farewell to the family of the Ptolemies. Augustus, after leading Selene, the daughter of Cleopatra and Antony, through the streets of Rome in his triumph, had given her in marriage to the younger Juba, the historian of Africa; and about the same time he gave to the husband the kingdom of Mauritania, the inheritance of his father. His son Ptolemy succeeded him on the throne, but was

A RELIEF FROM SAQQÂRA.

soon turned out of his kingdom. We trace the last of the Ptolemies in his travels through Greece and Asia Minor by the inscriptions remaining to his honour. The citizens of Xanthus in Lycia set up a monument to him; and at Athens his statue was placed beside that of Philadelphus in the gymnasium of Ptolemy, near the temple of Theseus, where he was honoured as of founder's kin. He was put to death by Caligula. Drusilla, another grandchild of Cleopatra and Antony, married Antonius Felix, the procurator of Judæa, after the death of his first wife, who was also named Drusilla. These are the last notices that we meet with of the royal family of Egypt.

As soon as the news of Caligula's death (A. D. 41) reached Egypt, the joy of the Jews knew no bounds. They at once flew to arms to revenge themselves on the Alexandrians, whose streets were again the seat of civil war. The governor did what he could to quiet both parties, but was not wholly successful till the decree of the new emperor reached Alexandria. In this Claudius granted to the Jews the full rights of citizenship, which they had enjoyed under the Ptolemies, and which had been allowed by Augustus; he left them to choose their own high priest, to enjoy their own religion without hindrance, and he repealed the laws of Caligula under which they had been groaning. At this time the Jewish alabarch in Egypt was Demetrius, a man of wealth and high birth, who had married Mariamne, the daughter of the elder Agrippa.

The government under Claudius was mild and just, at least as far as a government could be in which every tax-gatherer, every military governor, and every sub-prefect was supposed to enrich himself by his appointment. Every Roman officer, from the general down to the lowest tribune, claimed the right of travelling through the country free of expense, and seizing the carts and cattle of the villagers to carry him forward to the next town, under the pretence of being a courier on the public service. But we have a decree of the ninth year of this reign, carved on the temple in the Great Oasis, in which

Cneius Capito, the prefect of Egypt, endeavours to put a stop to this injustice. He orders that no traveller shall have the privilege of a courier unless he has a proper warrant, and that then he shall only claim a free lodging; that clerks in the villages shall keep a register of all that is taken on account of the public service; and that if anybody make an unjust claim he shall pay four times

EGYPTIAN THRESHING - MACHINE.

the amount to the informer and six times the amount to the emperor. But royal decrees could do little or nothing where there were no judges to enforce them; and the people of Upper Egypt must have felt this law as a cruel insult when they were told that they might take up their complaints to Basilides, at Alexandria. The employment of the informer is a full acknowledgment of the weakness of this absolute government, and that the prefect had not the power to enforce his own decrees; and, when we compare this law with that of Alexander on his conquest of the country, we have no difficulty in seeing why Egypt rose under the Ptolemies and sunk under the selfish policy of Augustus.

Claudius was somewhat of a scholar and an author; he wrote several volumes both in Greek and in Latin. The former he might perhaps think would be chiefly valued in Alexandria; and when he founded a new college in that city, called after himself the Claudian Museum, he ordered that on given days every year his history of Carthage should be publicly read in one museum, and his history of Italy in the other; thus securing during his reign an attention to his writings which their merits alone would not have gained.

Under the government of Claudius the Egyptians were again allowed to coin money; and in his first year begins that historically important series in which every coin is dated with the year of the emperor's reign. The coins of the Ptolemies were strictly Greek in their workmanship, and the few Egyptian characters that we see upon them are so much altered by the classic taste of the die-engraver that we hardly know them again. But it is far otherwise with the coins of the emperors, which are covered with the ornaments, characters, and religious ceremonies of the native Egyptians; and, though the style of art is often bad, they are scarcely equalled by any series of coins whatever in the service they render to the historian.

It was in this reign that the route through Egypt to India first became really known to the Greeks and Romans. The historian Pliny, who died in 79 A. D., has left us a contemporary account of these early voyages. "It will not be amiss," he says in his *Natural History*, "to set forth the whole of the route from Egypt, which has been stated to us of late, upon information on which reliance may be placed and is here published for the first time. The subject is one well worthy of our notice, seeing that in no year does India drain our empire of less than five hundred and fifty millions of sesterces [or two million dollars], giving back her own wares in exchange, which are sold among us at fully one hundred times their cost price.

"Two miles distant from Alexandria is the town of Heliopolis. The distance thence to Koptos, up the Nile, is three hundred and eight miles; the voyage is performed, when the Etesian winds are blowing, in twelve days. From Koptos the journey is made with the aid of camels, stations being arranged at intervals for the supply of fresh water. The first of these stations is called Hydreuma, and is distant twenty-two miles; the second is situate on a mountain at a distance of one day's journey from the last; the third is at a second Hydreuma, distant from Koptos ninety-five miles; the fourth is on a mountain; the next to that is another Hydreuma, that of Apollo, and is distant from Koptos one hundred and eighty-four miles; after which there is another on a mountain; there is then another station at a place called the New Hydreuma, distant from Koptos two hundred and thirty miles; and next to it there is another called the Old Hydreuma, where a detachment is always on guard, with a caravansary that affords lodging for two thousand persons. The last is distant from the New Hydreuma seven miles. After leaving it, we come to the city of Berenicê, situate upon a harbour of the Red Sea, and distant from Koptos two hundred and fifty-seven miles. The greater part of this distance is generally travelled by night, on account of the extreme heat, the day being spent at the stations; in consequence of which it takes twelve days to perform the whole journey from Koptos to Berenicê.

"Passengers generally set sail at midsummer before the rising of the Dog-star, or else immediately after, and in about thirty days arrive at Ocelis in Arabia, or else at Cane, in the region which bears frankincense. To those who are bound for India, Ocelis is the best place for embarkation. If the wind called Hippolus happens to be blowing, it is possible to arrive in forty days at the nearest mart of India, Muziris by name [the modern Mangalore]. This, however, is not a very desirable place for disembarkation, on account of the pirates which frequent its vicinity, where they occupy a place, Nitrias; nor, in fact, is it very rich in articles of merchandise. Besides, the roadstead for shipping is a considerable distance from the shore, and the cargoes have to be conveyed in boats, either for loading or discharging. At the moment that I am writing these pages," continues Pliny, "the name of the king of the place is Cælobotras. Another part, and a much more convenient one, is that which lies in the territory of the people called Neacyndi, Barace by name. Here King Pandian used to reign, dwelling at a considerable distance from the mart in the interior, at a city known as Modiera. The district from which pepper is carried down to Barace in boats hollowed out of a single tree, is known as Cottonara. None of these names of nations, ports, and cities are to be found in any of the former writers, from which circumstance it would appear that the localities have since changed their names. Travellers set sail from India on their return to Europe, at the beginning of the Egyptian month Tybus, which is our December, or, at all events, before the sixth day of the Egyptian month Mechir, the same as our ides of January: if they do this, they can go and return in the same year. They set sail from India with a south-east wind, and, upon entering the Red Sea, catch the south-west or south."

The places on the Indian coast which the Egyptian merchant vessels then reached are verified from the coins found there; and as we know the course of the trade-wind by which they arrived, we also know the part of Africa where they left the shore and braved the dangers of the ocean. A hoard of Roman gold coins of these reigns has been dug up in our own days near Calicut, under the roots of a banyan-tree. It had been there buried by an Alexandrian merchant on his arrival from this voyage, and left safe under the cover of the sacred tree to await his return from a second journey. But he died before his return, and his secret died with him. The products of the Indian trade were chiefly silk, diamonds, and other precious stones, ginger, spices, and some scents. The state of Ethiopia was then such that no trade came down the Nile to Syênê; and the produce of southern Africa was brought by coasting vessels to Berenicê. These products were ivory, rhinoceros teeth, hippopotamus skins, tortoise shell, apes, monkeys, and slaves, a list which throws a sidelight both on the pursuits of the natives and the tastes of the ultimate purchasers.

The Romans in most cases collected the revenues of a province by means of a publican or farmer, to whom the taxes were let by auction; but such was the importance of Egypt that the same jealousy which made them think its government too great to be trusted to a man of high rank, made them think its revenues too large to be trusted to one farmer. The smaller branches of the Egyptian revenue were, however, let out as usual, and even the collection of the customs of the whole of the Red Sea was not thought too much to trust to one citizen. Annius Plocamus, who farmed them in this reign, had a little fleet under his command to collect them with; and, tempted either by trade or plunder, his ships were sometimes as far out as the south coast of Arabia. On one occasion one of his freedmen in the command of a vessel was carried by a north wind into the open ocean, and after being fifteen days at sea found himself on the coast of Ceylon. This island was not then wholly new to the geographers of Egypt and Europe. It had been heard of by the pilots in the voyage of Alexander the Great; Eratosthenes had given it a place in his map; and it had often been reached from Africa by the sailors of the Red Sea in wickerwork boats made of papyrus; but this was the first time it had been visited by a European.

AN ARAB GIRL.

In the neighbourhood of the above-mentioned road from Koptos to Berenicê were the porphyritic quarries and the emerald mines, which were briskly worked under the Emperor Claudius. The mountain was now named the Claudian Mountain.

As this route for trade became known, the geographers began to understand the wide space that separates India from Africa. Hitherto, notwithstanding a few voyages of discovery, it had been the common opinion that Persia was in the neighbourhood of Ethiopia. The Greeks had thought that the Nile rose in India, in opposition to the Jews, who said that it was the river Gihon of the garden of Eden, which made a circuit round the whole of the land of Cush, or Ethiopia. The names of these countries got misused accordingly; and even after the mistake was cleared up we sometimes find Ethiopia called India.

The Egyptian chemists were able to produce very bright dyes by methods then unknown to Greece or Rome. They dipped the cloth first into a liquid of one colour, called a mordant, to prepare it, and then into a liquid of a second colour; and it came out dyed of a third colour, unlike either of the former. The ink with which they wrote the name of a deceased person on the mummy-cloth, like our own marking-ink, was made with nitrate of silver. Their knowledge of chemistry was far greater than that of their neighbours, and the science is even now named from the country of its birth. The later Arabs called it Alchemia, *the Egyptian art*, and hence our words alchemy and chemistry. So also Naphtha, or *rock oil*, from the coast of the Red Sea; and Anthracite, or *rock fuel*, from the coast of Syria, both bear Egyptian names. To some Egyptian stones the Romans gave their own names; as the black glassy obsidian from Nubia they called after Obsidius, who found it; the black Tiberian marble with white spots, and the Augustan marble with regular wavy veins, were both named after the emperors. Porphyry was now used for statues for the first time, and sometimes to make a kind of patchwork figure, in which the clothed parts were of the coloured stone, while the head, hands, and feet were of white marble. And it was thought that diamonds were nowhere to be found but in the Ethiopian gold mines.

Several kinds of wine were made in Egypt; some in the Arsinoïte nome on the banks of the lake Mœris; and a poor Libyan wine at Antiphræ on the coast, a hundred miles from Alexandria. Wine had also been made in Upper Egypt in small quantities a very long time, as we learn from the monuments; but it was produced with difficulty and cost and was not good; it was not valued by the Greeks. It was poor and thin, and drunk only by those who were feverish and afraid of anything stronger. That of Anthylla, to the east of Alexandria, was very much better. But better still were the thick luscious Tæniotic and the mild delicate Mareotic wines. This last was first grown at Plinthine, but afterwards on all the banks of the lake Mareotis. The Mareotic wine was white and sweet and thin, and very little heating or intoxicating. Horace had carelessly said of Cleopatra that she was drunk with Mareotic wine; but

Lucan, who better knew its quality, says that the headstrong lady drank wine far stronger than the Mareotic. Near Sebennytus three kinds of wine were made; one bitter named Peuce, a second sparkling named Æthalon, and the third Thasian, from a vine imported from Thasus. But none of these Egyptian wines was thought equal to those of Greece and Italy. Nor were they made in quantities large enough or cheap enough for the poor;

FARMING IN EGYPT.

and here, as in other countries, the common people for their intoxicating drink used beer or spirits made from barley. The Egyptian sour wine, however, made very good vinegar, and it was then exported for sale in Rome.

During this half-century that great national work, the lake of Mœris, by which thousands of acres had been flooded and made fertile, and the watering of the lower country regulated, was, through the neglect of the embankments, at once destroyed. The latest traveller who mentions it is Strabo, and the latest geographer Pomponius Mela. By its means the province of Arsinoë was made one of the most fruitful and beautiful spots in Egypt. Here only does the olive grow wild. Here the vine will grow. And by the help of this embanked lake the province was made yet more fruitful. But before Pliny wrote, the bank had given way, the pent-up waters had made for themselves a channel into the lake now called Birket el Kurun, and the two small pyramids, which had hitherto been surrounded by water, then stood on dry ground. Thus was the country slowly going to ruin by the faults of the government, and ignorance in the foreign rulers. But, on the other hand, the beautiful temple of Latopolis, which had been begun under the Ptolemies, was finished in this reign; and bears the name of Claudius with those of some later emperors on its portico and walls.

In the Egyptian language the word for a year is *Bait*, which is also the name of a bird. In hieroglyphics this word is spelt by a palm-branch *Bai* and the letter T, followed sometimes by a circle as a picture of the year. Hence arose among a people fond of mystery and allegory a mode of speaking of the year under the name of a palm-branch or of a bird; and they formed a fable out of a mere confusion of words. The Greeks, who were not slow to copy Egyptian mysticism, called this fabulous bird the *Phœnix* from their own name for the palm-tree. The end of any long period of time they called the return of the phœnix to earth. The Romans borrowed the fable, though perhaps without understanding the allegory; and in the seventh year of this reign, when the emperor celebrated the secular games at Rome, at the end of the eighth century since the city was built, it was said that the phœnix had come to Egypt and was thence brought to Rome. This was in the consulship of Plautius and Vitellius; and it would seem to be only from mistakes in the name that Pliny places the event eleven years earlier, in the consulship of Plautius and Papinius, and that Tacitus places it thirteen years earlier in the consulship of Fabius and Vitellius. This fable is connected with some of the remarkable epochs in Egyptian history. The story lost nothing by travelling to a distance. In Rome it was said that this wonderful bird was a native of Arabia, where it lived for five hundred years, that on its death a grub came out of its body which in due time became a perfect bird; and that the new phœnix brought to Egypt the bones of its parent in the nest of spices in which it had died, and laid them on the altar in the temple of the sun in Heliopolis. It then returned to Arabia to live in its turn for five hundred years, and die and give life again to another as before. The Christians saw in this story a type of the resurrection; and Clement, Bishop of Rome, quotes it as such in his Epistle to the Corinthians.

We find the name of Claudius on several of the temples of Upper Egypt, particularly on that of Apollinopolis Magna, and on the portico of the great temples of Latopolis, which were being built in this reign.

In the beginning of the reign of Nero, 55 A. D., an Egyptian Jew, who claimed to be listened to as a prophet, raised the minds of his countrymen into a ferment of religious zeal by preaching about the sufferings of their brethren in Judæa; and he was able to get together a body of men, called in reproach the Sicarii, or *ruffians*, whose numbers are variously stated at four thousand and thirty thousand, whom he led out of Egypt to free the holy city from the bondage of the heathen. But Felix, the Roman governor, led against them the garrison of Jerusalem, and easily scattered the half-armed rabble. By such acts of religious zeal on the part of the Jews they were again brought to blows with the Greeks of Alexandria. The Macedonians, as the latter still called themselves, had met in public assembly to send an embassy to Rome, and some Jews who entered the meeting, which as citizens they had a full right to do, were seized and ill-treated by them as spies. They would perhaps have even been put to death if a large body of their countrymen had not run to their rescue. The Jews attacked the assembled Greeks with stones and lighted torches, and would have burned the amphitheatre and all that were in it, if the prefect, Tiberius Alexander, had not sent some of the elders of their own nation to calm their angry feelings. But, though the mischief was stopped for a time, it soon broke out again; and the prefect was forced to call out the garrison of two Roman legions and five thousand Libyans before he could re-establish peace in the city. The Jews were always the greatest sufferers in these civil broils; and Josephus says that fifty thousand of his countrymen were left dead in the streets of Alexandria. But this number is very improbable, as the prefect was a friend to the Jewish nation, and as the Roman legions were not withdrawn to the camp till they had guarded the Jews in carrying away and burying the bodies of their friends.

It was a natural policy on the part of the emperors to change a prefect whenever his province was disturbed by rebellion, as we have seen in the case of Flaccus, who was recalled by Caligula. It was easier to send a new governor than to inquire into a wrong or to redress a grievance; and accordingly in the next year C. Balbillus was sent from Rome as prefect of Egypt. He reached Alexandria on the sixth day after leaving the Straits of Sicily, which was spoken of as the quickest voyage known. The Alexandrian ships were better built and better manned than any others, and, as a greater number of vessels sailed every year between that port and Puteoli on the coast of Italy than between any other two places, no voyage was better understood or more quickly performed. They were out of sight of land for five hundred miles between Syracuse and Cyrene. Hence we see that the quickest rate of sailing, with a fair wind, was at that time about one hundred and fifty miles in the twenty-four hours. But these ships had very little power of bearing up against the wind; and if it were contrary the voyage became tedious. If the captain on sailing out of the port of Alexandria found the wind westerly, and was unable to creep along the African coast to Cyrene, he stood over to the coast of Asia Minor, in hopes of there finding a more favourable wind. If a storm arose, he ran into the nearest port, perhaps in Crete, perhaps in Malta, there to wait the return of fair weather. If winter then came on, he had to lie by till spring. Thus a vessel laden with Egyptian wheat, leaving Alexandria in September, after the harvest had been brought down to the coast, would sometimes spend five months on its voyage from that port to Puteoli. Such was the case with the ship bearing the children of Jove as its figure-head, which picked up the Apostle Paul and the historian Josephus when they had been wrecked together on the island of Malta; and such perhaps would have been the

EGYPTIAN THRESHING MACHINE.

case with the ship which they before found on the coast of Lycia, had it been able to reach a safe harbour, and not been wrecked at Malta.

The rocky island of Malta, with the largest and safest harbour in the Mediterranean, was a natural place for ships to touch at between Alexandria and Italy. Its population was made up of those races which had sailed upon its waters first from Carthage and then from Alexandria; it was a mixture of Phœnicians, Egyptians, and

Greco-Egyptians. To judge from the skulls turned up in the burial-places, the Egyptians were the most numerous, and here as elsewhere the Egyptian superstitions conquered and put down all the other superstitions. While the island was under the Phœnicians, the coins had the head of the Sicilian goddess on one side, and on the other the Egyptian trinity of Isis, Osiris, and Nepthys. When it was under the Greek rule the head on the coins received an Egyptian head-dress, and became that of the goddess Isis, and on the other side of the coin was a winged figure of Osiris. It was at this time governed by a Roman governor. The large temple, built with barbarian rudeness, and ornamented with the Phœnician palm-branch, was on somewhat of a Roman plan, with a circular end to every room. But it was dedicated to the chief god of Egypt, and is even yet called by its Greek name Hagia Chem, *the temple of Chem.* The little neighbouring island of Cossyra, between Sicily and Carthage, also shows upon its coins clear traces of its taste for Egyptian customs.

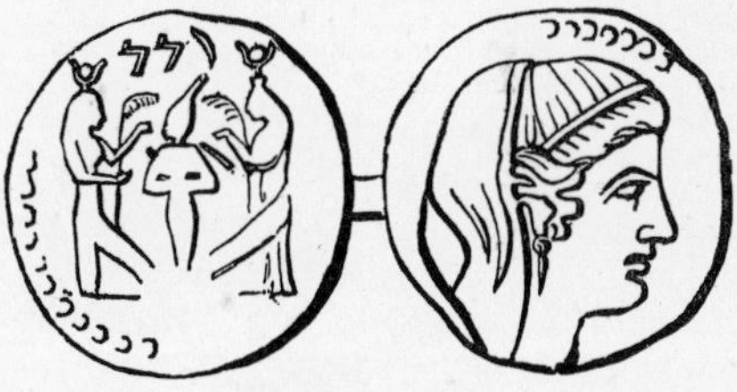

MALTESE COIN.

The first five years of this reign, the *quinquennium Neronis*, while the emperor was under the tutorship of the philosopher Seneca, became in Rome proverbial for good government, and on the coinage we see marks of Egypt being equally well treated. In the third year we see on a coin the queen sitting on a throne with the word *agreement*, as if to praise the young emperor's good feeling in following the advice of his mother Agrippina. On another the emperor is styled *the young good genius*, and he is represented by the sacred basilisk crowned with the double crown of Egypt. The new prefect, Balbillus, was an Asiatic Greek, and no doubt received his Roman names of Tiberius Claudius on being made a freedman of the late emperor. He governed the country mildly and justly; and the grateful inhabitants declared that under him the Nile was more than usually bountiful, and that its waters always rose to their just height. But in the latter part of the reign the Egyptians smarted severely under that cruel principle of a despotic monarchy that every prefect, every sub-prefect, and even every deputy tax-gatherer, might be equally despotic in his own department. On a coin of the thirteenth year of the reign of this ruler, we see a ship with the word *emperor-bearer*, being that in which he then sailed into Greece, or in which the Alexandrians thought that he would visit their city. But if they had really hoped for his visit as a pleasure, they must have thought it a danger escaped when they learned his character; they must have been undeceived when the prefect Cæcinna Tuscus was punished with banishment for venturing to bathe in the bath which was meant for the emperor's use if he had come on his projected visit.

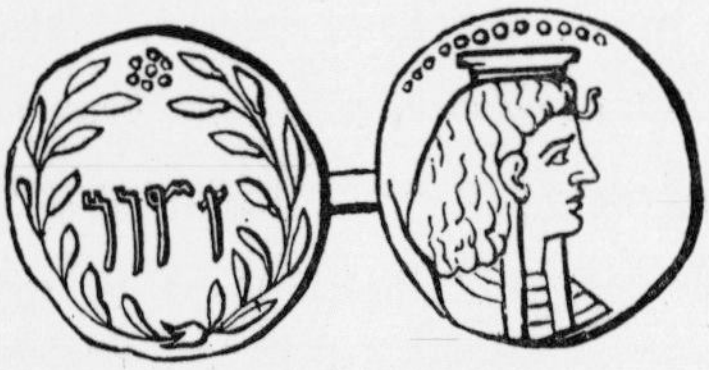

COIN OF COSSYRA.

During the first century and a half of Roman sway in Egypt the school of Alexandria was nearly silent. We have a few poems by Leonides of Alexandria, one of which is addressed to the Empress Poppæa, as the wife of Jupiter, on his presenting a celestial globe to her on her birthday. Pamphila wrote a miscellaneous history of entertaining stories, and her lively, simple style makes us very much regret its loss. Chæremon, a Stoic philosopher, had been, during the last reign, at the head of the Alexandrian library, but he was removed to Rome as one of the tutors to the young Nero. He is ridiculed by Martial for writing in praise of death, when, from age and poverty, he was less able to enjoy life. We still possess a most curious though short account by him of the monastic habits of the ancient Egyptians. He also wrote on hieroglyphics, and a small fragment containing his opinion of the meanings of nineteen characters still remains to us. But he is not always right; he thinks the characters were used allegorically for thoughts, not for sounds; and fancies that the priests used them to keep secret the real nature of the gods.

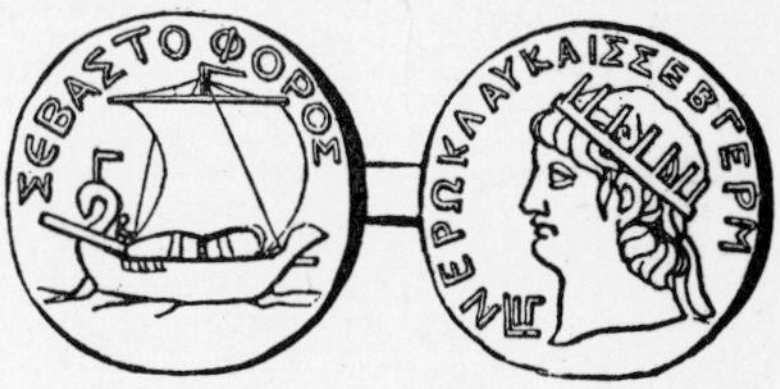

COIN OF NERO.

He was succeeded at the museum by his pupil Dionysius, who had the charge of the library till the reign of Trajan. Dionysius was also employed by the prefect as a secretary of state, or, in the language of the day, secretary to the embassies, epistles, and answers. He was the author of the *Periegesis*, and aimed at the rank of a poet by writing a treatise on geography in heroic verse. From this work he is named Dionysius Periegetes. While careful to remind us that his birthplace Alexandria was a Macedonian city, he gives due honour to Egypt and the Egyptians. There is no river, says he, equal to the Nile for carrying fertility and adding to the happiness of the land. It divides Asia from Libya, falling between rocks at Syênê, and then passing by the old and famous city of Thebes, where Memnon every morning salutes his beloved Aurora as she rises. On its banks dwells a rich and glorious race of men, who were the first to cultivate the arts of life; the first to make trial of the plough and sow their seed in a straight furrow; and the first to map the heavens and trace the sloping path of the sun.

According to the traditions of the church, it was in this reign that Christianity was first brought into Egypt by the Evangelist Mark, the disciple of the Apostle Peter. Many were already craving for religious food more real than the old superstitions. The Egyptian had been shaken in his attachment to the sacred animals by Greek ridicule. The Greek had been weakened in his belief of old Homer's gods by living with men who had never heard of them. Both were dissatisfied with the scheme of explaining the actions of their gods by means of allegory. The crumbling away of the old opinions left men more fitted to receive the new religion from Galilee. Mark's preaching converted crowds in Alexandria; but, after a short stay, he returned to Rome, in about the eleventh year of this reign, leaving Annianus to watch over the growing church. Annianus is usually called the first bishop of Alexandria; and Eusebius, who lived two hundred years later, has given us the names of his successors in an unbroken chain. If we would inquire whether the early converts to Christianity in Alexandria were Jews, Greeks, or Egyptians, we have nothing to guide us but the names of these bishops. Annianus, or Annaniah, as his name was written by the Arabic historians, was very likely a Jew; indeed, the Evangelist Mark would begin by addressing himself to the Jews, and would leave the care of the infant church to one of his own nation. In the platonic Jews, Christianity found a soil so exactly suited to its reception that it is only by the dates that the Therapeutæ of Alexandria and their historian Philo are proved not to be Christian; and, again, it was in the close union between the platonic Jews and the platonists that Christianity found its easiest path to the ears and hearts of the pagans. The bishops that followed seem to have been Greek converts. Before the death of Annaniah, Jerusalem had been destroyed by the Roman armies, and the Jews sunk in their own eyes and in those of their fellow-citizens throughout the empire; hence the second bishop of Alexandria was less likely to be of Hebrew blood; and it was long before any Egyptians aimed at rank in the church. But though the spread of Christianity was rapid, both among the Greeks and the Egyptians, we must not hope to find any early traces of it in the historians. It was at first embraced by the unlearned and the poor, whose deeds and opinions are seldom mentioned in history; and we may readily believe the scornful reproach of the unbelievers, that it was chiefly received by the unfortunate, the unhappy, the despised, and the sinful. When the white-robed priestesses of Ceres carried the sacred basket through the streets of Alexandria, they cried out, "Sinners away, or keep your eyes to the ground; keep your eyes to the ground!" When the crier, standing on the steps of the portico in front of the great temple, called upon the pagans to come near and join in the celebration of their mysteries, he cried out, "All ye who are clean of hands and pure of heart, come to the sacrifice; all ye who are guiltless in thought and deed, come to the sacrifice." But many a repentant sinner and humble spirit must have drawn back in distrust from a summons which to him was so forbidding, and been glad to hear the good tidings of mercy offered by Christianity to those who labour and are heavy laden, and to the broken-hearted who would turn away from their wickedness. While such were the chief followers of the gospel, it was not likely to be much noticed by the historians; and we must wait till it forced its way into the schools and the palace before we shall find many traces of the rapidity with which it was spreading.

During these reigns the Ethiopian Arabs kept up their irregular warfare against the southern frontier. The tribe most dreaded were the Blemmyes, an uncivilised people, described by the affrighted neighbours as having no heads, but with eyes and mouth on the breast; and it was under that name that the Arabs spread during each century farther and farther into Egypt, separating

ETHIOPIAN ARABS.

the province from the more cultivated tribes of Upper Ethiopia or Meroë. The cities along the banks of the Nile in Lower Ethiopia, between Nubia and Meroë, were ruined by being in the debatable land between the two nations. The early Greek travellers had counted about twenty cities on each side of the Nile between Syênê and Meroë; but when, in a moment of leisure, the Roman government proposed to punish and stop the inroads of these troublesome neighbours, and sent forward a tribune with a guard of soldiers, he reported on his return that the whole country was a desert, and that there was scarcely a city inhabited on either side of the Nile beyond Nubia. But he had not marched very far. The interior of Africa was little known; and to seek for the fountain of the Nile was another name for an impossible or chimerical undertaking.

But Egypt itself was so quiet as not to need the presence of so large a Roman force as usual to keep it in obedience; and when Vespasian, who commanded Nero's armies in Syria, found the Jews more obstinate in their rebellion and less easily crushed than he expected, the emperor sent the young Titus to Alexandria, to lead to his father's assistance all the troops that could be spared. Titus led into Palestine through Arabia two legions, the Fifth and the Tenth, which were then in Egypt.

We find a temple of this reign in the oasis of Dakleh, or the Western Oasis, which seems to have been a more flourishing spot in the time of the Romans than when Egypt itself was better governed. It is so far removed from the cities in the valley of the Nile that its position, and even existence, was long unknown to Europeans, and to such hiding-places as this many of the Egyptians fled, to be farther from the tyranny of the Roman tax-gatherers.

Hitherto the Roman empire had descended for just one hundred years through five emperors like a family inheritance; but, on the death of Nero, the Julian and Claudian families were at an end, and Galba, who was raised to the purple by the choice of the soldiers, endeavoured to persuade the Romans and their dependent provinces that they had regained their liberties. The Egyptians may have been puzzled by the word *freedom*, then struck upon the coins by their foreign masters, but must have been pleased to find it accompanied with a redress of grievances.

Galba began his reign with the praiseworthy endeavour of repairing the injustice done by his cruel predecessor. He at once recalled the prefect of Egypt, and appointed in his place Tiberius Julius Alexander, an Alexandrian, a son of the former prefect of that name; and thus Egypt was under the government of a native prefect. The peaceable situation of the Great Oasis has saved a long Greek inscription of the decree which was now issued in redress of the grievances suffered under Nero. It is a proclamation by Julius Demetrius, the commander of the Oasis, quoting the decree of Tiberius Julius Alexander, the new prefect of Egypt.

The prefect acknowledges that the loud complaints with which he was met on entering upon his government were well founded, and he promises that the unjust taxes shall cease; that nobody shall be forced to act as a provincial tax-gatherer; that no debts shall be cancelled or sales made void under the plea of money owing to the revenue; that no freeman shall be thrown into prison for debt, unless it be a debt due to the royal revenue, and that no private debt shall be made over to the tax-gatherer, to be by him collected as a public debt; that no property settled on the wife at marriage shall be seized for taxes due from the husband; and that all new charges and claims which had grown up within the last five years shall be repealed. In order to discourage informers, whom the prefects had much employed, and by whom the families in Alexandria were much harassed, and to whom he laid the great falling off in the population of that city, he orders, that if anybody should make three charges and fail in proving them, he shall forfeit half his property and lose the right of bringing an action at law. The land had always paid a tax in proportion to the number of acres overflowed and manured by the waters of the Nile; and the husbandmen had latterly been frightened by the double threat of a new measurement of the land, and of making it at the same time pay according to the ancient registers of the overflow when the canals had been more open and more acres flooded; but the prefect promises that there shall be no new measurements, and that they shall only be taxed according to the actual overflow. In 69 A. D. Galba was murdered, after a reign of seven months. Some of his coins, however, are dated in the second year of his reign, according to the Alexandrian custom of counting the years. They called the 29th of August, the first new year's day after the sovereign came to the throne, the first day of his second year.

Otho was then acknowledged as emperor by Rome and the East, while the hardy legions of Germany thought themselves entitled to choose for themselves. They set up their own general, Vitellius. The two legions in Egypt sided with the four legions in Syria under Mucianus, and the three legions which, under Vespasian, were carrying on the memorable war against the Jews; and all took the oaths to Otho. We find no hieroglyphical inscriptions during this short reign of a few weeks, but there are many Alexandrian coins to prove the truth of the historian; and some of them, like those of Galba, bear the unlooked-for word *freedom*. In the few weeks which then passed between the news of Otho's death and of Vespasian being raised to the purple in Syria, Vitellius was acknowledged in Egypt; and the Alexandrian mint struck a few coins in his name with the figure of Victory. But as soon as the legions of Egypt heard that the Syrian army had made choice of another emperor, they withdrew their allegiance from Vitellius, and promised it to his Syrian rival.

EGYPTIAN COIN OF GALBA.

Vespasian was at Cæsarea, in command of the army employed in the Jewish war, when the news reached him that Otho was dead, and that Vitellius had been raised to the purple by the German legions, and acknowledged at Rome; and, without wasting more time in refusing the honour than was necessary to prove that his soldiers were in earnest in offering it, he allowed himself to be proclaimed emperor, as the successor of Otho. He would not, however, then risk a march upon Rome, but he sent to Alexandria to tell Tiberius Alexander, the governor of Egypt, what he had done; he ordered him to claim in his name the allegiance of that great province, and added that he should soon be there himself. The two Roman legions in Egypt much preferred the choice of the Eastern to that of the Western army, and the Alexandrians, who had only just acknowledged Vitellius, readily took the oath to be faithful to Vespasian. This made it less necessary for him to hasten thither, and he only reached Alexandria in time to hear that Vitellius had been murdered after a reign of eight months, and that he himself had been acknowledged as emperor by Rome and the Western legions. His Egyptian coins in the first year of his reign, by the word *peace*, point to the end of the civil war.

When Vespasian entered Alexandria, he was met by the philosophers and magistrates in great pomp. The philosophers, indeed, in a city where, beside the officers of government, talent formed the only aristocracy, were a very important body; and Dion, Euphrates, and Apollonius had been useful in securing for Vespasian the allegiance of the Alexandrians. Dion was an orator, who had been professor of rhetoric, but he had given up that study for philosophy. His orations, or declamations, gained for him the name of Chrysostom, or *golden-mouthed.* Euphrates, his friend, was a platonist, who afterwards married the daughter of the prefect of Syria, and removed to Rome. Apollonius of Tyana, the most celebrated of these philosophers, was one of the first who gained his eminence from the study of Eastern philosophy, which was then rising in the opinions of the Greeks as highly worth their notice. He had been travelling in the East; and, boasting that he was already master of all the fabled wisdom of the Magi of Babylon and of the Gymnosophists of India, he was come to Egypt to compare this mystic philosophy with that of the hermits of Ethiopia and the Thebaid. Addressing himself as a pupil to the priests, he willingly yielded his belief to their mystic claims; and, whether from being deceived or as a deceiver, whether as an enthusiast or as a cheat, he pretended to have learned all the supernatural knowledge which they pretended to teach. By the Egyptians he was looked upon as the favourite of Heaven; he claimed the power of working miracles by his magical arts, and of foretelling events by his knowledge of astrology. In the Thebaid he was so far honoured that at the bidding of the priests one of the sacred trees spoke to him, as had been their custom from of old with favourites, and in a clear and rather womanly voice addressed him as a teacher from heaven.

It was to witness such practices as these, and to learn the art of deceiving their followers, that the Egyptian priests were now consulted by the Greeks. The oracle at Delphi was silent, but the oracle of Ammon continued to return an answer. The mystic philosophy of the East had come into fashion in Alexandria, and the priests were more celebrated as magicians than as philosophers. They would tell a man's fortune and the year that he was to die by examining the lines of his forehead. Some of them even undertook, for a sum of money, to raise the dead to life, or, rather, to recall for a time to earth the unwilling spirits, and make them answer any questions that might be put to them. Ventriloquism was an art often practised in Egypt, and perhaps invented there. By this the priests gained a power over the minds of the listeners, and could make them believe that a tree, a statue, or a dead body, was speaking to them.

The Alexandrian men of letters seldom erred by wrapping themselves up in pride to avoid the fault of meanness; they usually cringed to the great. Apollonius was wholly at the service of Vespasian, and the emperor repaid the philosopher by flattery as well as by more solid favours. He kept him always by his side during his stay in Egypt; he acknowledged his rank as a prophet, and tried to make further use of him in persuading the Egyptians of his own divine right to the throne. Vespasian begged him to make use of his prayers that he might obtain from God the empire which he had as yet hardly grasped; but Apollonius, claiming even a higher mission from Heaven than Vespasian was granting to him, answered, with as much arrogance as flattery, "I have myself already made you emperor." With the intimacy between Vespasian and Apollonius begins the use of gnostic emblems on the Alexandrian coins. The imperial pupil was not slow in learning from such a master; and the people were as ready to believe in the emperor's miracles as in the philosopher's. As Vespasian was walking through the streets of Alexandria, a man well known as having a disease in his eyes threw himself at his feet and begged of him to heal his blindness. He had been told by the god Serapis that he should regain his sight if the emperor would but deign to spit upon his eyelids. Another man, who had lost the use of a hand, had been told by the same god that he should be healed if the emperor would but trample on him with his feet. Vespasian at first laughed at them and thrust them off; but at last he so far yielded to their prayers, and to the flattery of his friends, as to have the physicians of Alexandria consulted whether it was in his power to heal these unfortunate men. The physicians, like good courtiers, were not so unwise as to think it impossible; besides, it seemed meant by the god as a public proof of Vespasian's right to the throne; if he were successful the glory would be his, and if he failed the laugh would be against the cripples. The two men were therefore brought before him, and in the face of the assembled citizens he trampled on one and spit on the other; and his flatterers declared that he had healed the maimed and given sight to the blind.

Vespasian met with further wonders when he entered the temple of Serapis to consult the god as to the state and fortunes of the empire. He went into the inner sanctuary alone, and, to his surprise, there he beheld the old Basilides, the freedman of Claudius, one of the chief men of Alexandria, whom he knew was then lying dangerously ill, and several days' journey from the city. He inquired of the priests whether Basilides had been in the temple, and was assured that he had not. He then asked whether he had been in Alexandria; but nobody had seen him there. Lastly, on sending messengers, he learned that he was on his death-bed eighty miles off. With this miracle before his eyes, he could not distrust the answers which the priests gave to his questions.

From Alexandria Vespasian sent back Titus to finish the siege of Jerusalem. The Jewish writer Joseph, the son of Matthias, or Flavius Josephus, as he called himself when he entered the service of the emperor, was then in Alexandria. He had been taken prisoner by Vespasian, but had gained his freedom by the betrayal of his country's cause. He joined the army of Titus and marched to the overthrow of Jerusalem. Notwithstanding the obstinate and heroic struggles of the Jews, Judæa was wholly conquered by the Romans, and Jerusalem and its other fortresses either received Roman garrisons or were dismantled. The Temple was overthrown in the month of September, A. D. 70. Titus made slaves of ninety-seven thousand men, many of whom he led with him into Egypt, and then sent them to work in the mines. These were soon followed by a crowd of other brave Jews, who chose rather to quit their homes and live as wanderers in Egypt than to own Vespasian as their king. They knew no lord but Jahveh; to take the oaths or to pay tribute to Cæsar was to renounce the faith of their fathers. But they found no safety in Egypt. Their Greek brethren turned against them, and handed six hundred of them up to Lupus, the governor of Egypt, to be punished; and their countryman Josephus brands them all with the name of Sicarii. They tried to hide themselves in Thebes and other cities less under the eyes of the Roman governor. They were, however, followed and taken, and the courage with which the boys and mere children bore their sufferings, sooner than acknowledge Vespasian for their king, drew forth the praise of even the time-serving Josephus.

The Greek Jews of Egypt gained nothing by this treachery towards their Hebrew brethren; they were themselves looked down upon by the Alexandrians, and distrusted by the Romans. The emperor ordered Lupus to shut up the temple at Onion, near Heliopolis, in which, during the last three hundred years, they had been allowed to have an altar, in rivalry to the Temple of Jerusalem. Even Josephus, whose betrayal of his countrymen might have saved him from their enemies, was sent with many others in chains to Rome, and was only set free on his making himself known to Titus. Indeed, when the Hebrew Jews lost their capital and their rank as a nation, their brethren felt lowered in the eyes of their fellow-citizens, in whatever city they dwelt, and in Alexandria they lost all hope of keeping their privileges; although the emperor refused to repeal the edict which granted them their citizenship, an edict to which they always appealed for protection, but often with very little success.

The Alexandrians were sadly disappointed in Vespasian. They had been among the first to acknowledge him as emperor while his power was yet doubtful, and they looked for a sum of money as a largess; but to their sorrow he increased the taxes, and re-established some which had fallen into disuse. They had a joke against him, about his claiming from one of his friends the trifling debt of six oboli; and, upon hearing of their witticisms, he was so angry that he ordered this sum of six oboli to be levied as a poll-tax upon every man in the city, and he only remitted the tax at the request of his son Titus. He went to Rome, carrying with him the nickname of Cybiosactes, *the scullion*, which the Alexandrians gave him for his stinginess and greediness, and which they had before given to Seleucus, who robbed the tomb of Alexander the Great, at Alexandria, of its famous golden sarcophagus.

Titus saw the importance of pleasing the people; and his wish to humour their ancient prejudices, at the ceremony of consecrating a new bull as Apis, brought some blame upon him. He there, as became the occasion, wore the state crown, and dazzled the people of Memphis with his regal pomp; but, while thus endeavouring to strengthen his father's throne, he was by some accused of grasping at it for himself.

The great temple of Kneph, at Latopolis, which had been the work of many reigns and perhaps many centuries, was finished under Vespasian. It is a building worthy of the best times of Egyptian architecture. It has a grand portico, upheld by four rows of massive columns, with capitals in the form of papyrus flowers. On the ceiling is a zodiac, like that at Tentyra; and, though many other kings' names are carved on the walls, that of Vespasian is in the dedication over the entrance.

Of the reign of Titus in Egypt we find no trace beyond his coins struck each year at Alexandria, and his name carved on one or two temples which had been built in former reigns.

Of the reign of Domitian (81—96 A. D.) we learn something from the poet Juvenal, who then held a military post in the province; and he gives us a sad account of the state of lawlessness in which the troops lived under his commands. All quarrels between soldiers and citizens were tried by the officers according to martial law; and justice was very far from being even-handed between the Roman and the poor Egyptian. No witness was bold enough to come forward and say anything against a soldier, while everybody was believed who spoke on his behalf. Juvenal was at a great age when he was sent into Egypt; and he felt that the command of a cohort on the very borders of the desert was a cruel banishment from the literary society of Rome. His death in the camp was hastened by his wish to return home. As what Juvenal chiefly aimed at in his writings was to lash the follies of the age, he, of course, found plenty of amusement in the superstitions and sacred animals of Egypt. But he sometimes takes a poet's liberty, and when he tells us that man's was almost the only flesh that they ate without sinning, we need not believe him to the letter. He gives a lively picture of a fight which he saw between the citizens of two towns. The towns of Ombos and Tentyra, though about a hundred miles apart, had a long-standing quarrel about their gods. At Ombos they worshipped the crocodile and the crocodile-headed god Savak, while at Tentyra they worshipped the goddess Hâthor, and were celebrated for their skill in catching and killing crocodiles. So, taking advantage of a feast or holiday, they marched out for a fight. The men of Ombos were beaten and put to flight; but one of them, stumbling as he ran away, was caught and torn to pieces, and, as Juvenal adds, eaten by the men of Tentyra. Their worship of beasts, birds, and fishes, and even growing their gods in the garden, are pleasantly hit off by him; they left nothing, said he, without worship, but the goddess of chastity. The mother goddess, Isis, the queen of heaven, was the deity to whom they bowed with the most tender devotion, and to swear by Isis was their favourite oath; and hence the leek, in their own language named Isi, was no doubt the vegetable called a god by the satiric Juvenal.

At the same time also the towns of Oxyrrhynchos and Cynopolis, in the Heptanomos, had a little civil war about the animals which they worshipped. Somebody at Cynopolis was said to have caught an oxyrrhynchus fish in the Nile and eaten it; and so the people of Oxyrrhynchos, in revenge, made an attack upon the dogs, the gods of Cynopolis. They caught a number of them, killed them in sacrifice to their offended fish-god, and ate them. The two parties then flew to arms and fought several battles; they sacked one another's cities in turns, and the war was not stopped till the Roman troops marched to the spot and punished them both.

But we gain a more agreeable and most likely a more true notion of the mystical religion and philosophy of the Egyptians in these days from the serious enquiries of Plutarch, who, instead of looking for what he could laugh at, was only too ready to believe that he saw wisdom hidden under an allegory in all their superstitions. Many of the habits of the priests, such as shaving the whole body, wearing linen instead of cotton, and refusing some meats as impure, seem to have arisen from a love of cleanliness; their religion ordered what was useful. And it also forbade what was hurtful; so to stir the fire with a sword was displeasing to the gods, because it spoilt the temper of the metal. None but the vulgar now looked upon the animals and statues as gods; the priests believed that the unseen gods, who acted with one mind and with one providence, were the authors of all good; and though these, like the sun and moon, were called in each country by a different name, yet, like those luminaries, they were the same over all the world. Outward ceremonies in religion were no longer thought enough without a good life; and, as the Greeks said, that beard and cloak did not make a philosopher, so the Egyptians said that white linen and a tonsure would not make a follower of Isis. All the sacrifices to the gods had a secondary meaning, or, at least, they tried to join a moral aim to the outward act; as on the twentieth day of the month, when they ate honey and figs in honour of Thot, they sang "Sweet is truth." The Egyptians, like most other Eastern polytheists, held the doctrine which was afterwards called Manicheism; they believed in a

SCENE IN A SEPULCHRAL CHAMBER.

good and in a wicked god, who governed the world between them. Of these the former made himself threefold, because three is a perfect number, and they adopted into their religion that curious metaphysical opinion that everything divine is formed of three parts; and accordingly, on the Theban monuments we often see the gods in groups of three. They worshipped Osiris, Isis, and Horus under the form of a right-angled triangle, in which Horus was the side opposite to the right angle. The favourite part of their mythology was the lamentation of Isis for the death of her husband Osiris. By another change the god Horus, who used to be a crowned king of manly stature, was now a child holding a finger to his mouth, and thereby marking that he had not yet learned to talk. The Romans, who did not understand this Egyptian symbol for youthfulness, thought that in this character he was commanding silence; and they gave the name of Harpocrates, *Horus the powerful*, to a god of silence. Horus was also often placed as a child in the arms of his mother Isis; and thus by the loving nature of the group were awakened the more tender feelings of the worshipper. The Egyptians, like the Greeks, had always been loud in declaring that they were beloved by their gods; but they received their favours with little gratitude, and hardly professed that they felt any love towards the gods in return. But after the time of the Christian era, we meet with more kindly feelings even among the pagans. We find from the Greek names of persons that they at least had begun to think their gods deserving of love, and in this group of the mother and child, such a favourite also in Christian art, we see in what direction these more kindly feelings found an entrance into the Egyptian religion. As fast as opinion was raising the great god Serapis above his fellows and making the wrathful judge into the ruler of the world, so fast was the same opinion creating for itself a harbour of refuge in the child Horus and its mother.

The deep earnestness of the Egyptians in the belief of their own religion was the chief cause of its being adopted by others. The Greeks had borrowed much from it. Though in Rome it had been forbidden by law, it was much cultivated there in private; and the engraved rings on the fingers of the wealthy Romans which bore the figures of Harpocrates and other Egyptian gods easily escaped the notice of the magistrate. But the superstitious Domitian, who was in the habit of consulting astrologers and Chaldæan fortune-tellers, allowed the Egyptian worship. He built at Rome a temple to Isis, and another to Serapis; and such was the eagerness of the citizens for pictures of the mother goddess with her child in her arms that, according to Juvenal, the Roman painters all lived upon the goddess Isis. For her temple in the Campus Martius, holy water was even brought from the Nile to purify the building and the votaries; and a regular college of priests was maintained there by their zeal and at their cost, with a splendour worthy of the Roman capital. Domitian, also, was somewhat of a scholar, and he sent to Alexandria for copies

HARPOCRATES.

of their books, to restore the public library at Rome which had been lately burnt; while his garden on the banks of the Tiber was richer in the Egyptian winter rose than even the gardens of Memphis and Alexandria.

During this century the coinage continues one of the subjects of chief interest to the antiquary. In 92 A. D., in the eleventh year of his reign, when Domitian took upon himself the tribunitian power at Rome for a second period of ten years, the event was celebrated in Alexandria with a triumphal procession and games in the hippodrome, of all which we see clear traces on the Egyptian coins.

COINS OF DOMITIAN.

The coinage is almost the only trace of Nerva (96—98 A. D.) having reigned in Egypt; but it is at the same time enough to prove the mildness of his government. The Jews who by their own law were of old required to pay half a shekel, or a didrachm, to the service of their temple, had on their conquest been made to pay that sum as a yearly tribute to the Ptolemies, and afterwards to the emperors. It was a poll-tax levied on every Jew throughout the empire. But Nerva had the humanity to relieve them from this insulting tribute, and well did he deserve the honour of having it recorded on the coins struck in his reign.

The coinage of the eleventh year of his successor, Trajan (98—117 A. D.), is very remarkable for its beauty, its technical skill, and variety, even more so than that of the eleventh year of Domitian. The coins have hitherto proclaimed, in a manner unmistakably plain to those who study numismatics, the games and conquests of the emperors, the bountiful overflow of the Nile, and sometimes the worship of Serapis; but we now enter upon the most brilliant and most important period of the Egyptian coinage, and find a rich variety of fables taken both from Egyptian and Greek mythology. The coins of Rome in this and the following reigns show the wealth, good taste, and learning of the nation, but they are surpassed by the coins of Egypt. While history is nearly silent, and the buildings and other proofs of Roman good government have perished, the coins alone are quite enough to prove the well-being of the people. Among the Egyptian coins those of Trajan, Hadrian, and the Antonines equal in number those of all the other emperors together, while in beauty they far surpass them. They are mostly of copper, of a small size, and thick, weighing about one hundred and ten grains, and some larger of two hundred and twenty grains; the silver coins are less common, and of mixed metal.

COIN OF NERVA.

Though the Romans, while admiring and copying everything that was Greek, affected to look upon the Egyptians as savages, who were only known to be human beings by their power of speech, still the Egyptian physicians were held by them in the highest repute. The more wealthy Romans often sailed to Alexandria for the benefit of their advice. Pliny the Elder, however, thought that of the invalids who went to Egypt for their health more were cured by the sea voyage than by the physicians on their arrival. One of Cicero's physicians was an Egyptian. Pliny the Younger repaid his Egyptian oculist,

TRINITY OF ISIS, HORUS, AND NEPHTHYS.

Harpocrates, by getting a rescript from the emperor to make him a Roman citizen. But the statesman did not know under what harsh laws his friend was born, for the grant was void in the case of an Egyptian, the emperor's rescript was bad as being against the law; and Pliny had again to beg the greater favour that the Egyptian might first be made a citizen of Alexandria, without which the former favour was useless. Thus, even in Alexandria, a conquered province governed by the despotic will of a military emperor, there were still some laws or principles which the emperor found it not easy to break. The courts of justice, those to whom the edicts were addressed and by whom they were to be explained and carried into effect, claimed a power in some cases above the emperor; and the first article in the Roman code was that an imperial rescript, by whomsoever or howsoever obtained, was void if it was against the law. As the lawyers and magistrates formed part of the body of citizens, the Alexandrians had so far a share in the government of their own affairs; but this was an advantage that the Egyptians lost by being under the power of the Greek magistrates.

Trajan always kept in the public granaries of Rome a supply of Egyptian grain equal to seven times the *canon*, or yearly gift to the poor citizens; and in this prudent course he was followed by all his successors,

COINS OF TRAJAN.

until the store was squandered by the worthless Elagabalus. One year, when the Nile did not rise to its usual height, and much of the grain land of the Delta, instead of being moistened by its waters and enriched by its mud, was left a dry, sandy plain, the granaries of Rome were unlocked to feed the city of Alexandria. The Alexandrians then saw the unusual sight of ships unloading their cargoes of wheat in their harbour, and the Romans boasted that they took the Egyptian tribute in grain, not because they could not feed themselves, but because the Egyptians had nothing else to send them.

Alexandria under the Romans was still the centre of the trading world, not only having its own great trade in grain, but being the port through which the trade of India and Arabia passed to Europe, and at which the Syrian vessels touched in their way to Italy. The harbour was crowded with masts and strange prows and uncouth sails, and the quays always busy with loading and unloading; while in the streets might be seen men of all languages and all dresses, copper-coloured Egyptians, swarthy Jews, lively, bustling Greeks, and haughty Italians, with Asiatics from the neighbouring coasts of Syria and Cilicia, and even dark Ethiopians, painted Arabs, Bactrians, Scythians, Persians, and Indians, all gay with their national costumes. Alexandria was a spot in which Europe met Asia, and each wondered at the strangeness of the other.

Of the Alexandrians themselves we receive a very unfavourable account from their countryman, Dion Chrysostom. With their wealth, they had those vices which usually follow or cause the loss of national independence. They were eager for nothing but food and horse-races. They were grave and quiet in their sacrifices and listless in business, but in the theatre or in the stadium men, women, and children were alike heated into passion, and overcome with eagerness and warmth of feeling. A scurrilous song or a horse-race would so rouse them into a quarrel that they could not hear for their own noise, nor see for the dust raised by their own bustle in the hippodrome; while all those acts of their rulers, which in a more wholesome state of society would have called for notice, passed by unheeded. They cared more for the tumble of a favourite charioteer than for the sinking state of the nation. The ready employment of

EGYPTIAN WIG (BRITISH MUSEUM).

ridicule in the place of argument, of wit instead of graver reason, of nicknames as their most powerful weapon, was one of the worst points in the Alexandrian character. Frankness and manliness are hardly to be looked for under a despotic government where men are forbidden to speak their minds openly; and the Alexandrians made use of such checks upon their rulers as the law allowed them. They lived under an absolute monarchy tempered only by ridicule. Though their city was four hundred years old, they were still colonists and without a mother-country. They had very little faith in anything great or good, whether human or divine. They had few cherished prejudices, no honoured traditions, sadly little love of fame, and they wrote no histories. But in luxury and delicacy they set the fashion to their conquerors. The wealthy Alexandrian walked about Rome in a scarlet robe, in summer fanning himself with gold, and displaying on his fingers rings carefully suited to the season; as his hands were too delicate to carry his heavier jewels in the warm weather. At the supper tables of the rich, the Alexandrian singing boys were much valued; the smart young Roman walked along the Via Sacra humming an Alexandrian tune; the favourite comic actor, the delight of the city, whose jokes set the theatre in a roar, was an Alexandrian; the Retiarius, who, with no weapon but a net, fought against an armed gladiator in the Roman forum, and came off conqueror in twenty-six such battles, was an Alexandrian; and no breed of fighting-cocks was thought equal to those reared in the suburbs of Alexandria.

In the reign of Augustus the Roman generals had been defeated in their attacks on Arabia; but under Trajan, when the Romans were masters of all the countries which surround Arabia Nabatæa, and when Egypt was so far quiet that the legions could be withdrawn without danger to the provinces, the Arabs could hold out no longer, and the rocky fastness of Petra was forced to receive a Roman garrison. The event was as usual commemorated on the coins of Rome; and for the next four hundred years that remarkable Arab city formed part of the Roman empire; and Europeans now travelling through the desert from Mount Sinai to Jerusalem are agreeably surprised at coming upon temples, carved out of the solid rock, ornamented with Corinthian columns of the age of the Antonines.

In the twelfth year of this reign, when Lucius Sulpicius Simius was prefect, some additions which had been made to the temple at Panopolis in the Thebaid were dedicated in the name of the emperor; and in the nineteenth year, when Marcus Rutilius Lupus was prefect, a new portico in the oasis of Thebes was in the same manner dedicated to Serapis and Isis. A small temple, which had been before built at Denderah, near the great temple of Venus, was in the first year of this reign dedicated to the Empress Plotina, under the name of the great goddess, the Younger Venus.

The canal from the Nile near Bubastis to the Bitter Lakes, which had been first made by Necho, had been either finished or a second time made by Philadelphus; and in this reign that great undertaking was again renewed. But the stream of the Nile was deserting the Bubastite branch, which was less navigable than formerly; and the engineers now changed the greater part of the canal's bed. They thought it wiser to bring water from a higher part of the Nile, so that the current in the canal might run into the Red Sea instead of out, and its waters might still be fresh and useful to agriculture. It now began at Babylon opposite Memphis and entered the Red Sea at a town which, taking its name from the locks, was called Clysmon, about ten miles to the south of Arsinoë. This latter town was no longer a port, having been separated from the sea by the continual advance of the sands. We have no knowledge of how long the care of the imperial prefects kept this new canal open and in use. It was perhaps one of the first of the Roman works that went to decay; and, when we find the Christian pilgrims sailing along it seven centuries later, on their way from England to the holy sepulchre. it had been again opened by the Muhammedan conquerors of Egypt.

ANTONINIAN TEMPLE NEAR SINAI.

Writings which some now regard as literary forgeries appeared in Alexandria about this time. They prophesied the re-establishment of the Jews at Jerusalem, and, as the wished-for time drew near, all the eastern provinces of the Roman empire were disturbed by rebellious risings of the Jews. Moved by the religious enthusiasm which gave birth to the writings, the Jews of Egypt in the eighteenth year of this reign (116 A. D.) were again roused into a quarrel with their Greek fellow-citizens; and in the next year, the last of the reign, they rose against their Roman governors in open rebellion, and they were not put down till the prefect Lupus had brought his forces against them. After this the Jews of Cyrene marched through the desert into Egypt, under the command of Lucuas, to help their brethren; and the rebellion took the regular form of a civil war, with all its usual horrors. The emperor sent against the Jews an army followed by a fleet, which, after numerous skirmishes and battles, routed them with great slaughter, and drove numbers of them back into the desert, whence they harassed the village as robbers. By these unsuccessful appeals to force, the Jews lost all right to those privileges of citizenship which they always claimed, and which had been granted by the emperors, though usually refused by the Alexandrians. The despair and disappointment of the Jews seem in many cases to have turned their minds to the Christian view of the Old Testament prophecies; henceforth, says Eusebius, the Jews embraced the Christian religion more readily and in greater numbers.

In A. D. 122, the sixth year of the reign of Hadrian, Egypt was honoured by a visit from the emperor. He was led to Egypt at that time by some riots of a character more serious than usual, which had arisen between two cities, probably Memphis and Heliopolis, about a bull, as to whether it was to be Apis or Mnevis. Egypt had been for some years without a sacred bull; and when at length the priests found one, marked with the mystic spots, the inhabitants of those two cities flew to arms, and the peace of the province was disturbed by their religious zeal, each claiming the bull as their own.

Hadrian also undertook a voyage up the Nile from Alexandria in order to explore the wonders of Egypt. This was the fashion then, for the ancient monuments and the banks of this mysterious river offered just as many attractions at that time as they have done to all nations since the expedition of Napoleon. That animal-worship, which had remained unchanged for centuries, a riddle of human religion, was bound to excite the curiosity of strangers. In this divinisation of animals lay the greatest contempt for human understanding, and it was a bitter satire on the apotheosis of kings and emperors. For what was the divinity of Sesostris, of Alexander, of Augustus, or Hadrian compared with the heavenly majesty of the ox Apis, or the holy cats, dogs, kites, crocodiles, and god-apes? Egypt was at this epoch already a museum of the Pharaoh-time and its enbalsamed culture. Strange buildings, rare sculptures, hieroglyphics, and pictures still filled the ancient towns, even though these had lost their splendour. Memphis and Heliopolis, Bubastis, Abydos, Saïs, Tanis, and the hundred-gated Thebes had long fallen into ruin, although still inhabited.

The emperor's escort must have been an extraordinary sight as it steered up the stream on a fleet of dahabiehs. The emperor was accompanied by students of the museum, interpreters, priests, and astrologers. Amongst his followers were Verus and the beautiful Antinous.

The Empress Sabina also accompanied him; she had the poetess Julia Balbilla amongst her court ladies. They landed wherever there was anything of interest to be seen, and there was more in those days than there is now. They admired the great pyramids, the colossal sphinx, and the sacred town of Memphis. This city, the ancient royal seat of the Pharaohs, and even in Strabo's time the second town in Egypt, was not yet buried under the sand of the desert; its disappearance had, however, already begun. Under the Ptolemies it had given much of the material of her temples and palaces for the building of Alexandria. The great palace of the Pharaohs had long been destroyed, but there still remained many notable monuments, such as the temple of Phtah, the pyramids, the necropolis, and the Serapeum, and they retained their ancient cult. The town was still the chief seat of the Egyptian hierarchy and the residence of Apis; for this very reason the Roman government had destined it to be one of her strong military stations, for here a legion was quartered. The emperor could walk through the time-worn avenues of sphinxes which led to the wonderful vaults where the long succession of divine animals was buried, each like a Pharaoh, in a magnificent granite sarcophagus. Hadrian could admire the beautifully sculptured tomb of Di, an Egyptian officer of the fifth dynasty, with less trouble than we must experience now; for now the palaces, the pictures of the gods, and almost all the pyramids are swallowed up in sand. Miserable Arab villages, such as Saqqâra, have fixed themselves in the ruins of Memphis, and from a thick palm grove one can look with astonishment upon the torso of the powerful Ramses II. lying solitary there, the last witness to the glory of the temple of Phtah, before which this colossus once had its stand. In the neighbourhood of Memphis lay Heliopolis, the town of the sun-god, with its ancient temple, and a school of Egyptian wisdom, in which Plato is supposed to have studied.

In Heliopolis the worship of the god Ra was preserved, the centre of which was the holy animal Mnevis, a rival or comrade of Apis. Cambyses had partly destroyed the temple and even the obelisks which the Pharaohs had in the course of centuries erected to the sun-god; nowhere in Egypt existed so many of these monuments as here and in Thebes. Hadrian saw many of them lying half-burnt on the ground just as Strabo had done. On the site of Heliopolis, now green with wheat-fields, only a single obelisk has remained upright, which is considered as the oldest of all, and was erected in the twelfth dynasty by Ûsirtasen I.

The royal assemblage had arrived in the course of their journey at Besa, a place on the right bank of the river, opposite Hermopolis, when a strange event occurred. This was the death of Hadrian's favourite, Antinous, a young Greek from Claudiopolis, who had been degraded to the position of Ganymede to the emperor on account of his beauty. It is not known where the emperor first came across the youth; possibly in his native land, Bithynia. Not till he came to Egypt did he become his inseparable companion, and this must have been a deep offence to his wife. The unfortunate queen was delivered in Besa from his hated presence, for Antinous was drowned there in the Nile.

His death was surrounded by mystery. Was it accident? Was he a victim? Hadrian's humanity protects him from the suspicion that he sacrificed his victim in cold blood, as Tiberius had once sacrificed the beautiful Hypatus in Capri. Had the fantastic youth sacrificed himself of his own free will to the death divinities in order to save the emperor's life? Had the Egyptian priests foreseen in the stars some danger threatening Hadrian, only to be averted by the death of his favourite? Such an idea commended itself to the superstition of the time, especially in this land and by the mysterious Nile. It corresponded, too, with the emperor's astrological arts. Was Antinous certain when he plunged into the waves of the Nile that he would arise from them as a god? Hadrian asserts in his memoirs that it was an accident, but no one believed him. The divine honours which he paid to the dead youth lead us to suppose that they formed the reward of a self-sacrifice, which, according to the custom of those times, constituted a highly moral action, and was looked upon as heroic devotion. At any rate, we will assume that this sacrifice sank into the Nile without Hadrian's will. Hadrian mourned for Antinous with unspeakable pain and "womanly tears." Now he was Achilles by the corpse of Patroklus, or Alexander by the pyre of the dead Hephaistus. He had the youth splendidly buried in Besa. This most extraordinary intermezzo of all Nile journeys supplied dying heathendom with a new god, and art with its last ideal form. Probably, also, during the burial, far-sighted courtiers already saw the star of Antinous shining in Egypt's midnight sky, and then Hadrian saw it himself.

In the mystical land of Egypt, life might still be poetical even in the clear daylight of Roman universal history in the reign of Hadrian. The death of the young Bithynian seems to have occurred in October, 130. The emperor continued his journey as soon as he had given orders for a splendid town to be erected on the site of

COMMEMORATIVE COIN OF ANTINOUS.

Besa, in honour of his friend. In November, 130, the royal company is to be found amongst the ruins of Thebes.

Thebes, the oldest town in Egypt, had been first put in the shade by Memphis, and then destroyed by Cambyses. Since the time of the Ptolemies, it had been called Diospolis, and Ptolemais had taken its place as capital of the Thebaid. Already in Strabo's time it was split up. It formed on either side of the Nile groups of gigantic temples and palaces, monuments, and royal graves similar to those scattered to-day amongst Luxor, Karnak, Medinet-Habu, Deir-el-Bahari, and Kurna.

In Hadrian's time the Rameseum, the so-called grave of Osymandias, on the western bank of the Nile, the wonderful building of Ramses II., must still have been in good repair. These pylons, pillars, arcades, and courts, these splendid halls with their sculpture-covered walls, appear even to have influenced the Roman art in the time of the emperors. Their reflex influence has been even seen in Trajan's forum, in which the chief thing was the emperor's tomb.

In Alexandria the emperor mixed freely with the professors of the museum, asking them questions and answering theirs in return; and he dropped his tear of pity on the tomb of the great Pompey, in the form of a Greek epigram, though with very little point. He laid out large sums of money in building and ornamenting the city, and the Alexandrians were much pleased with his behaviour. Among other honours that they paid him, they changed the name of the month December, calling it the month Hadrian; but as they were not followed by the rest of the empire the name soon went out of use. The emperor's patronage of philosophy was rather at the cost of the Alexandrian museum, for he enrolled among its paid professors men who were teaching from school to school in Italy and Asia Minor. Thus Polemon of Laodicea, who taught oratory and philosophy at Rome, Laodicea, and Smyrna, and had the right of a free passage for himself and his servants in any of the public ships whenever he chose to move from city to city for the purposes of study or teaching, had at the same time a salary from the Alexandrian museum. Dionysius of Miletus also received his salary as a professor in the museum while teaching philosophy and mnemonics at Miletus and Ephesus. Pancrates, the Alexandrian poet, gained his salary in the museum by the easy task of a little flattery. On Hadrian's return to Alexandria from the Thebaid, the poet presented to him a rose-coloured lotus, a flower well known in India, though less common in Egypt than either the blue or white lotus, and assured him that it had sprung out of the blood of the lion slain by his royal javelin at a lion-hunt in Libya. The emperor was pleased with the compliment, and gave him a place in the museum; and Pancrates in return named the plant the lotus of Antinous. Pancrates was a warm admirer of the mystical opinions of the Egyptians which were then coming into note in Alexandria. He was said to have lived underground in holy solitude or converse with the gods for twenty-three years, and during that time to have been taught magic by the goddess Isis, and thus to have gained the power of working miracles. He learned to call upon the queen of darkness by her Egyptian name Hecate, and when driving out evil spirits to speak to them in the Egyptian language. Whether these Greek students of the Eastern mysticism were deceivers or deceived, whether they were led by a love of notoriety or of knowledge, is in most cases doubtful, but they were surrounded by a crowd of credulous admirers, who

ROSE - COLOURED LOTUS.

formed a strange contrast with the sceptics and critics of the museum.

Among the Alexandrian grammarians of this reign was Apollonius Dyscolus, so called perhaps from a moroseness of manner, who wrote largely on rhetoric, on the Greek dialects, on accents, prosody, and on other branches of grammar. In the few pages that remain of his numerous writings, we trace the love of the marvellous which was then growing among some of the philosophers. He tells us many remarkable stories, which he collected rather as a judicious inquirer than as a credulous believer; such as of second sight; an account of a lad who fell asleep in the field while watching his sheep, and then slept for fifty-seven years, and awoke to wonder at the strangeness of the changes that had taken place in the meanwhile; and of a man who after death used from time to time to leave his body, and wander over the earth as a spirit, till his wife, tired of his coming back again so often, put a stop to it by having his mummy burnt. He gives us for the first time Eastern tales in a Greek dress, and we thus learn the source from which Europe gained much of its literature in the Middle Ages. The Alexandrian author of greatest note at this time was the historian Appian, who tells us that he had spent some years in Rome practising as a lawyer, and returned to Egypt on being appointed to a high post in the government of his native city. There he wrote his Roman history.

In this reign the Jews, forgetful of what they had just suffered under Trajan, again rose against the power of

Rome; and, when Judæa rebelled against its prefect, Tinnius Rufus, a little army of Jews marched out of Egypt and Libya, to help their brethren and to free the holy land (130 A. D.). But they were everywhere routed and put down with resolute slaughter.

Travellers, on reaching a distant point of a journey,

VOCAL STATUE OF AMENHOTHES.

or on viewing any remarkable object of their curiosity, have at all times been fond of carving or scribbling their names on the spot, to boast of their prowess to after-comers; and never had any place been more favoured with memorials of this kind than the great statue of Amenhôthes at Thebes. This colossal statue, fifty-three feet high, was famed, as long as the Egyptian priesthood lasted, for sending forth musical sounds every morning at sunrise, when first touched by the sun's rays; and no traveller ever visited Thebes without listening for these remarkable notes. The journey through Upper Egypt was at this time perfectly open and safe, and the legs and feet of the statue are covered with names, and inscriptions in prose and verse, of travellers who had visited it at sunrise during the reigns of Hadrian and the Antonines. From these curious memorials we learn that Hadrian visited Thebes a second time with his queen, Sabina, in the fifteenth year of his reign. When the empress first visited the statue she was disappointed at not hearing the musical sounds; but, on her hinting threats of the emperor's displeasure, her curiosity was gratified on the following morning. This gigantic statue of hard gritstone had formerly been broken in half across the waist, and the upper part thrown to the ground, either by the shock of an earthquake or the ruder shock of Persian zeal against the Egyptian religion; and for some centuries past the musical notes had issued from the broken fragments. Such was its fallen state when the Empress Sabina saw it, and when Strabo and Juvenal and Pausanias listened to its sounds; and it was not till after the reign of Hadrian that it was again raised upright like its companion, as travellers now see it.

From this second visit, and a longer acquaintance, Hadrian seems to have formed a very poor opinion of the Egyptians and Egyptian Jews; and the following curious letter, written in 134 A. D. to his friend Servianus, throws much light upon their religion as worshippers of Serapis, at the same time that it proves how numerous the Christians had become in Alexandria, even within

The Slumber Song

From the painting by P. Grot. Johann

Grotjohann Dssldf. 88

seventy years of the period during which the evangelist Mark is believed to have preached there:

"Hadrian Augustus to Servianus, the consul, greeting:

"As for Egypt, which you were praising to me, dearest Servianus, I have found its people wholly light, wavering, and flying after every breath of a report. Those who worship Serapis are Christians, and those who call themselves bishops of Christ are devoted to Serapis. There is no ruler of a Jewish synagogue, no Samaritan, no presbyter of the Christians, who is not a mathematician, an augur, and a soothsayer. The very patriarch himself, when he came into Egypt, was by some said to worship Serapis, and by others to worship Christ. As a race of men, they are seditious, vain, and spiteful; as a body, wealthy and prosperous, of whom nobody lives in idleness. Some blow glass, some make paper, and others linen. There is work for the lame and work for the blind; even those who have lost the use of their hands do not live in idleness. Their one god is nothing; Christians, Jews, and all nations worship him. I wish this body of men was better behaved, and worthy of their number; for as for that they ought to hold the chief place in Egypt. I have granted everything unto them; I have restored their old privileges, and have made them grateful by adding new ones."

Among the crowd of gods that had formerly been worshipped in Egypt, Serapis had latterly been rising above the rest. He was the god of the dead, who in the next world was to reward the good and punish the wicked; and in the growing worship of this one all-seeing judge we cannot but trace the downfall of some of the evils of polytheism. A plurality in unity was another method now used to explain away the polytheism. The oracle when consulted about the divine nature had answered, "I am Ra, and Horus, and Osiris;" or, as the Greeks translated it, Apollo, and Lord, and Bacchus; "I rule the hours and the seasons, the wind and the storms, the day and the night; I am king of the stars and myself an immortal fire." Hence arose the opinion which seems to have been given to Hadrian, that the Egyptians had only one god, and his mistake in thinking that the worshippers of Serapis were Christians. The emperor, indeed, himself, though a polytheist, was very little of an idolater; for, though he wished to add Christ to the number of the Roman gods, he on the other hand ordered that the temples built in his reign should have no images for worship; and in after ages it was common to call all temples without statues Hadrian's temples. But there were other and stronger reasons for Hadrian's classing the Christians with the Egyptian astrologers. A Christian heresy was then rising into notice in Egypt in that very form, taking its opinions from the philosophy on which it was engrafted. Before Christianity was

EGYPTIAN ORACLE.

preached in Alexandria, there were already three religions or forms of philosophy belonging to the three races of men who peopled that busy city; first, the Greek philosophy, which was chiefly platonism; secondly, the mysticism of the Egyptians; and lastly, the religion of the Jews. These were often more or less mixed, as we see them all united in the works of Philo-Judæus; and in the writings of the early converts we usually find Christianity clothed in one or other of these forms, according to the opinions held by the writers before their conversion. The first Christian teachers, the apostolic fathers as they are called, because they had been hearers of the apostles themselves, were mostly Jews; but among the Egyptians and Greeks of Alexandria their religion lost much of its purely moral caste, and became, with the former, an astrological mysticism, and with the latter an abstract speculative theology. It is of the Egyptian Jews that Hadrian speaks in his letter just quoted; many of them had been already converted to Christianity, and their religion had taken the form of Gnosticism.

Gnosticism, or Science, for the name means no more, was not then new in Alexandria, nor were its followers originally Christians. It was the proud name claimed for their opinions by those who studied the Eastern philosophy of the Magi; and Egypt seems to have been as much its native soil as India. The name of Gnostic, says Weber, was generally given to those who distinguished between belief on authority and gnosis, *i. e.*, between the ordinary comprehension and a higher knowledge only granted to a few gifted or chosen ones. They were split up into different sects, according as they approached more nearly the Eastern theosophy or the platonic philosophy; but in general the Eastern conception, with its symbols and unlimited fantasy, remained dominant. The " creed of those who know " never reached actual monotheism, the conception of one personal god, who created everything according to his own free will and rules over everything with unlimited wisdom and love. The god of the Gnostics is a dark, mysterious being which can only arrive at a consciousness of itself through a manifold descending scale of forces, which flow from the god himself. The visible world was created out of dead and evil matter by Demiurgos, the divine workmaster, a production and subordinate of the highest god. Man, too, is a production of this subordinate creator, a production subject to a blind fate, and a prey to those powers which rule between heaven and earth, without free-will, the only thing which makes the ideas of sin and responsibility possible. Matter is the seat of evil, and as long as man stands under the influence of this matter, he is in the hands of evil and knows no freedom. Redemption can only reach him through those higher beings of light, which free man from the power of matter and translate him into the kingdom of light. According to the Gnostic teaching, Christ is one of these beings of light; he is one of the highest who appeared on earth, and is transformed into a mythical, allegorical being, with his human nature, his sufferings and death completely suppressed. The redeemed soul is then as a kind of angel, or ideal being, brought in triumph into the idealistic realm of light as soon as it has purified itself to the nature of a spirit, by means of penitence, chastisements, and finally the death of the physical body. Hence the Gnostics attached little importance to the means of mercy in the Church, to the Bible, or the sacraments; they allowed the Church teaching to exist as a necessary conception for the people, but they placed their own teachings far above it as mysterious or secret teachings. As regards their morals and mode of life, the Gnostics generally went to extremes. It was due to Gnosticism that art and science found an entrance into the Church. It preserved the Church from becoming stereotyped in form; but, built up entirely on ideas and not on historical facts, it died from its own hollowness and eccentricity.

We still possess the traces of the Gnostic astrology in a number of amulets and engraved gems, with the word *Abraxas* or rather *Abrasax* and other emblems of their superstition, which they kept as charms against diseases and evil spirits. The word *Abra-sax* may be translated *Hurt me not.* To their mystic rites we may trace many of the reproaches thrown upon Christianity, such as that the Christians worshipped the head of an ass, using the animal's Koptic name *Eeo*, to represent the name of ΙΑΩ, or Jahveh. To the same source we may also trace some of the peculiarities of the Christian fathers, such as St. Ambrose calling Jesus "the good scarabæus, who rolled up before him the hitherto unshapen mud of our bodies;" a thought which seems to have been borrowed as much from the hieroglyphics as from the insect's habits; and perhaps from the Egyptian priests in some cases, using the scarabæus to denote the god Horus-Ra, and sometimes the word *only-begotten.* We trace this thought on the Gnostic gems where we see a winged griffin rolling before him a wheel, the emblem of eternity. He sits like a conqueror on horseback, trampling under foot the serpent of old, the spirit of sin and death. His horse is in the form of a ram, with an eagle's head and the crowned asp or basilisk for its tail. Before him stands the figure of victory giving him a crown; above are written the words Alpha and Omega, and below perhaps the word ΙΑΩ, Jahveh.

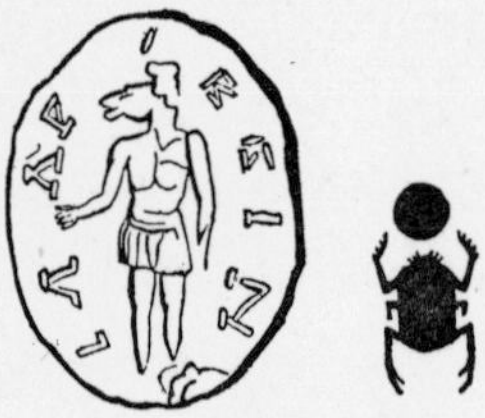

KOPTIC CHARM AND SCARABÆUS.

So far we have seen the form which Christianity at first took among the Egyptians; but, as few writings by these Gnostics have come down to our time, we chiefly know their opinions from the reproaches of their enemies. It was not till the second generation of Gnostic teachers were spreading their heresies that the Greek philosophers began to embrace Christianity, or the Christians to study Greek literature; but as soon as that was the case we have an unbroken chain of writings, in which we find Christianity more or less mixed with the Alexandrian form of platonism.

The philosopher Justin, after those who had talked with the apostles, is the earliest Christian writer whose works have reached us. He was a Greek, born in Samaria; but he studied many years in Alexandria under philosophers of all opinions. He did not, however, at once find in the schools the wisdom he was in search for. The Stoic could teach him nothing about God; the Peripatetic wished to be paid for his lessons before he gave them; and the Pythagorean proposed to begin with music and mathematics. Not content with these, Justin turned to the platonist, whose purer philosophy seemed to add wings to his thoughts, and taught him to mount aloft towards true wisdom. While turning over in his mind what he had thus learned in the several schools, dissatisfied with the philosopher's views, he chanced one day to meet with an old man walking on the seashore near Alexandria, to whom he unbosomed his thoughts, and by whom he was converted to Christianity.

Justin tells us that there were no people, whether Greeks or barbarians, or even dwellers in tent and waggons, among whom prayers were not offered up to the heavenly father in the name of the crucified Jesus. The Christians met every Sunday for public worship, which began with a reading from the prophets, or from the memoirs of the apostles called the gospels. This was followed by a sermon, a prayer, the bread and wine, and a second prayer. Justin's quotations prove that he is speaking of the New Testament, which within a hundred years of the crucifixion was read in all the principal cities in which Greek was spoken. Justin died as a martyr in 163 A. D.

GNOSTIC GEM.

The platonic professorship in Alexandria had usually been held by an Athenian, and for a short time Athenagoras of Athens taught that branch of philosophy in the museum; but he afterwards embraced the Christian religion, and then taught Christianity openly in Alexandria. He enjoys with Justin the honour of being one of the first men of learning who were converted, and, like Justin, his chief work is an apology for the Christians, addressed to the emperor, Marcus Aurelius. Athenagoras confines himself in his defence to the resurrec-

GEMS SHOWING SYMBOL OF DEATH AND THE WORD ΙΑΩ (JAVEH).

tion from the dead and the unity of the Deity, the points chiefly attacked by the pagans.

Hadrian's Egyptian coins are remarkable both for number and variety. In the sixth year of the reign we see a ship with spread sails, most likely in gratitude for the emperor's safe arrival in Egypt. In the eighth year we see the head of the favourite Antinous, who had been placed among the gods of the country. In the eleventh year, when the emperor took up the tribunitial power at Rome for a second period of ten years, we find a series of coins, each bearing the name of the nome or district in which it was coined. This indeed is the most remarkable year of the most remarkable reign in the whole history of coinage; we have numerous coins for every year of this reign, and, in this year, for nearly every nome in Egypt. Some coins are strongly marked with the favourite opinion of the Gnostics as to the opposition between good and evil. On one we have the war between the serpent of good and the serpent of evil,

HADRIAN'S EGYPTIAN COINS.

distinguished by their different forms and by the emblems of Isis and Serapis; on others the heads of Isis and Serapis, the principles of love and fear; while on a third these two are united into a trinity by Horus, who is standing on an eagle instead of having an eagle's head, as represented on previous coins.

The beginning of the reign of Antoninus Pius (A. D. 138) was remarkable as being the end of the Sothic period of one thousand four hundred and sixty years; the movable new year's day of the calendar had come round to the place in the natural year from which it first began to move in the reign of Menophres or Thûtmosis III.; it had come round to the day when the dog-star rose heliacally. If the years had been counted from the beginning of this great year, there could have been no doubt when it came to an end, as from the want of a leap year the new year's day must have been always moving one day in four years; but no satisfactory reckoning of the years had been kept, and, as the end of the period was only known by observation, there was some little doubt about the exact year. Indeed, among the Greek astronomers, Dositheus said the dog-star rises heliacally twenty-three days after midsummer, Meton twenty-eight days, and Euctemon thirty-one days; they thus left a doubt of thirty-two years as to when the period should end, but the statesmen placed it in the first year of the reign of Antoninus. This end of the Sothic period was called the return to the phœnix, and had been looked forward to by the Egyptians for many years, and is well marked on the coins of this reign. The coins for the first eight years teem with astronomy. There are several with the goddess Isis in a boat, which we know, from the zodiac in the Memnonium at Thebes, was meant for the heliacal rising of the dog-star. In the second and in the sixth year we find on the coins the remarkable word AION, *the age* or *period*, and an ibis with a glory of rays round its head, meant for the bird phœnix. In the seventh year we see Orpheus playing on his lyre while all the animals of the forest are listening, thus pointing out the return of the golden age. In the eighth year we have the head of

Serapis circled by the seven planets, and the whole within the twelve signs of the zodiac; and on another coin we have the sun and moon within the signs of the zodiac. A series of twelve coins for the same year tells us that the house of the sun, in the language of the astrologers, is in the lion, that of the moon in the crab, the houses of Venus in the scales and the bull, those of Mars in the scorpion and the ram, those of Jupiter in the archer and the fishes, those of Saturn in the sea-goat and aquarius, those of Mercury in the virgin and the twins. On the coins of the same year we have the eagle and thunder-bolt, the sphinx, the bull Apis, the Nile and crocodile, Isis nursing the child Horus, the hawk-headed Aroëris, and the winged sun. On coins of other years we have a camelopard, Horus sitting on the lotus-flower, and a sacrifice to Isis, which was celebrated on the last day of the year.

The coins also tell us of the bountiful overflow of the Nile, and of the goodness of the harvests that followed; thus, in the ninth, tenth, thirteenth, and seventeenth years, we see the river Nile in the form of an old man leaning on a crocodile, pouring corn and fruit out of a cornucopia, while a child by his side, with the figures 16, tells us that in those years the waters of the Nile rose at Memphis to the wished-for height of sixteen cubits. From these latter coins it would seem that but little change had taken place in the soil of the Delta by the yearly deposit of mud; Herodotus says that sixteen cubits was the wished-for rise of the Nile at Memphis when he was there. And we should almost think that the seasons were more favourable to the husbandman during the reign of an Antonine than of a Caligula, did we not set it down to the canals being better cleansed by the care of the prefect, and to the mildness of the government leaving the people at liberty to enjoy the bounties of nature, and at the same time making them more grateful in acknowledging them.

The mystic emblems on the coins are only what we

COINS OF ANTONINUS PIUS.

might look for from the spread of the Gnostic opinions, and the eagerness with which the Greeks were copying the superstitions of the Egyptians; and, while astrology was thus countenanced by the state, of course it was not less followed by the people. The poor Jews took to it as a trade. In Alexandria the Jewess, half beggar, half fortune-teller, would stop people in the streets and interpret dreams by the help of the Bible, or sit under a sacred tree like a sibyl, and promise wealth to those who consulted her, duly proportioned to the size of the coin by which she was paid. We find among the Theban ruins pieces of papyrus with inscriptions, describing the positions of the heavens at particular hours in this reign, for the astrologers therewith to calculate the nativities of the persons then born. On one is a complete horoscope, containing the places of the sun, moon, and every planet, noted down on the zodiac in degrees and minutes of a degree; and with these particulars the mathematician undertook to foretell the marriage, fortune, and death of the person who had been born at the instant when the heavenly bodies were so situated; and, as the horoscope was buried in the tomb with the mummy, we must suppose that it was thought that the prognostication would hold good even in the next world.

But astrology was not the only end to which mathematics were then turned. Claudius Ptolemy, the astronomer and geographer, was at that time the ornament of the mathematical school of Alexandria. In his writings he treats of the earth as the centre of the heavens, and the sun, moon, and planets as moving in circles and epicycles round it. This had been the opinion of some of the early astronomers; but since this theory of the heavens received the stamp of his authority, it is now always called the Ptolemaic system.

In this reign was made a new survey of all the military roads in the Roman empire, called the *Itinerary of Antoninus*. It included the great roads of Egypt, which were only six in number. One was from Contra-Pselcis in Nubia along the east bank of the Nile, to Babylon opposite Memphis, and there turning eastward through

Heliopolis and the district of the Jews to Clysmon, where Trajan's canal entered the Red Sea. A second, from Memphis to Pelusium, made use of this for about thirty miles, joining it at Babylon, and leaving it at Scenæ Veteranorum. By these two roads a traveller could go from Pelusium to the head of the Red Sea; but there was a shorter road through the desert which joined the first at Serapion, about fifty miles from Clysmon, instead of at Scenæ Veteranorum, which was therefore about a hundred miles shorter. A fourth was along the west bank of the Nile from Hiera Sycaminon in Nubia to Alexandria, leaving the river at Andropolis, about sixty miles from the latter city. A fifth was from Palestine to Alexandria, running along the coast of the Mediterranean from Raphia to Pelusium, and thence, leaving the coast to avoid the flat country, which was under water during the inundation; it joined the last at Andropolis. The sixth road was from Koptos on the Nile to Berenicê on the Red Sea. These six were probably the only roads under the care of the prefect. Though Syênê was the boundary of the province of Egypt, the Roman power was felt for about one hundred miles into Nubia, and we find the names of the emperors on several temples between Syênê and Hiera Sycaminon. But beyond this, though we find inscriptions left by Roman travellers, the emperors seem never to have aimed at making military roads, or holding any cities against the inroads of the Blemmyes and other Arabs.

To this survey we must add the valuable geographical knowledge given by Arrian in his voyage round the shores of the Red Sea, which has come down to us in an interesting document, wherein he mentions the several seaports and their distances, with the tribes and cities near the coast. The trade of Egypt to India, Ethiopia, and Arabia was then most valuable, and carried on with great activity; but, as the merchandise was in each case carried only for short distances from city to city, the traveller could gain but little knowledge of where it came from, or even sometimes of where it was going. The Egyptians sent coarse linen, glass bottles, brazen vessels,

STATUE OF THE NILE.

brass for money, and iron for weapons of war and hunting; and they received back ivory, rhinoceros' teeth, Indian steel, Indian ink, silks, slaves, tortoise-shell, myrrh, and other scents, with many other Eastern articles of high price and little weight. The presents which the merchants made to the petty kings of Arabia were chiefly horses, mules, and gold and silver vases. Beside this, the ports on the Red Sea carried on a brisk trade among themselves in grain, expressed oil, wicker boats, and sugar. Of sugar, or honey from the cane, this is perhaps the earliest mention found in history; but Arrian does not speak of the sugar-cane as then new, nor does he tell us where it was grown. Had sugar been then seen for the first time he would certainly have said so; it must have been an article well known in the Indian trade. While passing through Egypt on his travels, or while living there and holding some post under the prefect, the historian Arrian has left us his name and a few lines of poetry carved on the foot of the great sphinx near the pyramids.

At this time also the travellers continued to carve their names and their feelings of wonder on the foot of the musical statue at Thebes and in the deep empty tombs of the Theban kings. These inscriptions are full of curious information. For example, it has been doubted whether the Roman army was provided with medical officers. Their writers have not mentioned them. But part of the Second Legion was at this time stationed at Thebes; and one Asclepiades, while cutting his name in a tomb which once held some old Theban, has cleared up the doubt for us, by saying that he was physician to the Second Legion.

Antoninus made a hippodrome, or race-course, for the amusement of the citizens of Alexandria, and built two gates to the city, called the gate of the sun and the gate of the moon, the former fronting the harbour and the latter fronting the lake Mareotis, and joined by the great street which ran across the whole width of the city. But this reign was not wholly without trouble; there was a rebellion in which the prefect Dinarchus lost his life, and for which the Alexandrians were severely punished by the emperor.

The coins of Marcus Aurelius, the successor of Antoninus Pius, have a rich variety of subjects, falling not far short of those of the last reign. On those of the fifth year, the bountiful overflow of the Nile is gratefully acknowledged by the figure of the god holding a cornucopia, and a troop of sixteen children playing round him. It had been not unusual in hieroglyphical writing to express a thought by means of a figure which in the Koptic language had nearly the same sound; and we have seen this copied on the coins in the case of a Greek word, when the bird phœnix was used for the palm-

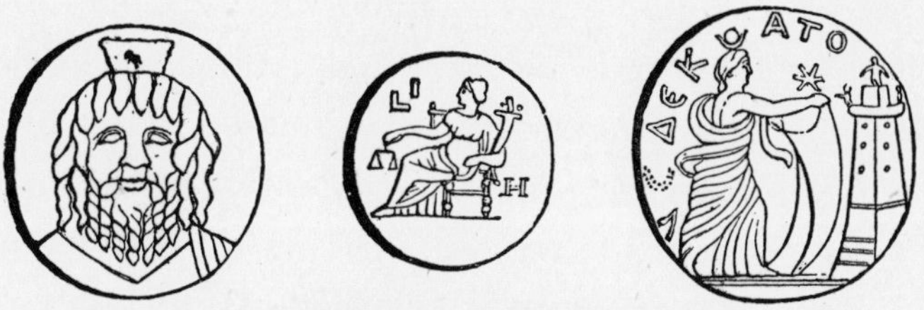

COINS OF MARCUS AURELIUS.

branch phœnix, or the hieroglyphical word *year;* and a striking instance may be noticed in the case of a Latin word, as the sixteen children or *cupids* mean sixteen *cubits*, the wished-for height of the Nile's overflow. The statue of the Nile, which had been carried by Vespasian to Rome and placed in the temple of Peace, was surrounded by the same sixteen children. On the coins of his twelfth year the sail held up by the goddess Isis is blown towards the Pharos lighthouse, as if in that year the emperor had been expected in Alexandria.

We find no coins in the eleventh or fourteenth years of this reign, which makes it probable that it was in the eleventh year (A. D. 172) that the rebellion of the native soldiers took place. These were very likely Arabs who had been admitted into the ranks of the legions, but having withdrawn to the desert they now harassed the towns with their marauding inroads, and a considerable time elapsed before they were wholly put down by Avidius Cassius at the head of the legions. But Cassius himself was unable to resist the temptations which always beset a successful general, and after this victory he allowed himself to be declared emperor by the legions of Egypt; and this seems to have been the cause of no coins being struck in Alexandria in the fourteenth year of the reign. Cassius left his son Mæcianus in Alexandria with the title of Pretorian Prefect, while he himself marched into Syria to secure that province. There the legions followed the example of their brethren in Egypt, and the Syrians were glad to acknowledge a general of the Eastern armies as their sovereign. But on Marcus leading an army into Syria he was met with the news that the rebels had repented, and had put Cassius to death, and he then moved his forces towards Egypt; but before his arrival the Egyptian legions had in the same manner put Mæcianus to death, and all had returned to their allegiance.

When Marcus arrived in Alexandria the citizens were agreeably surprised by the mildness of his conduct. He at once forgave his enemies; and no offenders were put to death for having joined in the rebellion. The severest punishment, even to the children of Cassius, was banishment from the province, but without restraint, and with the forfeiture of less than half their patrimony. In Alexandria the emperor laid aside the severity of the soldier, and mingled with the people as a fellow-citizen in the temples and public places; while with the professors in the museum he was a philosopher, joining them in their studies in the schools.

Rome and Athens at this time alike looked upon Alexandria as the centre of the world's learning. The library was then in its greatest glory; the readers were numerous, and Christianity had as yet raised no doubts about the value of its pagan treasures. All the wisdom of Greece, written on rolls of brittle papyrus or tough parchment, was ranged in boxes on the shelves. Of these writings the few that have been saved from the wreck of time are no doubt some of the best, and they are perhaps enough to guide our less simple taste towards the unornamented grace of the Greek model. But we often fancy those treasures most valuable that are beyond our reach, and hence when we run over the names of the authors in this library we think perhaps too much of those which are now missing. The student in the museum could have read the lyric poems of Alcæus and Stersichorus, which in matter and style were excellent enough to be judged not quite so good as Homer; the tender lamentations of Simonides; the warm breathings of Sappho, the tenth muse; the pithy iambics of Archilochus, full of noble flights and brave irregularities; the comedies of Menander, containing every kind of excellence; those of Eupolis and Cratinus, which were equal to Aristophanes; the histories of Theopompus, which in the speeches were as good as Thucydides; the lively, agreeable orations of Hyperides, the accuser of Demosthenes; with the books of travels, chronologies, and countless others of less merit for style and genius, but which, if they had been saved, would not have left Egypt wholly without a history.

The trade of writing and making copies of the old authors employed a great many hands in the neighbourhood of the museum. Two kinds of handwriting were in use. One was a running hand, with the letters joined

ALEXANDRIAN FORMS OF WRITING.

together in rather a slovenly manner; and the other a neat, regular hand, with the letters square and larger, written more slowly but read more easily. Those that wrote the first were called *quick-writers*, those that wrote the second were called *book-writers*. If an author was not skilled in the use of the pen, he employed a *quick-writer* to write down his words as he delivered them. But in order that his work might be published it was handed over to the *book-writers* to be copied out more neatly; and numbers of young women, skilled in penmanship, were employed in the trade of copying books for sale. For this purpose parchment was coming into use, though the old papyrus was still used, as an inexpensive though less lasting writing material.

Athenæus, if we may judge from his writings, was then the brightest of the Alexandrian wits and men of learning. We learn from his own pages that he was born at Naucratis, and was the friend of Pancrates, who lived under Hadrian, and also of Oppian, who died in the reign of Caracalla. His *Deipnosophist*, or table-talk of the philosophers, is a large work full of pleasing anecdotes and curious information, gathered from comic writers and authors without number that have long since been lost. But it is put together with very little skill. His industry and memory are more remarkable than his judgment or good taste; and the table-talk is too often turned towards eating and drinking. His amusing work is a picture of society in Alexandria, where everything frivolous was treated as grave, and everything serious was laughed at. The wit sinks into scandal, the humour is at the cost of morality, and the numerous quotations are chosen for their point, not for any lofty thoughts or noble feeling. Alexandria was then as much the seat of literary wit as it was of dry criticism; and Martial, the lively author of the *Epigrams*, had fifty years before remarked that there were few places in the world where he would more wish his verses to be repeated than on the banks of the Nile.

Nothing could be lower than the poetic taste in Alexandria at this time. The museum was giving birth to a race of poets who, instead of bringing forth thoughts out of their own minds, found them in the storehouse of the memory only. They wrote their patchwork poems by the help of Homer's lines, which they picked from all parts of the Iliad and Odyssey and so put together as to make them tell a new tale. They called themselves Homeric poets.

A SNAKE-CHARMER.

Lucian, the author of the *Dialogues*, was at that time secretary to the prefect of Egypt, and this philosopher found a broad mark for his humour in the religion of the Egyptians, their worship of animals and water-jars, their love of magic, the general mourning through the land on the death of the bull Apis, their funeral ceremonies, their placing of their mummies round the dinner-table as so many guests, and pawning a father or a brother when in want of money. So little had the customs changed that the young Egyptians of high birth still wore their long hair tied in one lock, and hanging over the right ear, as we see on the Theban sculptures fifteen centuries earlier. It was then a mark of royalty, but had since been adopted by many families of high rank, and continues to be used even in the twentieth century.

Before the end of this reign we meet with a strong proof of the spread of Christianity in Egypt. The number of believers made it necessary for the Bishop of Alexandria to appoint three bishops under him, to look after the churches in three other cities; and accordingly Demetrius, who then held that office, took upon himself the rank, if not the name, of Patriarch of Alexandria. A second proof of the spread of Christianity is the pagan philosophers thinking it necessary to write against it. Celsus, an Epicurean of Alexandria, was one of the first to attack it. Origen answered the several arguments of Celsus with skill and candour. He challenges his readers to a comparison between the Christians and pagans in point of morals, in Alexandria or in any other city. He argues in the most forcible way that Christianity had overcome all difficulties, and had spread itself far and wide against the power of kings and emperors, and he says that nobody but a Christian ever died a martyr to the truth of his religion. He makes good use of the Jewish prophecies; but he brings forward no proofs in support of the truth of the gospel history; they were not wanted,

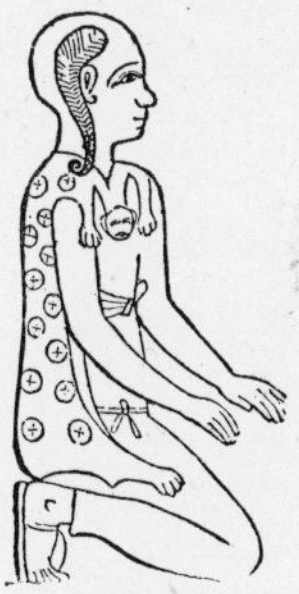

THE SIGN OF NOBILITY.

as Celsus and the pagans had not considered it necessary to call it into question.

Another proof of the number of Egyptian Christians is seen in the literary frauds of which their writers were guilty, most likely to satisfy the minds of those pagan converts that they had already made rather than from a wish to make new believers. About this time was written by an unknown Christian author a poem in eight books, named the *Sibylline Verses* which must not be mistaken for the pagan fragments of the same name. It is written in the form of a prophecy, in the style used by the Gnostics, and is full of dark sentences and half-expressed hints.

Another spurious Christian work of about the same time is the *Clementina*, or the *Recognitions of Clemens*, Bishop of Rome. It is an account of the travels of the Apostle Peter and his conversation with Simon Magus; but the author's knowledge of the Egyptian mythology, of the opinions of the Greek philosophers, and of the astrological rules by which fortunes are foretold from the planets' places, amply prove that he was an Egyptian or an Alexandrian. No name ranked higher among the Christians than that of Clemens Romanus; and this is only one out of several cases of Christian authors who wished to give weight to their own opinions by passing them upon the world as his writings.

Marcus Aurelius, who died in 181 A. D., had pardoned the children of the rebel general Avidius Cassius, but Commodus began his reign by putting them to death; and, while thus disregarding the example and advice of his father, he paid his memory the idle compliment of continuing his series of dates on his own coins. But the Egyptian coinage of Commodus clearly betrays the sad change that was gradually taking place in the arts of the country; we no longer see the former beauty and variety of subjects; and the silver, which had before been very much mixed with copper, was under Commodus hardly to be known from brass. Commodus was very partial to the Egyptian superstitions, and he adopted the tonsure, and had his head shaven like a priest of Isis, that he might more properly carry an Anubis staff in sacred processions, which continued to be a feature of the religious activities of the age.

CARTOUCHE OF COMMODUS.

Upper Egypt had latterly been falling off in population. It had been drained of all its hoarded wealth. Its carrying trade through Koptos to the Red Sea was much lessened. Any tribute that its temples received from the piety of the neighbourhood was small. Nubia was a desert; and a few soldiers at Syênê were enough to guard the poverty of the Thebaid from the inroads of the Blemmyes. It was no longer necessary to send criminals to the Oasis; it was enough to banish them to the neighbourhood of Thebes. Hence we learn but little of the state of the country. Now and then a traveller, after measuring the pyramids of Memphis and the underground tombs of Thebes, might venture as far as the cataracts, and watch the sun at noon on the longest day shining to the bottom of the sacred well at

Syênê, like the orator Aristides and his friend Dion. But such travellers were few; the majority of those who made this journey have left the fact on record.

The celebrated museum, which had held the vast library of the Ptolemies, had been burnt by the soldiers of Julius Cæsar in one of their battles with the Egyptian army in the streets of Alexandria; but the loss had been in part repaired by Mark Antony's gift of the library from Pergamus to the temple of Serapis. The new library, however, would seem to have been placed in a building somewhat separated from the temple, as when the temple of Serapis was burnt in the reign of Marcus Aurelius, and again when it was in part destroyed by fire in the second year of this reign we hear of no loss of books; and two hundred years later the library of the Serapium, it is said, had risen to the number of seven hundred thousand volumes. The temple-keeper to the great god Serapis, or one of the temple-keepers, at this time was Asclepiades, a noted boxer and wrestler, who had been made chief of the wrestling-ground and had received the high rank of the emperor's freedman. He set up a statue to his father Demetrius, an equally noted boxer and wrestler, who had been chief priest of the wrestling-ground and of the emperor's baths in the last reign. Another favourite in the theatre was Apolaustus of Memphis, who removed to Rome, where he was crowned as conqueror in the games, and as a reward made priest to Apollo and emperor's freedman.

THE ANUBIS STAFF.

The city of Canopus was still a large mart for merchandise, as the shallow but safe entrance to its harbour made it a favourite with pilots of the small trading vessels, who rather dreaded the rocks at the mouth of the harbour of Alexandria. A temple of Serapis which had lately been built at Canopus was dedicated to the god in the name of the Emperor Commodus; and there some of the grosser superstitions of the polytheists fled before the spread of Christianity and platonism in Alexandria. The Canopic jars, which held those parts of the body that could not be made solid in the mummy, and which had the heads of the four lesser gods of the dead on their lids, received their name from this city. The sculptures on the beautiful temples of Contra-Latopolis were also finished in this reign, and the emperor's names and titles were carved on the walls in hieroglyphics, with those of the Ptolemies, under whom the temple itself had been built. Commodus may perhaps not have been the last emperor whose name and praises were carved in hieroglyphics; but all the great buildings in the Thebaid, which add such value to the early history of Egypt, had ceased before his reign. Other buildings of a less lasting form were no doubt being built, such as the Greek temples at Antinoopolis and Ptolemais, which have long since been swept away; but the Egyptian priests, with their gigantic undertakings, their noble plan of working for after ages rather than for themselves, were nearly ruined, and we find no ancient building now standing in Egypt that was raised after the time of the dynasty of the Antonines.

But the poverty of the Egyptians was not the only cause why they built no more temples. Though the colossal statue of Amenhôthes uttered its musical notes every morning at sunrise, still tuneful amid the desolation with which it was surrounded, and the Nile was still worshipped at midsummer by the husbandman to secure its fertilising overflow; nevertheless, the religion itself for which the temples had been built was fast giving way before the silent spread of Christianity. The religion of the Egyptians, unlike that of the Greeks, was

CANOPIC JARS.

no longer upheld by the magistrate; it rested solely on the belief of its followers, and it may have merged into Christianity the faster for the greater number of truths which were contained in it than in the paganism of other nations. The scanty hieroglyphical records tell us little of thoughts, feelings, and opinions. Indeed that cumbersome mode of writing, which alone was used in religious matters, was little fitted for anything beyond the most material parts of their mythology. Hence we must not believe that the Egyptian polytheism was quite so gross as would appear from the sculptures; and indeed we there learn that they believed, even at the earliest times, in a resurrection from the tomb, a day of judgment, and a future state of rewards and punishments.

The priests made a great boast of their learning and philosophy, and could each repeat by heart those books of Thot which belonged to his own order. The singer, who walked first in the sacred processions, bearing the symbols of music, could repeat the books of hymns and the rules for the king's life. The soothsayer, who followed, carrying a clock and a palm-branch, the emblem of the year, could repeat the four astrological books; one on the moon's phases, one on the fixed stars, and two on their heliacal risings. The scribe, who walked next, carrying a book and the flat rule which held the ink and pen, was acquainted with the geography of the world and of the Nile, and with those books which describe the motions of the sun, moon, and planets, and the furniture of the temple and consecrated places. The master of the robes understood the ten books relating to education, to the marks on the sacred heifers, and to the worship of the gods, embracing the sacrifices, the first-fruits, the hymns, the prayers, the processions, and festivals. The prophet or preacher, who walked last, carrying in his arms the great water-pot, was the president of the temple, and learned in the ten books, called hieratic, relating to the laws, the gods, the management of the temples, and the revenue. Thus, of the forty-two chief books of Thot, thirty-six were learned by these priests, while the remaining six on the body, its diseases, and medicines, were learned by the Pastophori, priests who carried the image of the god in a small shrine. These books had been written at various times: some may have been very old, but some were undoubtedly new; they together formed the Egyptian bible. Apollonius, or Apollonides Horapis, an Egyptian priest, had lately published a work on these matters in his own language, named Shomenuthi, *the book of the gods*.

But the priests were no longer the earnest, sincere teachers as of old; they had invented a system of secondary meanings, by which they explained away the coarse religion of their statues and sacred animals.

RELIGIOUS PROCESSION.

They had two religions, one for the many and one for the few; one, material and visible, for the crowds in the outer courtyards, in which the hero was made a god and every attribute of deity was made a person; and another, spiritual and intellectual, for the learned in the schools and sacred colleges. Even if we were not told, we could have no doubt but the main point of secret knowledge among the learned was a disbelief in those very doctrines which they were teaching to the vulgar, and which they now explained among themselves by saying that they had a second meaning. This, perhaps, was part of the great secret of the goddess Isis, the secret of Abydos, the betrayer of which was more guilty than he who should try to stop the *baris* or sacred barge in the procession on the Nile. The worship of gods, before whose statues the nation had bowed with unchanging devotion for at least two thousand years was now drawing to a close. Hitherto the priests had been able to resist all new opinions. The name of Amon-Ra had at one time been cut out from the Theban monuments to make way for a god from Lower Egypt; but it had been cut in again when the storm passed by. The Jewish monotheism had left the crowd of gods unlessened. The Persian efforts had overthrown statues and broken open temples, but had not been able to introduce their worship of the sun. The Greek conquerors had yielded to the Egyptian mind without a struggle; and Alexander had humbly begged at the door of the temple to be acknowledged as a son of Amon. But in the fulness of time these opinions, which seemed as firmly based as the monuments which represented them, sunk before a religion which set up no new statues, and could command no force to break open temples.

SHRINE.

The Egyptian priests, who had been proud of the superiority of their own doctrines over the paganism of their neighbours, mourned the overthrow of their national religion. "Our land," says the author of Hermes Trismegistus, "is the temple of the world; but, as wise men should foresee all things, you should know that a time is coming when it will seem that the Egyptians have by an unfailing piety served God in vain. For when strangers shall possess this kingdom religion will be neglected, and laws made against piety and divine worship, with punishment on those who favour it. Then this holy seat will be full of idolatry, idols' temples, and dead men's tombs. O Egypt, Egypt, there shall remain of thy religion but vague stories which posterity will refuse to believe, and words graven in stone recounting thy piety. The Scythian, the Indian, or some other barbarous neighbour shall dwell in Egypt. The Divinity shall reascend into the heaven; and Egypt shall be a desert, widowed of men and gods."

The spread of Christianity among the Egyptians was such that their teachers found it necessary to supply them with a life of Jesus, written in their own language, that they might the more readily explain to them his claim to be obeyed, and the nature of his commands. The Gospel according to the Egyptians, for such was the name this work bore, has long since been lost, and was little quoted by the Alexandrians. It was most likely a translation from one of the four gospels, though it had some different readings suited to its own church, and contained some praise of celibacy not found in the New Testament; but it was not valued by the Greeks, and was lost on the spread of the Koptic translation of the whole New Testament.

The grave, serious Christians of Upper Egypt were very unlike the lively Alexandrians. But though the difference arose from peculiarities of national character, it was only spoken of as a difference of opinion. The Egyptians formed an ascetic sect in the church, who were called heretics by the Alexandrians, and named Docetæ, because they taught that the Saviour was a god, and did not really suffer on the cross, but was crucified only *in appearance.* They of necessity used the Gospel according to the Egyptians, which is quoted by Cassianus, one of their writers; many of them renounced marriage with the other pleasures and duties of social life, and placed their chief virtue in painful self-denial; and out of them sprang that remarkable class of hermits, monks, and fathers of the desert who in a few centuries covered Europe with monasteries.

It is remarkable that the translation of a gospel into Koptic introduced a Greek alphabet into the Koptic language. Though for all religious purposes the scribes continued to use the ancient hieroglyphics, in which we trace the first steps by which pictures are made to represent words and syllables rather than letters, yet for the common purposes of writing they had long since made use of the *enchorial* or common hand, in which the earlier system of writing is improved by the characters representing only letters, though sadly too numerous for each to have a fixed and well-known force. But, as the hieroglyphics were also always used for carved writing on all subjects, and the common hand only used on papyrus with a reed pen, the latter became wholly an indistinct running hand; it lost that beauty and regularity which the hieroglyphics, like the Greek and Roman characters, kept by being carved on stone, and hence it would seem arose the want of a new alphabet for the New Testament. This was made by merely adding to the Greek alphabet six new letters borrowed from the hieroglyphics for those sounds which the Greeks did not use; and the writing was then written from left to right like a European language instead of in either direction according to the skill or fancy of the scribe.

It was only upon the ancient hieroglyphics thus falling into disuse that the Greeks of Alexandria, almost for the first time, had the curiosity to study the principles on which they were written. Clemens Alexandrinus, who thought no branch of knowledge unworthy of his attention, gives a slight account of them, nearly agreeing with the results of our modern discoveries. He mentions the three kinds of writing; first, the *hieroglyphic;* secondly, the *hieratic*, which is nearly the same, but written with a pen, and less ornamental than the carved figures; and thirdly, the *demotic*, or common alphabetic writing. He then divides the hieroglyphic into the alphabetic and the symbolic; and lastly, he divides the symbolic characters into the imitative, the figurative, and those formed like riddles. As instances of these last we may quote, for the first, the three zigzag lines which by simple imitation mean "water;" for the second, the oval which mean "a name," because kings' names were written within ovals; and for the third, a cup with three anvils, which mean "Lord of Battles," because "cup" and "lord" have nearly the same sound *neb*, and "anvils" and "battles" have nearly the same sound *meshe*.

In this reign Pantænus of Athens, a Stoic philosopher, held the first place among the Christians of Alexandria. He is celebrated for uniting the study of heathen learning with a religious zeal which led him to preach Christianity in Abyssinia. He introduced a taste for philosophy among the Christians; and, though Athenagoras rather deserves that honour, he was called the founder of the catechetical school which gave birth to the series

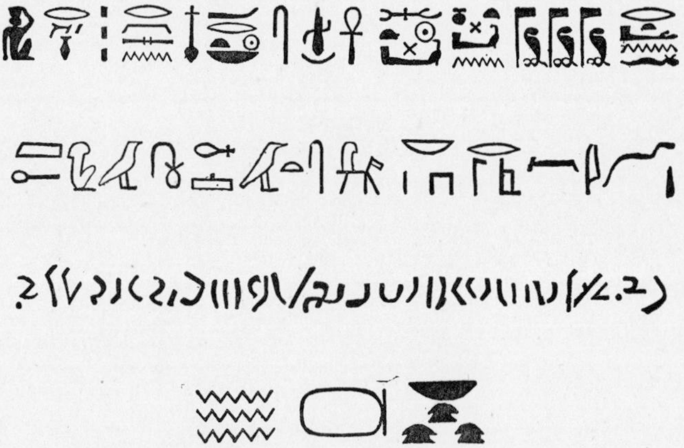

HIEROGLYPHIC, HIERATIC, AND DEMOTIC WRITING.

of learned Christian writers that flourished in Alexandria for the next century. To have been a learned man and a Christian, and to have encouraged learning among the catechists in his schools may seem deserving of no great praise. Was the religion of Jesus to spread ignorance and darkness over the world? But we must remember that a new religion cannot be introduced without some danger that learning and science may get forbidden, together with the ancient superstitions which had been taught in the same schools; we shall hereafter see that in the quarrels between pagans and Christians, and again between the several sects of Christians, learning was often reproached with being unfavourable to true religion; and then it will be granted that it was no small merit to have founded a school in which learning and Christianity went hand in hand for nearly two centuries. Pantænus has left no writings of his own, and is best known through his pupil or fellow-student, Clemens. He is said to have brought with him to Alexandria, from the Jewish Christians that he met with on his travels, a copy of St. Matthew's Gospel in the original Hebrew, a work now unfortunately lost, which, if we possessed it, would settle for us the disputed point, whether or no it contained all that now bears that Apostle's name in the Greek translation.

The learned, industrious, and pious Clemens, who, to distinguish him from Clemens of Rome, is usually called Clemens Alexandrinus, succeeded Pantænus in the catechetical school, and was at the same time a voluminous writer. He was in his philosophy a platonist, though sometimes called of the Eclectic school. He has left an Address to the Gentiles, a treatise on Christian behaviour called Pedagogus, and eight books of Stromata, or *collections*, which he wrote to describe the perfect Christian or Gnostic, to furnish the believer with a model for his imitation, and to save him from being led astray by the sects of Gnostics "falsely so called." By his advice, and by the imitation of Christ, the Christian is to step forward from faith, through love, to knowledge; from being a slave, he is to become a faithful servant and then a son; he is to become at last a god walking in the flesh.

Clemens was not wholly free from the mysticism which was the chief mark of the Gnostic sect. He thought much of the sacred power of numbers. Abraham had three hundred and eighteen servants when he rescued Lot, which, when written in Greek numerals thus, IHT formed the sacred sign for the name of Jesus. Ten was a perfect number, and is that of the commandments given to Moses. Seven was a glorious number, and there are seven Pleiades, seven planets, seven days in the week; and the two fishes and five barley loaves, with which the multitude were miraculously fed, together make the number of years of plenty in Egypt under Joseph. Clemens also quotes several lines in praise of the seventh day, which he says were from Homer, Hesiod, and Callimachus; but here there is reason to believe that he was deceived by the pious fraud of some zealous Jew or Christian, as no such lines are now to be found in the pagan poets.

During the reign of Pertinax, which lasted only three months (194 A. D.), we find no trace of his power in Egypt, except the money which the Alexandrians coined in his name. It seems to have been the duty of the prefect of the mint, as soon as he heard of an emperor's death, to lose no time in issuing coins in the name of his successor. It was one of the means to proclaim and secure the allegiance of the province for the new emperor.

During the reign of Commodus, Pescennius Niger had been at the head of the legion that was employed in

Upper Egypt in stopping the inroads of their troublesome neighbours, who already sometimes bore the name of Saracens. He was a hardy soldier, and strict in his discipline, while he shared the labours of the field and of the camp with the men under him. He would not allow them the use of wine; and once, when the troops that guarded the frontier at Syênê (Aswàn) sent to ask for it, he bluntly answered, "You have got the Nile to drink, and cannot possibly want more." Once, when a cohort had been routed by the Saracens, the men complained that they could not fight without wine; but he would not relax in his discipline. "Those who have just now beaten you," said Niger, "drink nothing but water." He gained the love and thanks of the people of Upper Egypt by thus bridling the lawlessness of the troops; and they gave him his statue cut in black basalt, in allusion to his name Niger. This statue was placed in his Roman villa.

But on the death of Pertinax, when Septimus Severus declared himself emperor in Pannonia, Niger, who was then in the province of Syria, did the same. Egypt and the Egyptian legions readily and heartily joined his party, which made it unnecessary for him to stay in that part of the empire; so he marched upon Greece, Thrace, and Macedonia. But there, after a few months, he was met by the army of his rival, who also sent a second army into Egypt; and he was defeated and slain at Cyzicus in Mysia, after having been acknowledged as emperor in Egypt and Syria for perhaps a year and a few months. We find no Alexandrian coins of Niger,

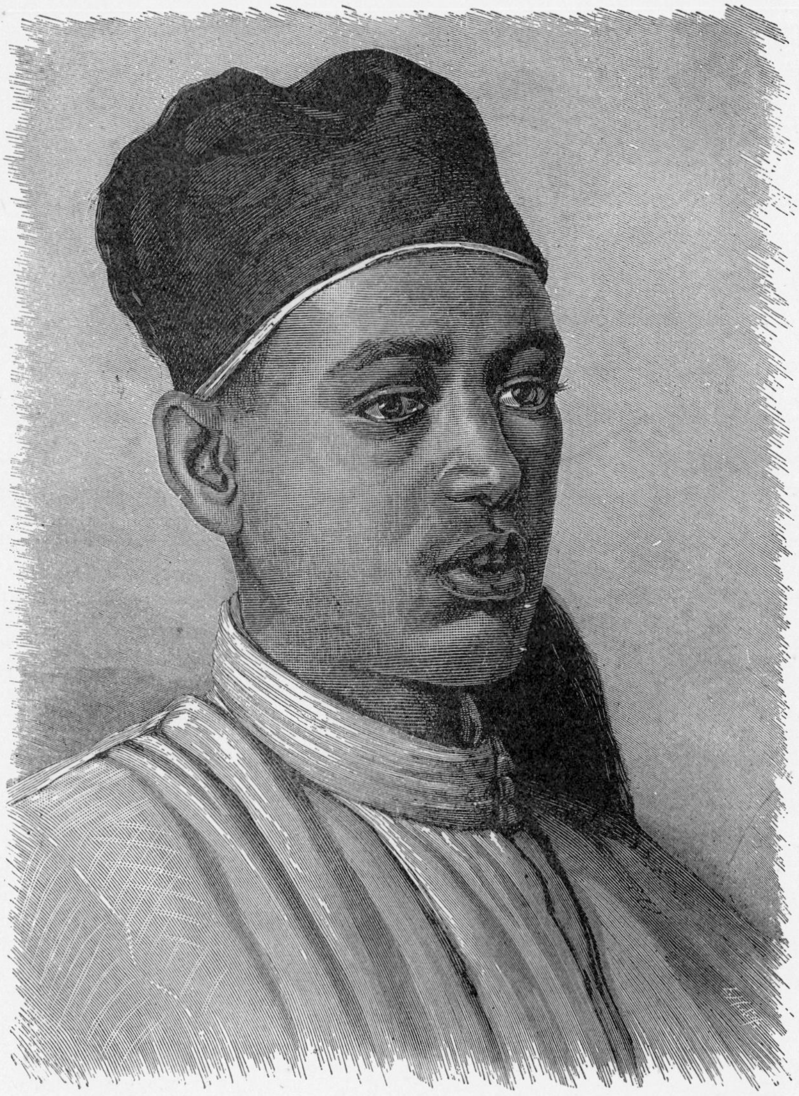

A NATIVE OF ASWAN.

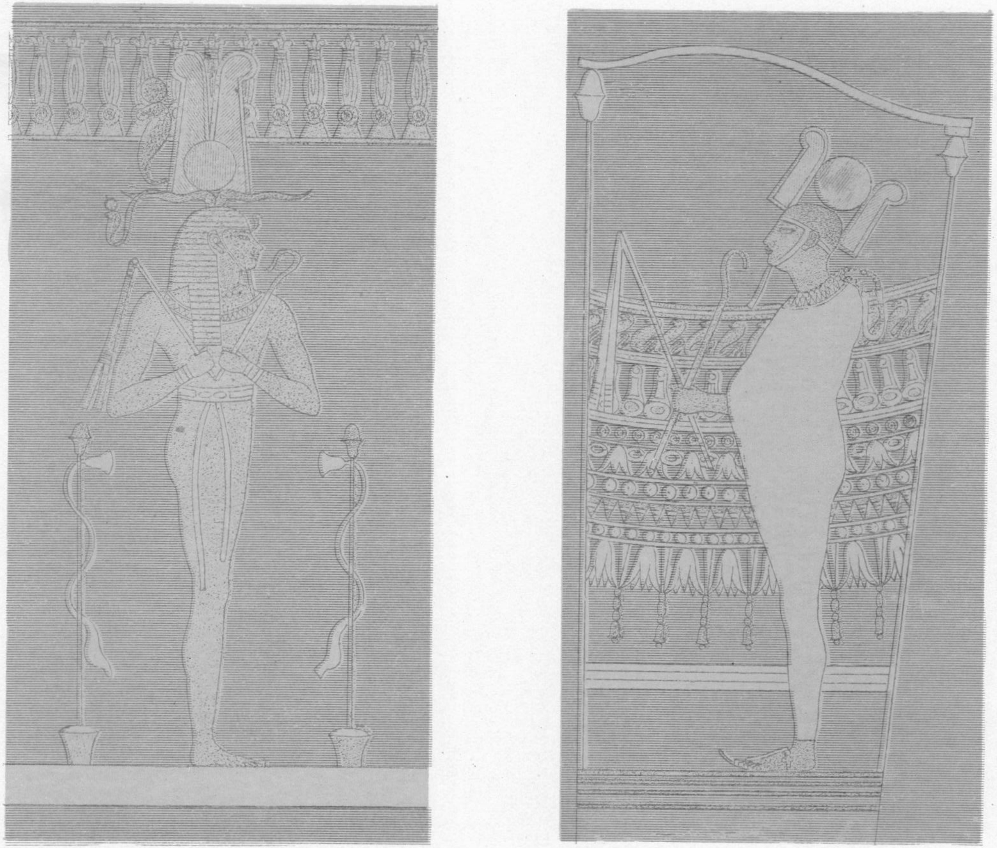

PAINTING AT THE ENTRANCE OF THE FIFTH TOMB OF THE KINGS
TO THE WEST, THEBES.

although we cannot allow a shorter space of time to his reign than one whole year, together with a few months of the preceding and following years. Within that time Severus had to march upon Rome against his first rival, Julian, to punish the prætorian guards, and afterwards to conquer Niger.

After the death of his rival, when Severus was the undisputed master of the empire, and was no longer wanted in the other provinces, he found leisure, in A. D. 196, to visit Egypt; and, like other active-minded travellers, he examined the pyramids of Memphis and the temples at Thebes, and laughed at the worship of Serapis and the Egyptian animals. His visit to Alexandria was marked by many new laws. Now that the Greeks of that city, crushed beneath two centuries of foreign rule, had lost any remains of courage or of pride that could make them feared by their Roman master, he relaxed part of the strict policy of Augustus. He gave them a senate and a municipal form of government, a privilege that had hitherto been refused in distrust to that great city, though freely granted in other provinces where rebellion was less dreaded. He also ornamented the city with a temple to Rhea, and with a public bath, which was named after himself the Bath of Severus.

Severus made a law, says the pagan historian, forbidding anybody, under a severe punishment, from becoming Jew or Christian. But he who gives the blow is likely to speak of it more lightly than he who smarts under it; and we learn from the historian of the Church that, in the tenth year of this reign, the Christians suffered persecution from their governors and their fellow-citizens. Among others who then lost their lives for their religion was Leonides, the father of Origen. He left seven orphan children, of whom the eldest, that justly celebrated writer, was only sixteen years old, but was already deeply read in the Scriptures, and in the great writers of Greece. As the property of Leonides was forfeited, his children were left in poverty; but the young Origen was adopted by a wealthy lady, zealous for the new religion, by whose help he was enabled to continue his studies under Clemens. In order to read the Old Testament in the original, he made himself master of Hebrew, which was a study then very unusual among the Greeks, whether Jews or Christians.

In this persecution of the Church all public worship was forbidden to the Christians; and Tertullian of Carthage eloquently complains that, while the emperor allowed the Egyptians to worship cows, goats, or crocodiles, or indeed any animal they chose, he only punished those that bowed down before the Creator and Governor of the world. Of course, at this time of trouble the catechetical school was broken up and scattered, so that there was no public teaching of Christianity in Alexandria. But Origen ventured to do that privately which was forbidden to be done openly; and, when the storm had blown over, Demetrius, the bishop, appointed him to that office at the head of the school which he had already so bravely taken upon himself in the hour of danger. Origen could boast of several pupils who added their names to the noble list of martyrs who lost their lives for Christianity, among whom the best known was Plutarch, the brother of Heraclas. Origen afterwards removed for a time to Palestine, and fell under the displeasure of his own bishop for being there ordained a presbyter.

In Egypt Severus seems to have dated the years of his reign from the death of Niger, though he had reigned in Rome since the deaths of Pertinax and Julian. His Egyptian coins are either copper, or brass plated with a little silver; and after a few reigns even those last traces of a silver coinage are lost in this falling country. In tracing the history of a word's meaning we often throw a light upon the customs of a nation. Thus, in Rome, gold was so far common that avarice was called the love of gold; while in Greece, where silver was the metal most in use, money was called *argurion.* In the same way it is curiously shown that silver was no longer used in Egypt by our finding that the brass coin of one hundred and ten grains weight, as being the only piece of money seen in circulation, was named an *argurion.*

The latter years of the reign of Caracalla were spent in visiting the provinces of his wide empire; and, after he had passed through Thrace and Asia Minor, Egypt had the misfortune to be honoured by a visit from its emperor. The satirical Alexandrians, who in the midst of their own follies and vices were always clever in lashing those of their rulers, had latterly been turning their unseemly jokes against Caracalla. They had laughed at his dressing like Achilles and Alexander the Great, while in his person he was below the usual height; and they had not forgotten his murder of his brother, and his talking of marrying his own mother. Some of these dangerous witticisms had reached his ears at Rome, and they were not forgotten. But Caracalla never showed his displeasure; and, as he passed through Antioch, he gave out that he was going to visit the city founded by Alexander the Great, and to consult the oracle in the temple of Serapis.

The Alexandrians in their joy got ready the hecatombs for his sacrifices; and the emperor entered their city through rows of torches to the sound of soft music, while the air was sweetened with costly scents, and the road scattered with flowers. After a few days he sacrificed in the temple of Serapis, and then visited the tomb of Alexander, where he took off his scarlet cloak, his rings, and his girdle covered with precious stones, and dutifully laid them on the sarcophagus of the hero. The Alexandrians were delighted with their visitor; and crowds flocked into the city to witness the daily and nightly shows, little aware of the unforgiving malice that was lurking in his mind.

The emperor then issued a decree that all the youths of Alexandria of an age to enter the army should meet him in a plain on the outside of the city; they had already a Macedonian and a Spartan phalanx, and he was going to make an Alexandrian phalanx. Accordingly the plain was filled with thousands of young men, who were ranged in bodies according to their height, their age, and their fitness for bearing arms, while their friends and relations came in equal numbers to be witnesses of their honour.

The emperor moved through their ranks, and was loudly greeted with their cheers, while the army which encircled the whole plain was gradually closing round the crowd and lessening the circle. When the ring was formed, Caracalla withdrew with his guards and gave the looked-for signal. The soldiers then lowered their spears and charged on the unarmed crowd, of whom a part were butchered and part driven headlong into the ditches and canals; and such was the slaughter that the waters of the Nile, which at midsummer are always red with the mud from the upper country, were said to have flowed coloured to the sea with the blood of the sufferers. Caracalla then returned to Antioch, congratulating himself on the revenge that he had taken on the Alexandrians for their jokes; not however till he had consecrated in the temple of Serapis the sword with which he boasted that he had slain his brother Geta.

Caracalla also punished the Alexandrians by stopping the public games and the allowance of grain to the citizens; and, to lessen the danger of their rebelling, he had the fortifications carried between the rest of the city and the great palace-quarter, the Bruchium, thus dividing Alexandria into two fortified cities, with towers on the walls between them. Hitherto, under the Romans as under the Ptolemies, the Alexandrians had been the trusted favourites of their rulers, who made use of them to keep the Egyptians in bondage. But under Caracalla that policy was changed; the Alexandrians were treated as enemies; and we see for the first time Egyptians taking their seat in the Roman senate, and the Egyptian religion openly cultivated by the emperor, who then built a temple in Rome to the goddess Isis.

On the murder of Caracalla in A. D. 217, Macrinus, who was thought to be the author of his death, was acknowledged as emperor; and though he only reigned for about two months, yet, as the Egyptian new year's day fell within that time, we find Alexandrian coins for the first and second years of his reign. The Egyptians pretended that the death of Caracalla had been foretold by signs from heaven; that a ball of fire had fallen on the temple of Serapis, which destroyed nothing but the sword with which Caracalla had slain his brother; and that an Egyptian named Serapion, who had been thrown into a lion's den for naming Macrinus as the future emperor, had escaped unhurt by the wild beasts.

Macrinus recalled from Alexandria Julian, the prefect of Egypt, and appointed to that post his friend Basilianus, with Marius Secundus, a senator, as second in command, who was the first senator that had ever held command in Egypt. He was himself at Antioch when Bassianus, a Syrian, pretending to be the son of Caracalla, offered himself to the legions as that emperor's successor. When the news reached Alexandria that the Syrian troops had joined the pretended Antoninus, the prefect Basilianus at once put to death the public couriers that brought the unwelcome tidings. But when, a few days afterwards, it was known that Macrinus had been defeated and killed, the doubts about his successor led to serious struggles between the troops and the Alexandrians. The Alexandrians could have had no love for a son of Caracalla; Basilianus and Secundus had before declared against him; but, on the other hand, the choice of the soldiers was guided by their brethren in Syria. The citizens flew to arms, and day after day was the battle fought in the streets of Alexandria between two parties, neither of whom was strong enough, even if successful, to have any weight in settling the fate of the Roman empire. Marius Secundus lost his life in the struggle. The prefect Basilianus fled to Italy to escape from his own soldiers; and the province of Egypt then followed the example of the rest of the East in acknowledging the new emperor.

For four years Rome was disgraced by the sovereignty of Elagabalus, the pretended son of Caracalla, and we find his coins each year in Alexandria. He was succeeded by the young Alexander, whose amiable virtues, however, could not gain for him the respect which he lost by the weakness of his government. The Alexandrians, always ready to lampoon their rulers, laughed at his wish to be thought a Roman; they called him the Syrian, the high priest, and the ruler of the synagogue. And well might they think slightly of his government, when a prefect of Egypt owed his appointment to the emperor's want of power to punish him. Epagathus had headed a mutiny of the prætorian guards in Rome, in which their general Ulpian was killed; and Alexander, afraid to punish the murderers, made the ringleader of the rebels prefect of Egypt in order to send him out of the way; so little did it then seem necessary to follow the cautious policy of Augustus, or to fear a rebellion in that province. But after a short time, when Epagathus had been forgotten by the Roman legion, he was removed to the government of Crete, and then at last punished with death.

In this reign Ammonius Saccas became the founder of a new and most important school of philosophy, that of the Alexandrian platonists. He is only known to us through his pupils, in whose writings we trace the mind and system of the teacher. The most celebrated of these pupils were Plotinus, Herennius, and Origen, a pagan writer, together with Longinus, the great master of the "sublime," who owns him his teacher in elegant literature. Ammonius was unequalled in the variety and depth of his knowledge, and was by his followers called heaven-taught. He aimed at putting an end to the triflings and quarrels of the philosophers by showing that all the great truths were the same in each system, and by pointing out where Plato and Aristotle agreed instead of where they differed; or rather by culling opinions out of both schools of philosophy, and by gathering together the scattered limbs of Truth, whose lovely form had been hewn to pieces and thrown to the four winds like the mangled body of Osiris.

Origen in the tenth year of this reign (A. D. 231) withdrew to Cæsarea, on finding himself made uncomfortable at Alexandria by the displeasure of Demetrius the bishop; and he left the care of the Christian school to Heraclas, who had been one of his pupils. Origen's opinions met with no blame in Cæsarea, where Christianity was not yet so far removed from its early simplicity as in Egypt.

The Christians of Syria and Palestine highly prized his teaching when it was no longer valued in Alexandria. He died at Tyre in the reign of Gallus.

On the death of Demetrius, Heraclas, who had just before succeeded Origen in the charge of the Christian school, was chosen Bishop of Alexandria; and Christianity had by that time so far spread through the cities of Upper and Lower Egypt that he found it necessary to ordain twenty bishops under him, while three had been found enough by his predecessor. From his being the head of the bishops, who were all styled fathers, Heraclas received the title of *Papa*, pope or grandfather, the title afterwards used by the bishops of Rome.

A MODERN SCRIBE.

Among the presbyters ordained by Heraclas was Ammonius Saccas, the founder of the platonic school; but he afterwards forsook the religion of Jesus; and we must not mistake him for a second Alexandrian Christian of the name of Ammonius, who can hardly have been the same person as the former, for he never changed his religion, and was the author of the *Evangelical Canons*, a work afterwards continued by Eusebius of Cæsarea.

On the death of the Emperor Alexander, in A. D. 235, while Italy was torn to pieces by civil wars and by its generals' rival claims for the purple, the Alexandrians seem to have taken no part in the struggles, but to have acknowledged each emperor as soon as the news reached them that he had taken the title. In one year we find Alexandrian coins of Maximin and his son Maximus, with those of the two Gordians, who for a few weeks reigned in Carthage, and in the next year we again have coins of Maximin and Maximus, with those of Balbinus and Pupienus, and of Gordianus Pius.

The Persians, taking advantage of the weakness in the empire caused by these civil wars, had latterly been harassing the eastern frontier; and it soon became the duty of the young Gordian to march against them in person. Hitherto the Roman armies had usually been successful; but unfortunately the Persians, or, rather, their Syrian and Arab allies, had latterly risen as much as the Romans had fallen off in courage and warlike skill. The army of Gordian was routed, and the emperor himself slain, either by traitors or by the enemy. Hereafter we shall see the Romans paying the just penalty for the example that they had set to the surrounding nations. They had taught them that conquest should be a people's chief aim, that the great use of strength was to crush a neighbour; and it was not long before Egypt and the other Eastern provinces suffered under the same treatment. So little had defeat been expected that the philosopher Plotinus had left his studies in Alexandria to join the army, in hopes of gaining for himself an insight into the Eastern philosophy that was so much talked of in Egypt. After the rout of the army he with difficulty escaped to Antioch, and thence he removed to Rome, where he taught the new platonism to scholars of all nations, including Serapion, the celebrated rhetorician, and Eustochius, the physician, from Alexandria.

SYMBOL OF EGYPT.

Philip, who is accused by the historians of being the author of Gordian's death, succeeded him on the throne in 244; but he is only known in the history of Egypt by his Alexandrian coins, which we find with the dates of each of the seven years of his reign, and these seem to prove that for one year he had been associated with Gordian in the purple. In the reign of Decius, which began in 249, the Christians of Egypt were again harassed by the zeal with which the laws against their religion were put in force. The persecution began by their fellow-citizens informing against them; but in the next year it was followed up by the prefect Æmilianus; and several Christians were summoned before the magistrate and put to death. Many fled for safety to the desert and to Mount Sinai, where they fell into a danger of a different kind; they were taken prisoners by the Saracens and carried away as slaves. Dionysius, the Bishop of Alexandria, himself fled from the storm, and was then banished to the village of Cephro in the desert. But his flight was not without some scandal to the Church, as there were not a few who thought that he was called upon by his rank at least to await, if not to court, the pains of martyrdom. Indeed, the persecution was less remarkable for the sufferings of the Christians than for the numbers who failed in their courage, and renounced Christianity under the threats of the magistrate. Dionysius, the bishop, who had shown no courage himself, was willing to pardon their weakness, and after fit proof of sorrow again to receive them as brethren. But his humanity offended the zeal of many whose distance from the danger had saved them from temptation; and it was found necessary to summon a council at Rome to settle the dispute. In this assembly the moderate party prevailed; and some who refused to receive back those who had once fallen away from the faith were themselves turned out of the Church.

Dionysius had succeeded Heraclas in the bishopric, having before succeeded him as head of the catechetical school. He was the author of several works, written in defence of the trinitarian opinions, on the one hand against the Egyptian Gnostics, who said that there were eight, and even thirty, persons in the Godhead, and, on the other hand, against the Syrian bishop, Paul of Samosata, on the Euphrates, who said that Jesus was a man, and that the Word and Holy Spirit were not persons, but attributes, of God.

But while Dionysius was thus engaged in a controversy with such opposite opinions, Egypt and Libya were giving birth to a new view of the trinity. Sabellius, Bishop of Ptolemais, near Cyrene, was putting forth the opinion that the Father, Son, and Holy Spirit were only three names for the one God, and that the creator of the world had himself appeared upon earth in the form of Jesus. Against this opinion Dionysius again engaged in controversy, arguing against Sabellius that Jesus was not the creator, but the first of created beings.

The Christians were thus each generation changing more and more, sometimes leaning towards Greek polytheism and sometimes towards Egyptian mysticism. As in each quarrel the most mysterious opinions were thought the most sacred, each generation added new mysteries to its religion; and the progress was rapid, from a practical piety, to a profession of opinions which they did not pretend to understand.

During the reigns of Gallus, of Æmilius Æmilianus, and of Valerian (A. D. 251—260), the Alexandrians coined money in the name of each emperor as soon as the news reached Egypt that he had made Italy acknowledge his title. Gallus and his son reigned two years and four months; Æmilianus, who rebelled in Pannonia, reigned three months; and Valerian reigned about six years.

Egypt, as a trading country, now suffered severely from the want of order and quiet government; and in particular since the reign of Alexander Severus it had been kept in a fever by rebellions, persecutions, and this unceasing change of rulers. Change brings the fear of change; and this fear checks trade, throws the labourer out of employment, and leaves the poor of the cities without wages and without food. Famine is followed by disease; and Egypt and Alexandria were visited in the reign of Gallus by a dreadful plague, one of those scourges that force themselves on the notice of the historian. It was probably the same disease that in a less frightful form had been not uncommon in that country and in the lower parts of Syria. The physician Aretæus describes it under the name of ulcers on the tonsils. It seems by the letters of Bishop Dionysius that in Alexandria the population had so much fallen off that the inhabitants between the ages of fourteen and eighty were not more than those between forty and seventy had been formerly, as appeared by old records then existing. The misery that the city had suffered may be measured by its lessened numbers.

During these latter years the eastern half of the empire was chiefly guarded by Odenathus of Palmyra, the brave and faithful ally of Rome, under whose wise rule his country for a short time held a rank among the empires of the world, which it never could have gained but for an union of many favourable circumstances. The city and little state of Palmyra is situated about midway between the cities of Damascus and Babylon. Separated from the rest of the world, between the Roman and the Parthian empires, Palmyra had long kept its freedom, while each of those great rival powers rather courted its friendship than aimed at conquering it. But, as the cause of Rome grew weaker, Odenathus wisely threw his weight into the lighter scale; and latterly, without aiming at conquest, he found himself almost the sovereign of those provinces of the Roman empire which were in danger of being overrun by the Persians. Valerian himself was conquered, taken prisoner, and put to

A HAREM WINDOW.

death by Sapor, King of Persia; and Gallienus, his son, who was idling away his life in disgraceful pleasures in the West, wisely gave the title of emperor to Odenathus, and declared him his colleague on the throne.

No sooner was Valerian taken prisoner than every province of the Roman empire, feeling the sword powerless in the weak hands of Gallienus, declared its own general emperor; and when Macrianus, who had been left in command in Syria, gathered together the scattered forces of the Eastern army, and made himself emperor of the East, the Egyptians owned him as their sovereign. As Macrianus found his age too great for the activity required of a rebel emperor, he made his two sons, Macrianus, junior, and Quietus, his colleagues; and we find their names on the coins of Alexandria, dated the first and second years of their reign. But Macrianus was defeated by Dominitianus at the head of a part of the army of Aureolus, who had made himself emperor in Illyricum, and he lost his life, together with one of his sons, while the other soon afterwards met with the same fate from Odenathus.

After this, Egypt was governed for a short time in the name of Gallienus; but the fickle Alexandrians soon made a rebel emperor for themselves. The Roman republic, says the historian, was often in danger from the headstrong giddiness of the Alexandrians. Any civility forgotten, a place in the baths not yielded, a heap of rubbish, or even a pair of old shoes in the streets, was often enough to throw the state into the greatest danger, and make it necessary to call out the troops to put down the riots. Thus, one day, one of the prefect's slaves was beaten by the soldiers, for saying that his shoes were better than theirs. On this a riotous crowd gathered round the house of Æmilianus to complain of the conduct of his soldiers. He was attacked with stones and such weapons as are usually within the reach of a mob. He had no choice but to call out the troops, who, when they had quieted the city and were intoxicated with their success, saluted him with the title of emperor; and hatred of Gallienus made the rest of the Egyptian army agree to their choice.

This was in the year 265. The new emperor called himself Alexander, and was even thought to deserve the name. He governed Egypt during his short reign with great vigour. He led his army through the Thebaid, and drove back the barbarians with a courage and activity which had latterly been uncommon in the Egyptian army. Alexandria then sent no tribute to Rome. "Well! cannot we live without Egyptian linen?" was the forced joke of Gallienus, when the Romans were in alarm at the loss of the usual supply of grain. But Æmilianus was soon beaten by Theodotus, the general of Gallienus, who besieged him in the strong quarter of Alexandria called the Bruchium, and then took him prisoner and strangled him.

During this siege the ministers of Christianity were able to lessen some of the horrors of war by persuading the besiegers to allow the useless mouths to quit the blockaded fortress. Eusebius, afterwards Bishop of Laodicea, was without the trenches trying to lessen the cruelties of the siege; and Anatolius, the Christian peripatetic, was within the walls, endeavouring to persuade the rebels to surrender. Gallienus in gratitude to his general would have granted him the honour of a proconsular triumph, to dazzle the eyes of the Alexandrians; but the policy of Augustus was not wholly forgotten, and the emperor was reminded by the priests that it was unlawful for the consular fasces to enter Alexandria.

The late Emperor Valerian had begun his reign with mild treatment of the Christians; but he was overpersuaded by the Alexandrians. He then allowed the power of the magistrate to be used, in order to check the Christian religion. But in this weakness of the empire Gallienus could no longer with safety allow the Christians to be persecuted for their religion. Both their numbers and their station made it dangerous to treat them as enemies; and the emperor ordered all persecution to be stopped. The imperial rescript for that purpose was even addressed to "Dionysius, Pinna, Demetrius, and the other bishops;" it grants them full indulgence in the exercise of their religion, and by its very address almost acknowledges their rank in the state. By this edict of Gallienus the Christians were put on a better footing than at any time since their numbers brought them under the notice of the magistrate.

When the bishop Dionysius returned to Alexandria, he found the place sadly ruined by the late siege. The middle of the city was a vast waste. It was easier, he says, to go from one end of Egypt to the other than to cross the main street which divided the Bruchium from the western end of Alexandria. The place was still marked with all the horrors of last week's battle. Then, as usual, disease and famine followed upon war. Not a house was without a funeral. Death was everywhere to be seen in its most ghastly form. Bodies were left unburied in the streets to be eaten by the dogs. Men ran away from their sickening friends in fear. As the sun set they felt in doubt whether they should be alive to

Egyptian Slave

From the painting by Siefert

see it rise in the morning. Cowards hid their alarms in noisy amusements and laughter. Not a few in very despair rushed into riot and vice. But the Christians clung to one another in brotherly love; they visited the sick; they laid out and buried their dead; and many of them thereby caught the disease themselves, and died as martyrs to the strength of their faith and love.

As long as Odenathus lived, the victories of the Palmyrenes were always over the enemies of Rome; but on his assassination, together with his son Herodes, though the armies of Palmyra were still led to battle with equal courage, its counsels were no longer guided with the same moderation. Zenobia, the widow of Odenathus, seized the command of the army for herself and her infant sons, Herennius and Timolaus; and her masculine courage and stern virtues well qualified her for the bold task that she had undertaken. She threw off the friendship of Rome, and routed the armies which Gallienus sent against her; and, claiming to be descended from Cleopatra, she marched upon Egypt, in 268 A. D., to seize the throne of her ancestors, and to add that kingdom to Syria and Asia Minor, which she already possessed.

COIN OF ZENOBIA.

Zenobia's army was led by her general, Zabda, who was joined by an Egyptian named Timogenes; and, with seventy thousand Palmyrenes, Syrians, and other barbarians, they routed the Roman army of fifty thousand Egyptians under Probatus. The unfortunate Roman general put an end to his own life; but nevertheless the

Palmyrenes were unsuccessful, and Egypt followed the example of Rome, and took the oaths to Claudius. For three years the coins of Alexandria bear the name of that emperor.

On the death of Claudius, his brother Quintillus assumed the purple in Europe (A. D. 270); and though he only reigned for seventeen days the Alexandrian mint found time to engrave new dies and to issue coined money in his name.

On the death of Claudius, also, the Palmyrenes renewed their attacks upon Egypt, and this second time with success. The whole kingdom acknowledged Zenobia as their queen; and in the fourth and fifth years of her reign in Palmyra we find her name on the Alexandrian coins. The Greeks, who had been masters of Egypt for six hundred years, either in their own name or in that of the Roman emperors, were then for the first time governed by an Asiatic. Palmyra in the desert was then ornamented with the spoils of Egypt; and travellers yet admire the remains of eight large columns of red porphyry, each thirty feet high, which stood in front of the two gates to the great temple. They speak for themselves, and tell their own history. From their material and form and size we must suppose that these columns were quarried between Thebes and the Red Sea, were cut into shape by Egyptian workmen under the guidance of Greek artists in the service of the Roman emperors; and were thence carried away by the Syrian queen to the oasis-city in the desert between Damascus and Babylon.

Zenobia was a handsome woman of a dark complexion, with an aquiline nose, quick, piercing eyes, and a masculine voice. She had the commanding qualities of Cleopatra, from whom her flatterers traced her descent, and she was without her vices. While Syriac was her native tongue, she was not ignorant of Latin, which she was careful to have taught to her children; she carried on her government in Greek, and could speak Koptic with the Egyptians, whose history she had studied and written upon. In her dress and manners she joined the pomp of the Persian court to the self-denial and military virtues of a camp. With these qualities, followed by a success in arms which they seemed to deserve, the world could not help remarking, that while Gallienus was wasting his time with fiddlers and players, in idleness that would have disgraced a woman, Zenobia was governing her half of the empire like a man.

COIN OF ATHENODORUS.

Zenobia made Antioch and Palmyra the capitals of her empire, and Egypt became for the time a province of Syria. Her religion like her language was Syriac. The name of her husband, Odenathus, means sacred to the goddess Adoneth, and that of her son, Vaballathus, means sacred to the goddess Baaleth. But as her troops were many of them Saracens or Arabs, a people nearly the same as the Blemmyes, who already formed part of the people of Upper Egypt, this conquest gave a new rank to that part of the population; and had the further result, important in after years, of causing them to be less quiet in their slavery to the Greeks of Alexandria.

But the sceptre of Rome had lately been grasped by the firmer hand of Aurelian, and the reign of Zenobia drew to a close. Aurelian at first granted her the title of his colleague in the empire, and we find Alexandrian coins with her head on one side and his on the other. But he lost no time in leading his forces into Syria, and, after routing Zenobia's army in one or two battles, he took her prisoner at Emessa. He then led her to Rome, where, after being made the ornament of his triumph, she was allowed to spend the rest of her days in quiet, having reigned for four years in Palmyra, though only for a few months in Egypt.

On the defeat of Zenobia it would seem that Egypt and Syria were still left under the government of one of her sons, with the title of colleague of Aurelian. The Alexandrian coins are then dated in the first year of Aurelian and the fourth of Vaballathus, or, according to the Greek translation of this name, of Athenodorus, who counted his years from the death of Odenathus.

The young Herodes, who had been killed with his father Odenathus, was not the son of Zenobia, but of a former wife, and Zenobia always acted towards him with the unkindness unfortunately too common in a step-mother. She had claimed the throne for her infant sons, Herennius and Timolaus; and we are left in doubt by the historians about Vaballathus; Vopiscus, who calls him the son of Zenobia, does not tell us who was his father. We know but little of him beyond his coins; but from these we learn that, after reigning one year with Aurelian, he aimed at reigning alone, took the title of Augustus, and dropped the name of Aurelian from his coins. This step was very likely the cause of his overthrow and death, which happened in the year 271.

On the overthrow of Zenobia's family, Egypt, which had been so fruitful in rebels, submitted to the Emperor Aurelian, but it was only for a few months. The Greeks of Alexandria, now lessened in numbers, were found to be no longer masters of the kingdom. Former rebellions in Egypt had been caused by the two Roman legions and the Greek mercenaries sometimes claiming the right to appoint an emperor to the Roman world; but Zenobia's conquest had raised the Egyptian and Arab population in their own opinion, and they were no longer willing to be governed by an Alexandrian or European master. In 272 A. D. they set up Firmus, a native of Seleucia, who took the title of emperor; and, resting his power on that part of the population that had been treated as slaves or barbarians for six hundred years, he aimed at the conquest of Alexandria.

Firmus was a man of great size and bodily strength, and, of course, barbarian manners. He had gained great riches by trade with India; and had a paper trade so profitable that he used to boast that he could feed an army on papyrus and glue. His house was furnished with glass windows, a luxury then but little known, and the squares of glass were fastened into the frames by means of bitumen. His chief strength was in the Arabs or Blemmyes of Upper Egypt, and in the Saracens who had lately been fighting against Rome under the standard of Zenobia. Firmus fixed his government at Koptos and Ptolemais, and held all Upper Egypt; but he either never conquered Alexandria, or did not hold it for many months, as for every year that he reigned in the Thebaid we find Alexandrian coins bearing the name of Aurelian. Firmus was at last conquered by Aurelian in person, who took him prisoner, and had him tortured and then put to death. During these troubles Rome had been thrown into alarm at the thoughts of losing the usual supply of Egyptian grain, as since the reign of Elagabalus the Roman granaries had never held more than was wanted for the year; but Aurelian hastened to send word to the Roman people that the country was again quiet, and that the yearly supplies, which had been delayed by the wickedness of Firmus, would soon arrive. Had Firmus raised the Roman legions in rebellion, he would have been honoured with the title of a rebel emperor; but, as his power rested on the Egyptians and Arabs, Aurelian only boasted that he had rid the world of a robber.

Another rebel emperor about this time was Domitius Domitianus; but we have no certain knowledge of the year in which he rebelled, nor, indeed, without the help of the coins should we know in what province of the whole Roman empire he had assumed the purple. The historian only tells us that in the reign of Aurelian the general Domitianus was put to death for aiming at a change. We learn, however, from the coins that he reigned for part of a first and a second year in Egypt;

Venders of Metal Ware

but the subject of his reign is not without its difficulties, as we find Alexandrian coins of Domitianus with Latin inscriptions, and dated in the third year of his reign. The Latin language had not at this time been used on the coins of Alexandria; and he could not have held Alexandria for any one whole year, as the series of Aurelian's coins is not broken. It is possible that the Latin coins of Domitianus may belong to a second and later usurper of the same name.

Aurelian had reigned in Rome from the death of Claudius; and, notwithstanding the four rebels to whom we have given the title of sovereigns of Egypt, money was coined in Alexandria in his name during each of those years. His coinage, however, reminds us of the troubled and fallen state of the country; and from this time forward copper, or, rather, brass, is the only metal used.

COIN OF DOMITIANUS WITH LATIN INSCRIPTION.

Aurelian left Probus in the command of the Egyptian army, and that general's skill and activity found full employment in driving back the barbarians who pressed upon the province on each of the three sides on which it was open to attack. His first battles were against the Africans and Marmaridæ, who were in arms on the side of Cyrene, and he next took the field against the Palmyrenes and Saracens, who still claimed Egypt in the name of the family of Zenobia. He employed the leisure of his soldiers in many useful works; in repairing bridges, temples, and porticoes, and more particularly in widening the trenches and keeping open the canals, and in such other works as were of use in raising and forwarding the yearly supply of grain to Rome. Aurelian increased the amount of the Egyptian tribute, which was paid in glass, paper, linen, hemp, and grain; the latter he increased by one-twelfth part, and he placed a larger number of ships on the voyage to make the supply certain.

The Christians were well treated during this reign, and their patriarch Nero so far took courage as to build the Church of St. Mary in Alexandria. This was probably the first church that was built in Egypt for the public service of Christianity, which for two hundred years had been preached in private rooms, and very often in secret. The service was in Greek, as, indeed, it was in all parts of Egypt: for it does not appear that Christian prayers were publicly read in the Egyptian language before the quarrel between the two churches made the Kopts unwilling to use Greek prayers. The liturgy there read was probably very nearly the same as that afterwards known as the *Liturgy of St. Mark.* This is among the oldest of the Christian liturgies, and it shows its country by the prayer that the waters of the river may rise to their just measure, and that rain may be sent from heaven to the countries that need it.

We learn from the historians that eight months were allowed to pass between the death of Aurelian and the choice of a successor; and during this time the power rested in the hands of his widow. The sway of a woman was never openly acknowledged in Rome, but the

Alexandrians and Egyptians were used to female rule, and from contemporary coins we learn that in Egypt the government was carried on in the name of the Empress Severina. The last coins of Aurelian bear the date of the sixth year of his reign, and the coins of Severina are dated in the sixth and seventh years. But after Tacitus was chosen emperor by his colleagues of the Roman senate, and during his short reign of six months (A. D. 276), his authority was obeyed by the Egyptian legions under Probus, as is fully proved by the Alexandrian coins bearing his name, all dated in the first year of his reign.

On the death of Tacitus, his brother Florian hoped to succeed to the imperial power, and was acknowledged in the same year by the senate and troops of Rome. But when the news reached Egypt it was at once felt by the legions that Probus, both by his own personal qualities and by the high state of discipline of the army under his command, and by his success against the Egyptian rebels, had a better claim to the purple than any other general. At first the opinion ran round the camp in a whisper, and at last the army spoke the general wish aloud; they snatched a purple cloak from a statue in one of the temples to throw over him, they placed him on an earthen mound as a tribunal, and against his will saluted him with the title of emperor. The choice of the Egyptian legions was soon approved of by Asia Minor, Syria, and Italy; Florian was put to death, and Probus

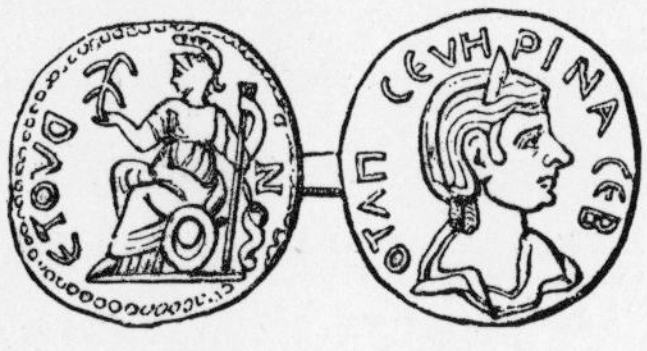

COIN OF SEVERINA.

shortly afterwards marched into Gaul and Germany, to quiet those provinces.

After a year or two, Probus was recalled into Egypt by hearing that the Blemmyes had risen in arms, and that Upper Egypt was again independent of the Roman power. Not only Koptos, which had for centuries been an Arab city, but even Ptolemais, the Greek capital of the Thebaid, was now peopled by those barbarians, and they had to be reconquered by Probus as foreign cities, and kept in obedience by Roman garrisons; and on his return to Rome he thought his victories over the Blemmyes of Upper Egypt not unworthy of a triumph.

By these unceasing wars, the Egyptian legions had lately been brought into a high state of discipline; and, confident in their strength, and in the success with which they had made their late general emperor of the Roman world, they now attempted to raise up a rival to him in the person of their present general Saturninus. Saturninus had been made general of the Eastern frontier by Aurelian, who had given him strict orders never to enter Egypt. "The Egyptians," says the historian, meaning, however, the Alexandrians, "are boastful, vain, spiteful, licentious, fond of change, clever in making songs and epigrams against their rulers, and much given to soothsaying and augury." Aurelian well knew that the loyalty of a successful general was not to be trusted in Egypt, and during his lifetime Saturninus never entered that province. But after his death, when Probus was called away to the other parts of the empire, the government of Egypt was added to the other duties of

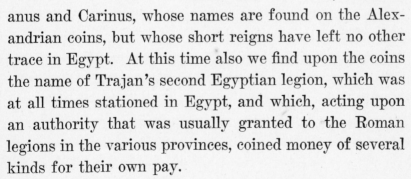

Saturninus; and no sooner was he seen there, at the head of an army that seemed strong enough to enforce his wishes, than the fickle Alexandrians saluted him with the title of emperor and Augustus. But Saturninus was a wise man, and shunned the dangerous honour; he had hitherto fought always for his country; he had saved the provinces of Spain, Gaul, and Africa from the enemy or from rebellion; and he knew the value of his rank and character too well to fling it away for a bauble. To escape from further difficulties he withdrew from Egypt, and moved his headquarters into Palestine. But the treasonable cheers of the Alexandrians could neither be forgotten by himself nor by his troops; he had withstood the calls of ambition, but he yielded at last to his fears; he became a rebel for fear of being thought one, and he declared himself emperor as the safest mode of escaping punishment. But he was soon afterwards defeated and strangled, against the will of the forgiving Probus.

COIN OF TRAJAN'S SECOND LEGION.

On the death of Probus, in A. D. 283, the empire fell to Carus and his sons, Numerianus and Carinus, whose names are found on the Alexandrian coins, but whose short reigns have left no other trace in Egypt. At this time also we find upon the coins the name of Trajan's second Egyptian legion, which was at all times stationed in Egypt, and which, acting upon an authority that was usually granted to the Roman legions in the various provinces, coined money of several kinds for their own pay.

The reign of Diocletian, beginning in A. D. 285, was one of suffering to the Egyptians; and in the fourth year the people rose against the Roman government, and gave the title of emperor to Achilleus, their leader in the rebellion. Galerius, the Roman general, led an army against the rebels, and marched through the whole of the Thebaid; but, though the Egyptians were routed whenever they were bold enough to meet the legions in battle, yet the rebellion was not very easily crushed. The Romans were scarcely obeyed beyond the spot on which their army was encamped. In the fourth year of the rebellion, A. D. 292, Diocletian came to Egypt, and the cities of Koptos and Busiris were besieged by the emperor in person, and wholly destroyed after a regular siege.

When Diocletian reached the southern limits of Egypt he was able to judge of the difficulty, and indeed the uselessness, of trying to hold any part of Ethiopia; and he found that the tribute levied there was less than the cost of the troops required to collect it. He therefore made a new treaty with the Nobatæ, as the people between the first and second cataracts were now called. He gave up to them the whole of Lower Ethiopia, or the province called Nubia. The valley for seventy miles above Syênê, which bore the name of the Dodecaschœnos, had been held by Augustus and his successors, and this was now given up to the original inhabitants. Diocletian strengthened the fortifications on the isle of Elephantine, to guard what was thenceforth the uttermost point of defence, and agreed to pay to the Nobatæ and Blemmyes a yearly sum of gold on the latter promising no longer to harass Upper Egypt with their marauding inroads, and on the former promising to forbid the Blemmyes from doing so. What remains of the Roman wall built against the inroads of these troublesome neighbours runs along the edge of the cultivated land on the east side of the river for some distance to the north of the cataract.

But so much was the strength of the Greek party lessened, and so deeply rooted among the Egyptians was their hatred of their rulers and the belief that they should then be able to throw off the yoke, that soon afterwards Alexandria declared in favour of Achilleus, and Diocletian was again called to Egypt to regain the capital. Such was the strength of the rebels that the city could not be taken without a regular siege. Diocletian surrounded it with a ditch and wall, and turned aside the canals that supplied the citizens with water. After a tedious siege of eight months, Alexandria was at last taken by storm in 297, and Achilleus was put to death. A large part of the city was burnt at the storming, nor would the punishment of the citizens have there ended, but for Diocletian's humane interpretation of an accident. The horse on which he sat stumbled as he entered the city with his troops, and he had the humanity to understand it as a command from heaven that he should stop the pillage of the city; and the citizens in gratitude erected near the spot a bronze statue of the horse to which they owed so much. This statue has long since been lost, but we cannot be mistaken in the place where it stood. The lofty column in the centre of the temple of Serapis, now well known by the name of Pompey's

Pillar,[1] once held a statue on the top, and on the base it still bears the inscription of the grateful citizens, "To the most honoured emperor, the saviour of Alexandria, the unconquerable Diocletian."

This rebellion had lasted more than nine years, and the Egyptians seemed never in want of money for the purposes of the war. Diocletian was struck with their riches, and he ordered a careful search to be made through Egypt for all writings on alchemy, an art which the Egyptians studied together with magic and astrology. These books he ordered to be burnt, under a belief that they were the great sources of the riches by which his own power had been resisted. Want and misery no doubt caused this rebellion, but the rebellion certainly caused more want and misery. The navigation of the Nile was stopped, the canals were no longer kept cleared, the fields were badly tilled, trade and manufactures were ruined. Since the rebellions against the Persians, Egypt had never suffered so much. It had been sadly changed by the troubles of the last sixty years, during which it had been six times in arms against Rome; and when the rebellion was put down by Diocletian, it was no longer the same country that it had been under the Antonines. The framework of society had been shaken, the Greeks had lessened in numbers, and still more in weight. The fall of the Ptolemies, and the conquest by Rome, did not make so great a change. The bright days of Egypt as a Greek kingdom began with the building of Alexandria, and they ended with the rebellions against Gallienus,

[1] See Volume X., page 317.

Aurelian and Diocletian. The native Egyptians, both Kopts and Arabs, now rise into more notice, as the Greek civilisation sinks around them. And soon the upper classes among the Kopts, to avoid the duty of maintaining a family of children in such troubled times, rush by thousands into monasteries and convents, and further lessen the population by their religious vows of celibacy.

In the twelfth year of the reign, that in which Alexandria rebelled and the siege was begun, the Egyptian coinage for the most part ceased. Henceforth, though money was often coined in Alexandria as in every other great city of the empire, the inscriptions were usually in Latin, and the designs the same as those on the coins of Rome. In taking leave of this long and valuable series of coins with dates, which has been our guide in the chronology of these reigns, we must not forget to acknowledge how much we owe to the labours of the learned Zoega. In his *Numi Ægypti Imperatorii*, the mere descriptions, almost without a remark, speak the very words of history.

The reign of Diocletian is chiefly remarkable for the new law which was then made against the Christians, and for the cruel severity with which it was put into force. The issuing of this edict in 304 A. D., which was to root out Christianity from the world, took place in the twentieth year of the reign, according to the Alexandrians, or in the nineteenth year after the emperor's first installation as consul, as years were reckoned in the other parts of the empire. The churches, which since the reign of Gallienus had been everywhere rising, were ordered to be destroyed and the Bibles to be burnt, while banishment, slavery, and death were the punishments threatened against those who obstinately clung to their religion. In no province of the empire was the persecution more severe than in Egypt; and many Christians fled to Syria, where the law, though the same, was more mildly carried into execution. But the Christians were too numerous to fly and too few to resist. The ecclesiastical writers present us with a sad tale of tortures and of death borne by those who refused to renounce their faith,—a tale which is only made less sad by the doubt how far the writers' feelings may have misled their judgment, and made them overstate the numbers.

But we may safely rely upon the account which Eusebius gives us of what he himself saw in Egypt. Many were put to death on the same day, some beheaded and some burnt. The executioners were tired, and the hearts of the pagan judges melted by the unflinching firmness of the Christians. Many who were eminent for wealth, rank, and learning chose to lay down their lives rather than throw a few grains of wheat upon the altar, or comply with any ceremony that was required of them as a religious test. The judges begged them to think of their wives and children, and pointed out that they were the cause of their own death; but the Christians were usually firm, and were beheaded for the refusal to take the test. Among the most celebrated of the Egyptian martyrs were Peter, Bishop of Alexandria, with Faustus, Dius, and Ammonius, presbyters under him; the learned Phileas, Bishop of Thmuis, Hesychius, the editor of the

Septuagint, and the Bishops Pachomius and Theodorus; though the pagans must have been still more surprised at Philoromus, the receiver-general of the taxes at Alexandria. This man, after the prefect of Egypt and the general of the troops, was perhaps the highest Roman officer in the province. He sat in public as a judge in Alexandria, surrounded by a guard of soldiers, daily deciding all causes relating to the taxes of Egypt. He was accused of no crime but that of being a Christian, which he was earnestly entreated to deny, and was at liberty indirectly to disprove by joining in some pagan sacrifice. The Bishops of Alexandria and Thmuis may have been strengthened under their trials by their rank in the church, by having themselves urged others to do their duty in the same case, but the receiver-general of the taxes could have had nothing to encourage him but the strength of his faith and a noble scorn of falsehood; he was reproached or ridiculed by all around him, but he refused to deny his religion, and was beheaded as a common criminal.

The ready ministers of this persecution were Culeianus, the prefect of the Thebaid, and Hierocles, the prefect of Alexandria. The latter was peculiarly well chosen for the task; he added the zeal of the theologian to the ready obedience of the soldier. He had written against the Christians a work named *Philalethes* (the lover of truth), which we now know only in the answer by Eusebius of Cæsarea. In this he denounced the apostles as impostors, and the Christian miracles as trifling; and, comparing them with the pretended miracles of Apollonius of Tyana, he pronounced the latter more numerous, more important, and better authenticated than the former by the evangelists; and he ridiculed the Christians for calling Jesus a god, while the pagans did not raise Apollonius higher than a man beloved by the gods.

This persecution under Diocletian was one of the most severe that the Christians ever underwent from the Romans. It did not, however, wholly stop the religious services, nor break up the regular government of the Church. In the catechetical school, Pierius, whom we have before spoken of as a man of learning, was succeeded by Theognostus and then by Serapion, whose name reminds us that the Egyptian party was gaining weight in the Alexandrian church. It can hardly have been for his superior learning, it may have been because his opinions were becoming more popular than those of the Greeks, that a professor with an Egyptian name was placed at the head of the catechetical school. Serapion was succeeded by Peter, who afterwards gained the bishopric of Alexandria and a martyr's crown. But these men were little known beyond their lecture-room. In the twentieth year of the reign, on the death of Peter, the Bishop of Alexandria, who lost his life as a martyr, the presbyters of the church met to choose a successor. Among their number was Arius, whose name afterwards became so famous in ecclesiastical history, and who had already, even before he was ordained a priest, offended many by the bold manner in which he stated his religious opinions. But upon him, if we may believe a partial historian, the majority of votes fell in the choice of a patriarch of Alexandria, and had he not himself modestly given way to the more ambitious Alexander, he might perhaps have been saved from the treatment which he afterwards suffered from his rival.

When, in the year 305, Diocletian and his colleague, Valerius Maximian, resigned the purple, Egypt with the rest of the East was given to Galerius, who had also as Cæsar been named Maximian on his Egyptian coins, while Constantius Chlorus ruled the West. Galerius in 307 granted some slight indulgence to the Christians without wholly stopping the persecution. But all favour was again withdrawn from them by his successor Maximin, who had indeed misgoverned Egypt for some years, under the title of Cæsar, before the rank of Augustus was granted to him. He encouraged private informers, he set townsman against townsman; and, as the wishes of the emperor are quickly understood by all under him, those who wished for his favour courted it by giving him an excuse for his cruelties. The cities sent up petitions to him, begging that the Christians might not be allowed to have churches within their walls. The history of these reigns indeed is little more than the history of the persecutions; and when the Alexandrian astronomers, dropping the era of Augustus, began to date from the first year of Diocletian, the Christian writers in the same way dated from the Era of the Martyrs.

It can be no matter of surprise to us that, in a persecution which threatened all classes of society, there should have been many who, when they were accused of being Christians, wanted the courage to undergo the pains of martyrdom, and escaped the punishment by joining in a pagan sacrifice. When the storm was blown over, these men again asked to be received into the Church, and their conduct gave rise to the very same quarrel that had divided the Christians in the reign of Decius. Meletius, a bishop of the Thebaid, was at the head of the party who would make no allowance for the weakness of their brethren, and who refused to grant to the repentant the forgiveness that they asked for. He had himself borne the same trials without bending, he had been sent as a criminal to work in the Egyptian mines, and had returned to Alexandria from his banishment, proud of his sufferings and furious against those who had escaped through cowardice. But the larger part of the bishops were of a more forgiving nature; they could not all boast of the same constancy, and the repentant Christians were re-admitted into communion with the faithful, while the followers of Meletius were branded with the name of heretics.

In Alexandria, Meletius soon found another and, as it proved, a more memorable occasion for the display of his zeal. He has the unenviable honour of being the author of the great Arian quarrel, by accusing of heresy Arius, at that time a presbyter of the church of Baucala near Alexandria, and by calling upon Alexander, the bishop, to inquire into his belief, and to condemn it if found unsound. Arius frankly and openly acknowledged his opinions: he thought Jesus a created being, and would speak of him in no higher terms than those used in the New Testament and Apostles' Creed, and defended his opinions by an appeal to the Scriptures. But he soon found that his defence was thought weak, and, without waiting to be condemned, he withdrew before the storm to Palestine, where he remained till summoned before the council of Nicæa in the coming reign.

It was during these reigns of trouble, about which history is sadly silent, when Greek learning was sinking, and after the country had been for a year or two in the power of the Syrians, that the worship of Mithra was brought into Alexandria, where superstitious ceremonies and philosophical subtleties were equally welcome. Mithra was the Persian god of the sun; and in the system of two gods, one good and the other wicked, he was the god of goodness. The chief symbol in his worship was the figure of a young hero in Phrygian cap and trousers, mounted on a sinking bull, and stabbing it in sacrifice to the god. In a deserted part of Alexandria, called the Mithrium, his rites were celebrated among ruins and rubbish; and his ignorant followers were as ignorantly accused of there slaying their fellow-citizens on his altars.

SYMBOL OF MITHRA.

It was about the same time that the eastern doctrine of Manicheism was said to have been brought into Egypt by Papus, and Thomas or Hermas. This sect, if sect it may be called, owed its origin to a certain Majus Mani, banished from Persia under the Sassanides; this Mani was a talented man, highly civilised through his studies and voyages in distant lands. In his exile he conceived the idea of putting himself forward as the reformer of the religions of all the peoples he had visited, and of reducing them all to one universal religion. Banished by the Christians, to whom he represented himself as the divinely inspired apostle of Jesus, in whom the Comforter had appeared, he returned to Persia, taking with him a book of the Gospels adorned by extraordinary paintings. Here he obtained at first the favour of the king and the people, till finally, after many changes of fortune, he was pursued by the magi, and convicted in a solemn disputation of falsifying religion; he was condemned to the terrible punishment of being flayed alive, after which his skin was to be stuffed and hung up over the gates of the royal city. His teaching consisted in a mixture of Persian and Christian-Gnostic views; its middle final point was the dualism of good and evil which rules in the world and in the human breast.

According to Mani's creed, there were originally two principles, God in His kingdom of light, and the demon with his kingdom of darkness, and these two principles existed independently of each other. The powers of evil fell into strife with each other, until, hurled away by their inward confusion, they reached the outermost edge of their own kingdom, and from there beheld the kingdom of light in all its glory. Now they ceased their strife among themselves and united to do battle to the kingdom of light. To meet them, God created the "original man," who, armed with the five pure elements, light, fire, air, water, and earth, advanced to meet the hostile powers. He was defeated, though finally saved; but a part of his light had thus made its way into the realm of darkness. In order gradually to regain this light, God caused the mother of life to create the visible world, in which that light lies hidden as a living power or world-soul awaiting its deliverance from the bonds of matter. In order to accomplish this redemption, two new beings of light proceed from God, viz.: Christ and the Holy Ghost, of whom the former, Christus Mithras, has his abode in the sun and moon, the latter in the ether diffused around the entire world. Both attract the powers of light which have sunk into the material world in order to lead them back, finally, into the everlasting realm of light. To oppose them, however, the demons created a new being, viz.: man, after the example of the "original man," and united in him the clearest light and the darkness peculiar to themselves, in order that the great strife might be renewed in his breast, and so man became the point of union of all the forces in the universe, the microcosm in which two principles ever strive for the mastery. Through the enticements of the material and the illusions of the demon, the soul of light was held in bondage in spite of its indwelling capacity for freedom, so that in heathenism and Judaism the "son of everlasting light," as the soul of the universe, was chained to matter. In order to accomplish this work of redemption more quickly, Christ finally leaves his throne at God's right hand, and appears on earth, truly in human form, but only with an apparent body; his suffering and death on the cross are but illusions for the multitude, although historical facts, and they serve at the same time as a symbol of the light imprisoned in matter, and as a typical expression of the suffering, poured out over the whole of nature (especially in the plant-world), of the great physical *weltschmerz.* Christ, through his teaching and power of attraction, began the deliverance of the light, so that one can truly say that the salvation of the world proceeds from rays which stream from the Cross; as, however, his teachings were conceived by the apostles in a Jewish sense, and the Gospels were disfigured, Mani appeared as the comforter promised by Christ to accomplish the victory. In his writings only is the pure truth preserved. Finally there will be a complete separation of the light from the darkness, and then the powers of darkness will fall upon each other again.

The ignorant in all ages of Christianity seem to have held nearly the same opinion in one form or other, thinking that sin has arisen either from a wicked being or from the wickedness of the flesh itself. The Jews alone proclaimed that God created good and God created evil. But we know of few writers who have ever owned themselves Manicheans, though many have been reproached as such; their doctrine is now known only in the works written against it. Of all heresies among the Christians this is the one most denounced by the ecclesiastical writers, and most severely threatened by the laws when the law makers became Christian; and of all the accusations of the angry controversialists this was the most reproachful. We might almost think that the numerous fathers who have written against the Manicheans must have had an easy victory when the enemy never appeared in the field, when their writings were scarcely answered, or their arguments denied; but perhaps a juster view would lead us to remark how much the writers, as well as the readers, must have felt the difficulty of accounting for the origin of evil, since men have run into such wild opinions to explain it.

Another heresy, which for a time made even as much noise as the last, was that of Hieracas of Leontopolis. Even in Egypt, where for two thousand years it had been the custom to make the bodies of the dead into mummies, to embalm them against the day of resurrection, a custom which had been usually practised by the Christians, this native Egyptian ventured to teach that nothing but the soul would rise from the dead, and that we must look forward to only a spiritual resurrection. Hieracas was a man of some learning, and, much to the vexation of those who opposed his arguments, he could repeat nearly the whole Bible by heart.

The Bishop Hesychius, the martyr in the late persecution, was one of the learned men of the time. He had published a new edition of the Septuagint Old Testament, and also of the New Testament. This edition was valued and chiefly used in Egypt, while that by Lucianus, who suffered in the same persecution, was read in Asia Minor from Constantinople to Antioch, and the older edition by Origen remained in use in Palestine. But such was the credit of Alexandria, as the chief seat of Christian learning, that distant churches sent there for copies of the Scriptures, foreign translations were mostly made from Alexandrian copies, and the greater number of Christians even now read the Bible according to the edition by Hesychius. We must, however, fear that these editors were by no means judicious in their labours. From the text itself we can learn that the early copiers of the Bible thought those manuscripts most valuable which were most full. Many a gloss and marginal note got written into the text. Their devotional feelings blinded their critical judgment; and they never ventured to put aside a modern addition as spurious. This mistaken view of their duty had of old guided the Hebrew copiers in Jerusalem; and though in Alexandria a juster criticism had been applied to the copies of Homer, it was not thought proper to use the

DOME PALM OF UPPER EGYPT.

same good sense when making copies of the Bible. So strong was the habit of grafting the additions into the text that the Greek translation became more copious than the Hebrew original, as the Latin soon afterwards became more copious than the Greek.

It was about this time, at least after Theodotion's translation of Daniel had received the sanction of the Alexandrian church, and when the teachers of Christianity found willing hearers in every city of Egypt, that the Bible was translated into the language of the country. We have now parts of several Koptic versions. They are translated closely, and nearly word by word from the Greek; and, being meant for a people among whom that language had been spoken for centuries, about one word in five is Greek. The Thebaic and Bashmuric versions may have been translated from the edition by Hesychius; but the Koptic version seems older, and its value to the Biblical critic is very great, as it helps us, with the quotations in Origen and Clemens, to distinguish the edition of the sacred text which was then used in Alexandria, and is shown in the celebrated Vatican manuscript, from the later editions used afterwards in Constantinople and Italy, when Christian literature flourished in those countries.

The Emperor Maximin died at Tarsus in A. D. 313, after being defeated by Licinius, who like himself had been raised to the rank of Augustus by Galerius, and to whom the empire of Egypt and the East then fell, while Constantine, the son of Constantius, governed Italy and the West. Licinius held his empire for ten years against the growing strength of his colleague and rival; but the ambition of Constantine increased with his power, and Licinius was at last forced to gather together his army in Thrace, to defend himself from an attack. His forces consisted of one hundred and fifty thousand foot, fifteen thousand horse, and three hundred and fifty triremes, of which Egypt furnished eighty. He was defeated near Adrianople; and then, upon a promise that his life should be spared, he surrendered to Constantine at Nicomedia. But the promise was forgotten and Licinius hanged, and the Roman world was once more governed by a single emperor.

AN ANCIENT EGYPTIAN NECKLACE.

CHAPTER II

THE CHRISTIAN PERIOD IN EGYPT

The Ascendency of the new religion: The Arian controversies: The Zenith of monasticism: The final struggle of Paganism: The decline of Alexandria.

THE PAPYRUS FLOWER.

COMING under the Roman sway, the Greek world underwent, not only politically but also intellectually, a complete change. As the Roman conquest had worn away all political differences and national divergences, and, by uniting the various races under the rule of the empire was bringing to its consummation the work begun by the Macedonian conqueror, it could not fail to influence the train of thought. On the one hand the political and ideal structure of Greek life was crumbling and bringing down the support and guiding principle supplied by the duties of citizenship and the devotion to the commonwealth. Man was thrown upon himself to find the principles of conduct. The customary morality and religion had been shaken in their foundations. The belief in the old gods and the old religion was undermined. Philosophy endeavoured to occupy the place left vacant by the gradual decay of the national religion. The individual, seeking for support and spiritual guidance, found it, or at least imagined he had found it, in philosophy. The conduct of life became the fundamental problem, and philosophy assumed a practical aspect. It aimed at finding a complete art of living. It had a thoroughly ethical stamp, and became more and more a rival of and opposed to religion. Such were the tendencies of the Stoic and Epicurean schools. The Roman rule was greatly favourable to such a development of thought. The Romans were a practical nation, had no conception of nor appreciation for purely theoretical problems, and demanded practical lessons and philosophical investigations which would serve as a guide for life. Thus the political tendency of the time towards practical wisdom had imparted a new direction to philosophical thought. Yet, as time went on, a deep feeling of dissatisfaction seized the ancient world in the midst of all the glories of the Roman rule. This huge empire could offer to the peoples, which it had welded into one mighty unit, no compensation for the loss of their national independence; it offered them no inner worth nor outer fortune. There was a complete discord running through the entire civilisation of the Græco-Roman world. The social condition of the empire had brought with it extreme contrasts in the daily life. The contrasts had become more pronounced. Abundance and luxury existed side by side with misery and starvation. Millions were excluded from the very necessaries of existence. With the sense of injustice and revolt against the existing inequality of the state of society, the hope for some future compensation arose. The millions excluded from the worldly possessions turned longingly to a better world. The thoughts of man were turned to something beyond terrestrial life, to heaven instead of earth. Philosophy, too, had failed to give complete satisfaction. Man had realised his utter inability to find knowledge in himself by his unaided efforts. He despaired to arrive at it without the help of some transcendental power and its kind assistance. Salvation was not to be found in man's own nature, but in a world beyond that of the senses. Philosophy could not satisfy the cultured man by the presentation of its ethical ideal of life, could not secure for him the promised happiness. Philosophy, therefore, turned to religion for help. At Alexandria, where, in the active work of its museum, all treasures of Grecian culture were garnered, all religions and forms of worship crowded together in the great throng of the commercial metropolis to seek a scientific clarification of the feelings that surged and stormed within them. The cosmopolitan spirit and broad-mindedness which had brought nations together under the Egyptian government, which had gathered scholars from all parts in the library and the museum, was favourable also to the fusion and reconciliation in the evolution of thought.

If Alexandria was the birthplace of that intellectual movement which has been described, this was not only the result of the prevailing spirit of the age, but was due to the influence of ideas; salvation could only be found in the reconciliation of ideas. The geographical centre of this movement of fusion and reconciliation was, however, in Alexandria. After having been the town of the museum and the library, of criticism and literary erudition, Alexandria became once again the meeting-place of philosophical schools and religious sects; communication had become easier, and various fundamentally different inhabitants belonging to distinct social groups met on the banks of the Nile. Not only goods and products of the soil were exchanged, but also ideas and thoughts. The mental horizon was widened, comparisons ensued, and new ideas were suggested and formed. This mixture of ideas necessarily created a complex spirit where two currents of thought, of critical scepticism and superstitious credulity, mixed and mingled. Another powerful factor was the close contact in which Occidentalism or Greek culture found itself with Orientalism. Here it was where the Greek and Oriental spirit mixed and mingled, producing doctrines and religious systems containing germs of tradition and science, of inspiration and reflection. Images and formulas, method and ecstasy, were interwoven and intertwined. The brilliant qualities of the Greek spirit, its sagacity and subtlety of intelligence, its lucidity and facility of expression, were animated and vivified by the Oriental spark, and gained new life and vigour. On the other hand, the contemplative spirit of the Orient, which is characterised by its aspiration towards the invisible and mysterious, would never have produced a coherent system or theory had it not been aided by Greek science. It was the latter that arranged and explained the Oriental traditions, loosed their tongues, and produced those religious doctrines and philosophical systems which culminated in Gnosticism, Neo-Platonism, the Judaism of Philo, and the Polytheism of Julian the Apostate.

It was the contemplative Oriental mind, with its tendency towards the supernatural and miraculous, with its mysticism and religion, and Greece with her subtle scrutinising and investigating spirit, which gave rise to the peculiar phase of thought prevalent in Alexandria during the first centuries of our era. It was tinctured with idealistic, mystic, and yet speculative and scientific colours. Hence the religious spirit in philosophy and the philosophic tendency in the religious system that are the characteristic features. "East and West," says Baldwin,[1] "met at Alexandria. The co-operative ideas of civilisations, cultures, and religions of Rome, Greece, Palestine, and the farther East found themselves in juxtaposition. Hence arose a new problem, developed partly by Occidental thought, partly by Oriental aspiration. Religion and philosophy became inextricably mixed, and the resultant doctrines consequently belong

[1] Baldwin: Dictionary of Philosophy.

to neither sphere proper, but are rather witnesses of an attempt at combining both. These efforts naturally came from two sides. On the one hand, the Jews tried to accommodate their faith to the results of Western culture, in which Greek culture predominated. On the other hand, thinkers whose main impulse came from Greek philosophy attempted to accommodate their doctrines to the distinctively religious problems which the Eastern nations had brought with them. From whichever side the consequences be viewed, they are to be characterised as theosophical rather than purely philosophical, purely religious, or purely theological."

The reign of Constantine the Great, who became sole ruler of the East and West in 323, after ten years' joint government with Licinius, is remarkable for the change which was then wrought in the religion and philosophy of the empire by the emperor's embracing the Christian faith. His conversion occurred in 312, and on his coming to the united sovereignty the Christians were at once released from every punishment and disability on account of their religion, which was then more than tolerated; they were put upon a nearly equal footing with the pagans, and every minister of the Church was released from the burden of civil and military duties. Whether the emperor's conversion arose from education, from conviction, or from state policy, we have no means of knowing; but Christianity did not reach the throne before it was the religion of a most important class of his subjects, and the Egyptian Christians soon found themselves numerous enough to call the Greek Christians heretics, as the Greek Christians had already begun to designate the Jewish.

The Greeks of Alexandria had formed rather a school of philosophy than a religious sect. Before Alexander's conquest the Greek settlers at Naucratis had thought it necessary to have their own temples and sacrifices; but since the building of Alexandria they had been smitten with the love of Eastern mysticism, and content to worship in the temples of Serapis and Mithra, and to receive instruction from the Egyptian priests. They had supported the religion of the conquered Egyptians without wholly believing it; and had shaken by their ridicule the respect for the very ceremonies which they upheld by law. Polytheism among the Greeks had been further shaken by the platonists; and Christianity spread in about equal proportions among the Greeks and the Egyptians. Before the conversion of Constantine the Egyptian church had already spread into every city of the province, and had a regular episcopal government. Till the time of Heraclas and Dionysius, the bishops had been always chosen by the votes of the presbyters, as the archdeacons were by the deacons. Dionysius in his public epistles joins with himself his fellow-presbyters as if he were only the first among equals; but after that time some irregularities had crept into the elections, and latterly the Church had become more monarchical. There was a patriarch in Alexandria, with a bishop in every other large city, each assisted by a body of priests and deacons. They had been clad in faith, holiness, humility, and charity; but Constantine robed them in honour, wealth, and power; and to this many of them soon added pride, avarice, and ambition.

This reign is no less remarkable for the religious quarrel which then divided the Christians, which set church against church and bishop against bishop, as soon as they lost that great bond of union, the fear of the pagans. Jesus of Nazareth was acknowledged by Constantine as a divine person; and, in the attempt then made by the Alexandrians to arrive at a more exact definition of his nature, while the emperor was willing to be guided by the bishops in his theological opinions, he was able to instruct them all in the more valuable lessons of mutual toleration and forbearance. The followers of early religions held different opinions, but distinguished themselves apart only by outward modes of worship, such as by sacrifices among the Greeks and Romans, and among the Jews and Egyptians by circumcision, and abstinence from certain meats. When Jesus of Nazareth introduced his spiritual religion of repentance and amendment of life, he taught that the test by which his disciples were to be known was their love to one another. After his death, however, the Christians gave more importance to opinions in religion, and towards the end of the third century they proposed to distinguish their fellow-worshippers in a mode hitherto unknown to the world, namely, by the profession of belief in certain opinions; for as yet there was no difference in their belief of historic facts. This gave rise to numerous metaphysical discussions, particularly among the more speculative and mystical.

At about this time the chief controversy was as to whether Christ was of the *same*, or of *similar* substance with God the Father, this being the dispute which divided Christendom for centuries. This dispute and others not quite so metaphysical were brought to the ears of the emperor by Alexander, Bishop of Alexandria, and Arius, the presbyter. The bishop had been enquiring into the belief of the presbyter, and the latter had argued against his superior and against the doctrine of the *consubstantiality* of the Father and the Son. The emperor's letter to the theologians, in this first ecclesiastical quarrel that was ever brought before a Christian monarch, is addressed to Alexander and Arius, and he therein tells them that they are raising useless questions, which it is not necessary to settle, and which, though a good exercise for the understanding, only breed ill-will, and should be kept by each man in his own breast. He regrets the religious madness which has seized all Egypt; and lastly he orders the bishop not to question the priest as to his belief, and orders the priest, if questioned, not to return an answer. But this wise letter had no weight with the Alexandrian divines. The quarrel gained in importance from being noticed by the emperor; the civil government of the country was clogged; and Constantine, after having once interfered, was persuaded to call a council of bishops to settle the Christian faith for the future. Nicæa in Bithynia was chosen as the spot most convenient for Eastern Christendom to meet in; and two hundred and fifty bishops, followed by crowds of priests, there met in council from Greece, Thrace, Asia

Minor, Syria, Arabia, Egypt, and Libya, with one or two from Western Europe.

At this synod, held in the year 325, Athanasius, a young deacon in the Alexandrian church, came for the first time into notice as the champion of Alexander against Arius, who was then placed upon his trial. All the authority, eloquence, and charity of the emperor were needed to quell the tumultuous passions of the assembly. It ended its stormy labours by voting what was called the Homoousian doctrine, that Jesus was of one substance with God. They put forth to the world the celebrated creed, named, from the city in which they met, the Nicene creed, and they excommunicated Arius and his followers, who were then all banished by the emperor. The meeting had afterwards less difficulty in coming to an agreement about the true time of Easter, and in excommunicating the Jews; and all except the Egyptians returned home with a wish that the quarrel should be forgotten and forgiven.

This first attempt among the Christians at settling the true faith by putting fetters on the mind, by drawing up a creed and punishing those that disbelieved it, was but the beginning of theological difficulties. These in Egypt arose as much from the difference of blood and language of the races that inhabited the country as from their religious belief; and Constantine must soon have seen that if as a theologian he had decided right, yet as a statesman he had been helping the Egyptians against the friends of his own Greek government in Alexandria.

After a reasonable delay, Arius addressed to the emperor a letter either of explanation or apology, asserting his full belief in Christianity, explaining his faith by using the words of the Apostles' Creed, and begging to be re-admitted into the Church. The emperor, either from a readiness to forgive, or from a change of policy, or from an ignorance of the theological controversy, was satisfied with the apology, and thereupon wrote a mild conciliatory letter to Athanasius, who had in the meantime been made Bishop of Alexandria, expressing his wish that forgiveness should at all times be offered to the repentant, and ordering him to re-admit Arius to his rank in the Church. But the young Athanasius, who had gained his favour with the Egyptian clergy, and had been raised to his high seat by his zeal shown against Arius, refused to obey the commands of the emperor, alleging that it was unlawful to re-admit into the Church anybody who had once been excommunicated. Constantine could hardly be expected to listen to this excuse, or to overlook this direct refusal to obey his orders. The rebellious Athanasius was ordered into the emperor's presence at Constantinople, and soon afterwards, in 335, called before a council of bishops at Tyre, where he was deposed and banished. At the same council, in the thirtieth year of this reign, Arius was re-admitted into communion with the Church, and after a few months he was allowed to return to Alexandria, to the indignation of the popular party in that city, while Athanasius remained in banishment during the rest of the reign, as a punishment for his disobedience.

This practice of judging and condemning opinions gave power in the Church to men who would otherwise have been least entitled to weight and influence. Athanasius rose to his high rank over the heads of the elder presbyters by his fitness for the harsher duties then required of an archbishop. Theological opinions became the watchwords of two contending parties; religion lost much of its empire over the heart; and the mild spirit of Christianity gave way to angry quarrels and cruel persecutions.

Another remarkable event of this reign was the foundation of the new city of Constantinople, to which the emperor removed the seat of his government. Rome lost much by the building of the new capital, although the emperors had for some time past ceased to live in Italy; but Alexandria lost the rank which it had long held as the centre of Greek learning and Greek thought, and it felt a blow from which Rome was saved by the difference of language. The patriarch of Alexandria was no longer the head of Greek Christendom. That rank was granted to the bishop of the imperial city; many of the philosophers who hung round the palace at Contantinople would otherwise have studied and taught in the museum; and the Greeks, by whose superiority Egypt had so long been kept in subjection, gradually became the weaker party. In the opinion of the historian, as in the map of the geographer, Alexandria had formerly been a Greek state on the borders of Egypt; but since the rebellion in the reign of Diocletian it was becoming more and more an Egyptian city; and those who in religion and politics thought and felt as Egyptians soon formed the larger half of the Alexandrians. The climate of Egypt was hardly fitted for the Greek race. Their numbers never could have been kept up by births alone, and they now began to lessen as the attraction to newcomers ceased. The pure Greek names hence-

THE ISLAND OF RHODHA.

forth become less common; and among the monks and writers we now meet with those named after the old gods of the country.

Constantine removed an obelisk from Egypt for the ornament of his new city, and he brought down another from Heliopolis to Alexandria; but he died before the second left the country, and it was afterwards taken by his son to Rome. These obelisks were covered with hieroglyphics, as usual, and we have a translation said to be made from the latter by Hermapion, an Egyptian priest. In order to take away its pagan character from the religious ceremony with which the yearly rise of the Nile was celebrated in Alexandria, Constantine removed the sacred cubit from the temple of Serapis to one of the Christian churches; and nothwithstanding the gloomy forebodings of the people, the Nile rose as usual, and the clergy afterwards celebrated the time of its overflow as a Christian festival.

The pagan philosophers under Constantine had but few pupils and met with but little encouragement. Alypius of Alexandria and his friend Iamblichus, however, still taught the philosophy of Ammonius and Plotinus. The only writings by Alypius now remaining are his *Introduction to Music;* in which he explains the notation of the fifteen modes or tones in their respective kinds of diatonic, chromatic, and enharmonic. His signs are said to be Pythagorean. They are in pairs, of which one is thought to represent the note struck on the lyre, and the other the tone of the voice to be sung thereto. They thus imply accord or harmony. The same signs are found in some manuscripts written over the syllables of ancient poems; and thereby scholars, learned at once in the Greek language, in the art of deciphering signs, and in the science of music, now chant the odes of Pindar in strains not dissimilar to modern cathedral psalmody.

Sopator succeeded Iamblichus as professor of platonism in Alexandria, with the proud title of successor to Plato. For some time he enjoyed the friendship of

Constantine; but, when religion made a quarrel between the friends, the philosopher was put to death by the emperor. The pagan account of the quarrel was that, when Constantine had killed his son, he applied to Sopator to be purified from his guilt; and when the platonist answered that he knew of no ceremony that could absolve a man from such a crime, the emperor applied to the Christians for baptism. This story may not be true, and the ecclesiastical historian remarks that Constantine had professed Christianity several years before the murder of his son; but then, as after his conversion he had got Sopator to consecrate his new city with a variety of pagan ceremonies, he may in the same way have asked him to absolve him from the guilt of murder.

On the death of Constantine, in 337, his three sons, without entirely dismembering the empire, divided the provinces of the Roman world into three shares. Constantine II., the eldest son, who succeeded to the throne of his father in Constantinople, and Constans, the youngest, who dwelt in Rome, divided Europe between them; while Constantius, the second son, held Syria, Mesopotamia, Armenia, and Egypt, of which possessions Antioch on the Orontes was at that time the capital. Thus Alexandria was doomed to a further fall. When governed by Rome it had still been the first of Greek cities; afterwards, when the seat of the empire was fixed at Constantinople, it became the second; but on this division of the Roman world, when the seat of government came still nearer to Egypt, and Antioch rose as the capital of the East, Alexandria fell to be the third among Greek cities. Egypt quietly received its political orders from Antioch. Its opinions also in some cases followed those of the capital, and it is curious to remark that the Alexandrian writers, when dating by the era of the creation, were now willing to consider the world ten years less old than they used, because it was so thought at Antioch. But it was not so with their religious opinions, and as long as Antioch and its emperor undertook to govern the Egyptian church there was little peace in the province.

The three emperors did not take the same side in the quarrel which under the name of religion was then unsettling the obedience of the Egyptians, and even in some degree troubling the rest of the empire. Constantius held the Arian opinions of Syria; but Constantine II. and Constans openly gave their countenance to the party of the rebellious Athanasius, who under their favour ventured to return to Alexandria, where, after an absence of two years and four months, he was received in the warmest manner by his admiring flock. But on the death of Constantine II., who was shortly afterwards killed in battle by his brother Constans, Constantius felt himself more master of his own kingdom; he deposed Athanasius, and summoned a council of bishops at Antioch to elect a new patriarch of Alexandria. Christian bishops, though they had latterly owed their ordination to the authority of their equals, had always received their bishoprics by the choice of their presbyters or of their flocks; and though they were glad to receive the support of the emperor, they were not willing to acknowledge him as their head. Hence, when the council at Antioch first elected Eusebius of Emisa into the bishopric of Alexandria, he chose to refuse the honour which they had only a doubtful right to bestow, rather than to venture into the city in the face of his popular rival. The council then elected Gregory, whose greater courage and ambition led him to accept the office.

The council of Antioch then made some changes in the creed. A few years later, a second council met in the same place, and drew up a creed more near to what we now call the Athanasian; but it was firmly rejected by the Egyptian and Roman churches. Gregory was no sooner elected to the bishopric than he issued his commands as bishop, though, if he had the courage, he had not at the time the power to enter Alexandria. But Syrianus, the general of the Egyptian troops, was soon afterwards ordered by the emperor to place him on his episcopal throne; and he led him into the city, surrounded by the spears of five thousand soldiers, and followed by the small body of Alexandrians that after this invasion of their acknowledged rights still called themselves Arians. Gregory entered Alexandria in the evening, meaning to take his seat in the church on the next day; but the people in their zeal did not wait quietly for the dreaded morning. They ran at once to the church, and passed the night there with Athanasius in the greatest anxiety. In the morning, when Gregory arrived at the church, accompanied with the troops, he found the doors barricaded and the building full of men and women, denouncing the sacrilege, and threatening resistance. But the general gave orders that the church should be stormed, and the new bishop carried in by force of arms; and Athanasius, seeing that all resistance was useless, ordered the deacons to give out a psalm, and they all marched out at the opposite door singing. After these acts of violence on the part of the troops, and of resistance on the part of the people, the whole city was thrown into an uproar, and the prefect was hardly strong enough to carry on the government; the regular supply of grain for the poor citizens of Alexandria, and for Constantinople, was stopped; and the blame of the whole thrown upon Athanasius. He was a second time obliged to leave Egypt, and he fled to Rome, where he was warmly received by the Emperor Constans and the Roman bishop. But the zeal of the Athanasian party would not allow Gregory to keep possession of the church which he had gained only by force; they soon afterwards set fire to it and burned it to the ground, choosing that there should be no church at all rather than that it should be in the hands of the Arians; and the Arian clergy and bishops, though supported by the favour of the emperor and the troops of the prefect, were everywhere throughout Egypt driven from their churches and monasteries.

During this quarrel it seems to have been felt by both parties that the choice of the people, or at least of the clergy, was necessary to make a bishop, and that Gregory had very little claim to that rank in Alexandria. Julius, the Bishop of Rome, warmly espoused the cause of Athanasius, and he wrote a letter to the Alexandrian church, praising their zeal for their bishop, and ordering them to re-admit him to his former rank, from which he had been deposed by the council of Antioch, but to which he had been restored by the Western bishops. Athanasius was also warmly supported by Constans, the emperor of the West, who at the same time wrote to his brother Constantius, begging him to replace the Alexandrian bishop, and making the additional threat that if he would not reinstate him he should be made to do so by force of arms.

Constantius, after taking the advice of his own bishops, thought it wisest to yield to the wishes or rather the commands of his brother Constans, and he wrote to Athanasius, calling him into his presence in Constantinople. But the rebellious bishop was not willing to trust himself within the reach of his offended sovereign; and it was not till after a second and a third letter, pressing him to come and promising him his safety, that he ventured within the limits of the Eastern empire. Strong in his high character for learning, firmness, and political skill, carrying with him the allegiance of the Egyptian nation, which was yielded to him much rather than to the emperor, and backed by the threats of Constans, Athanasius was at least a match for Constantius. At Constantinople the emperor and his subject, the Alexandrian bishop, made a formal treaty, by which it was agreed that, if Constantius would allow the Homoousian clergy throughout his dominions to return to their churches, Athanasius would in the same way throughout Egypt restore the Arian clergy; and upon this agreement Athanasius himself returned to Alexandria.

Among the followers of Athanasius was that important mixed race with whom the Egyptian civilisation chiefly rested, a race that may be called Koptic, but half Greek and half Egyptian in their language and religion as in their forefathers. But in feelings they were wholly opposed to the Greeks of Alexandria. Never since the last Nectanebo was conquered by the Persians, eight hundred years earlier, did the Egyptians seem so near to throwing off the foreign yoke and rising again as an independent nation. But the Greeks, who had taught them so much, had not taught them the arts of war; and the nation remained enslaved to those who could wield the sword. The return of Athanasius, however, was only the signal for a fresh uproar, and the Arians complained that Egypt was kept in a constant turmoil by his zealous activity. Nor were the Arians his only enemies. He had offended many others of his clergy by his overbearing manners, and more particularly by his following in the steps of Alexander, the late bishop, in claiming new and higher powers for the office of patriarch than had ever been yielded to the bishops of Alexandria before their spiritual rank had been changed into civil rank by the emperor's adoption of their religion. Meletius headed a strong party of bishops, priests, and deacons in opposing the new claims of the archiepiscopal see of Alexandria. His followers differed in no point of doctrine from the Athanasian party, but as they sided with the Arians they were usually called heretics.

By this time the statesmen and magistrates had gained a clear view of the change which had come over the political state of the empire, first by the spread of Christianity, and secondly by the emperor's embracing it. By supporting Christianity the emperors gave rank in the state to an organised and well-trained body, which immediately found itself in possession of all the civil power. A bishopric, which a few years before was a post of danger, was now a place of great profit, and secured to its possessor every worldly advantage of wealth, honour, and power. An archbishop in the capital, obeyed by a bishop in every city, with numerous

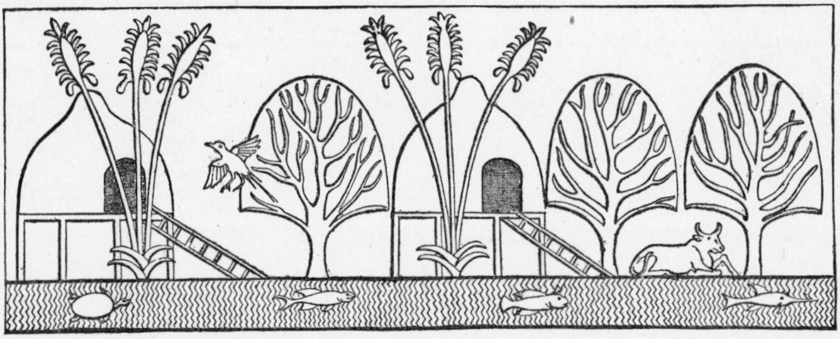

HOUSES BUILT ON PILES AT PUNT.

priests and deacons under them, was usually of more weight than the prefect. While Athanasius was at the height of his popularity in Egypt, and was supported by the Emperor of the West, the Emperor Constantius was very far from being his master. But on the death of Constans, when Constantius became sovereign of the whole empire, he once more tried to make Alexandria and the Egyptian church obedient to his wishes. He was, however, still doubtful how far it was prudent to measure his strength against that of the bishop, and he chose rather to begin privately with threats before using his power openly. He first wrote word to Athanasius, as if in answer to a request from the bishop, that he was at liberty, if he wished, to visit Italy; but he sent the letter by the hands of the notary Diogenes, who added, by word of mouth, that the permission was meant for a command, and that it was the emperor's pleasure that he should immediately quit his bishopric and the province. But this underhand conduct of the emperor only showed his own weakness. Athanasius steadily refused to obey any unwritten orders, and held his bishopric for upwards of two years longer, before Constantius felt strong enough to enforce his wishes. Towards the end of that time, Syrianus, the general of the Egyptian army, to whom this delicate task was entrusted, gathered together from other parts of the province a body of five thousand chosen men, and with these he marched quietly into Alexandria, to overawe, if possible, the rebellious bishop. He gave out no reason for his conduct; but the Arians, who were in the secret, openly boasted that it would soon be their turn to possess the churches. Syrianus then sent for Athanasius, and in the presence of Maximus the prefect again delivered to him the command of Constantius, that he should quit Egypt and retire into banishment, and he threatened to carry this command into execution by the help of the troops if he met with any resistance. Athanasius, without refusing to obey, begged to be shown the emperor's orders in writing; but this reasonable request was refused. He then entreated them even to give him, in their own handwriting, an order for his banishment; but this was also refused, and the citizens, who were made acquainted with the emperor's wishes and the bishop's firmness, waited in dreadful anxiety to see whether the prefect and the general would venture to enforce their orders. The presbytery of the church and the corporation of the city went up to Syrianus in solemn procession to beg him either to show a written authority for the banishment of their bishop, or to write to Constantinople to learn the emperor's pleasure. To this request Syrianus at last yielded, and gave his word to the friends of Athanasius that he would take no further steps till the return of the messengers which he then sent to Constantinople.

But Syrianus had before received his orders, which were, if possible, to frighten Athanasius into obedience, and, if that could not be done, then to employ force, but not to expose the emperor's written commands to the danger of being successfully resisted. He therefore only waited for an opportunity of carrying them into effect; and at midnight, on the ninth of February, A. D. 356, twenty-three days after the promise had been given, Syrianus, at the head of his troops, armed for the assault, surrounded the church where Athanasius and a crowded assembly were at prayers. The doors were forcibly and suddenly broken open, the armed soldiers rushed forward to seize the bishop, and numbers of his faithful friends were slain in their efforts to save him. Athanasius, however, escaped in the tumult; but though the general was unsuccessful, the bodies of the slain and the arms of the soldiers found scattered through the church in the morning were full proofs of his unholy attempt. The friends of the bishop drew up and signed a public declaration describing the outrage, and Syrianus sent to Constantinople a counter-protest declaring that there had been no disturbance in the city.

Athanasius, with nearly the whole of the nation for his friends, easily escaped the vengeance of the emperor; and, withdrawing for a third time from public life, he passed the remainder of this reign in concealment. He did not, however, neglect the interests of his flock. He encouraged them with his letters, and even privately visited his friends in Alexandria. As the greater part of the population was eager to befriend him, he was there able to hide himself for six years. Disregarding the scandal that might arise from it, he lived in the house of a young woman, who concealed him in her chamber, and waited on him with untiring zeal. She was then in the flower of her youth, only twenty years of age; and fifty years afterwards, in the reign of Theodosius II., when the name of the archbishop ranked with those of the apostles, this woman used to boast among the monks of Alexandria that in her youth she had for six years concealed the great Athanasius.

But though the general was not wholly successful, yet the Athanasian party was for the time crushed. Sebastianus, the new prefect, was sent into Egypt with orders to seize Athanasius dead or alive, wherever he should be found within the province; and under his protection the Arian party in Alexandria again ventured to meet in public, and proceeded to choose a bishop. They elected to this high position the celebrated George of

Cappadocia, a man who, while he equalled his more popular rival in learning and in ambition, fell far behind him in coolness of judgment, and in that political skill which is as much wanted in the guidance of a religious party as in the government of an empire.

George was born at Epiphania in Cilicia, and was the son of a clothier, but his ambition led him into the Church, as being at that time the fairest field for the display of talent; and he rose from one station to another till he reached the high post of Bishop of Alexandria. The fickle, irritable Alexandrians needed no such firebrand to light up the flames of discontent. George took no pains to conceal the fact that he held his bishopric by the favour of the emperor and the power of the army against the wishes of his flock. To support his authority, he opened his doors to informers of the worst description; anybody who stood in the way of his grasp at power was accused of being an enemy to the emperor. He proposed to the emperor to lay a house-tax on Alexandria, thereby to repay the expense incurred by Alexander the Great in building the city; and he made the imperial government more unpopular than it had ever been since Augustus landed in Egypt. He used the army as the means of terrifying the Homoousians into an acknowledgment of the Arian opinions. He banished fifteen bishops to the Great Oasis, besides others of lower rank. He beat, tortured, and put to death; the persecution was more cruel than any suffered from the pagans, except perhaps that in the reign of Diocletian; and thirty Egyptian bishops are said to have lost their lives while

George was patriarch of Alexandria. Most of these accusations, however, are from the pens of his enemies.

At this time the countries at the southern end of the Red Sea were becoming a little more known to Alexandria. Meropius, travelling in the reign of Constantine for curiosity and the sake of knowledge, had visited Auxum, the capital of the Hexumitæ, in Abyssinia. His companion Frumentius undertook to convert the people to Christianity and persuade them to trade with Egypt; and, as he found them willing to listen to his arguments, he came home to Alexandria to tell of his success and ask for support. Athanasius readily entered into a plan for spreading the blessings of Christianity and the power of the Alexandrian church. To increase the missionary's weight he consecrated him a bishop, and sent him back to Auxum to continue his good work. His progress, however, was somewhat checked by sectarian jealousy; for, when Athanasius was deposed by Constantius, Frumentius was recalled to receive again his orders and his opinions from the new patriarch. Constantius also sent an embassy to the Homeritæ on the opposite coast of Arabia, under Theophilus, a monk and deacon in the Church. The Homeritæ were of Jewish blood though of gentile faith, and were readily converted, if not to Christianity, at least to friendship with the emperor. After consecrating their churches, Theophilus crossed over to the African coast, to the Hexumitæ, to carry on the work which Frumentius had begun. There he was equally successful in the object of his embassy. Both in trade and in religion the Hexumitæ, who were also of

Jewish blood, were eager to be connected with the Europeans, from whom they were cut off by Arabs of a wilder race. He found also a little to the south of Auxum a settlement of Syrians, who were said to have been placed there by Alexander the Great. These tribes spoke the language called Ethiopic, a dialect of Arabic which was

TEMPLE OF ABU SIMBEL IN NUBIA.

not used in the country which we have hitherto called Ethiopia. The Ethiopic version of the Bible was about this time made for their use. It was translated out of the Greek from the Alexandrian copies, as the Greek version was held in such value that it was not thought necessary to look to the Hebrew original of the Old

Testament. But these well-meant efforts did little at the time towards making the Hexumitæ Christians. Distance and the Blemmyes checked their intercourse with Alexandria. It was not till two hundred years later that they could be said in the slightest sense to be converted to Christianity.

Though the origin of monastic life has sometimes been claimed for the Essenes on the shores of the Dead Sea, yet it was in Egypt that it was framed into a system, and became the model for the Christian world. It took its rise in the serious and gloomy views of religion which always formed part of the Egyptian polytheism, and which the Greeks remarked as very unlike their own gay and tasteful modes of worship, and which were readily engrafted by the Egyptian converts into their own Christian belief. In the reigns of Constantine and his sons, hundreds of Christians, both men and women, quitting the pleasures and trials of the busy world, withdrew one by one into the Egyptian desert, where the sands are as boundless as the ocean, where the sunshine is less cheerful than darkness, to spend their lonely days and watchful nights in religious meditation and in prayer. They were led by a gloomy view of their duty towards God, and by a want of fellow-feeling for their neighbour; and they seemed to think that pain and misery in this world would save them from punishment hereafter. The lives of many of these Fathers of the Desert were written by the Christians who lived at the same time; but a full account of the miracles which were said to have been worked in their favour, or by their means, would now only call forth a smile of pity, or perhaps even of ridicule.

" Prosperity and peace," says Gibbon, " introduced the distinction of the vulgar and the ascetic Christians. The loose and imperfect practice of religion satisfied the conscience of the multitude. The prince or magistrate, soldier or merchant, reconciled their fervent zeal, and implicit faith, with the exercise of their profession, the pursuit of their interest, and the indulgence of their passions; but the ascetics, who obeyed and abused the rigid precepts of the gospel, were inspired by the severe enthusiasm which represents man as a criminal and God as a tyrant. They seriously renounced the business and the pleasures of the age; abjured the use of wine, of flesh, and of marriage, chastised their body, mortified their affections, and embraced a life of misery, as the price of eternal happiness. The ascetics fled from a profane and degenerate world to perpetual solitude, or religious society. Like the first Christians of Jerusalem, they resigned the use, or the property, of their temporal possessions; established regular communities of the same sex and a similar disposition, and assumed the names of hermits, monks, or anchorites, expressive of their lonely retreat in a natural or artificial desert. They soon acquired the respect of the world, which they despised, and the loudest applause was bestowed on this divine philosophy, which surpassed, without the aid of science or reason, the laborious virtues of the Grecian schools. The monks might indeed contend with the Stoics in the contempt of fortune, of pain, and of death; the

Pythagorean silence and submission were revived in their servile discipline; and they disdained, as firmly as the Cynics themselves, all the forms and decencies of civil society. But the votaries of this divine philosophy aspired to imitate a purer and more perfect model. They trod in the footsteps of the prophets, who had retired to the desert; and they restored the devout and contemplative life, which had been instituted by the Essenians, in Palestine and Egypt. The philosophic eye of Pliny had surveyed with astonishment a solitary people who dwelt among the palm trees near the Dead Sea; who subsisted without money, who were propagated without women, and who derived from the disgust and repentance of mankind a perpetual supply of voluntary associates.

"Antony, an illiterate youth of the lower part of Thebaid, distributed his patrimony, deserted his family and native home, and executed his monastic penance with original and intrepid fanaticism. After a long and painful novitiate among the tombs and in a ruined tower, he boldly advanced into the desert three days' journey to the eastward of the Nile; discovered a lonely spot, which possessed the advantages of shade and water, and fixed his last residence on Mount Colzim near the Red Sea, where an ancient monastery still preserves the name and memory of the saint. The curious devotion of the Christians pursued him to the desert; and, when he was obliged to appear at Alexandria, in the face of mankind, he supported his fame with discretion and dignity. He enjoyed the friendship of Athanasius, whose doctrine he approved; and the Egyptian peasant respectfully declined a respectful invitation from the Emperor Constantine. The venerable patriarch (for Antony attained the age of 105 years) beheld the numerous progeny which had been formed by his example and his lessons. The prolific colonies of monks multiplied on the sands of Libya, upon the rocks of the Thebaid, and in the cities of the Nile. To the south of Alexandria, the mountain and adjacent desert of Nitria were peopled by five thousand anchorites; and the traveller may still investigate the ruins of fifty monasteries, which were planted in that barren soil by the disciples of Antony. In the Upper Thebaid, the vacant island of Tabenna was occupied by Pachomius and fourteen hundred of his brethren. That holy abbot successively founded nine monasteries of men and one of women; and the festival of Easter sometimes collected fifty thousand religious persons, who followed his angelic rules of discipline. The stately and populous city of Oxyrrhynchos, the seat of Christian orthodoxy, had devoted the temples, the public edifices, and even the ramparts, to pious and charitable uses, and the bishop, who might preach in twelve churches, computed ten thousand females and twenty thousand males of the monastic profession."

The monks borrowed many of their customs from the old Egyptian priests, such as shaving the head; and Athanasius in his charge to them orders them not to adopt the tonsure on the head, nor to shave the beard. He forbids their employing magic or incantations to assist their prayers. He endeavours to stop their emulation in fasting, and orders those whose strength of body enabled them to fast longest not to boast of it. But he orders them not even to speak to a woman, and wishes them not to bathe, as being an immodest act. The early Christians, as being a sect of Jews, had followed many Jewish customs, such as observing the Sabbath as well as the Lord's day; but latterly the line between the two religions had been growing wider, and Athanasius orders the monks not to keep holy the Jewish Sabbath. After a few years their religious duties were clearly laid down for them in several well-drawn codes.

One of the earliest of these ascetics was Ammon, who on the morning of his marriage is said to have persuaded his young wife of the superior holiness of a single life, and to have agreed with her that they should devote themselves apart to the honour of God in the desert. But, in thus avoiding the pleasures, the duties, and the temptations of the world, Ammon lost many of the virtues and even the decencies of society; he never washed himself, or changed his garments, because he thought it wrong for a religious man even to see himself undressed; and when he had occasion to cross a canal, his biographer tells us that attendant angels carried him over the water in their arms, lest, while keeping his vows, he should be troubled by wet clothes.

In the religious controversies, whether pagan or Christian, Rome had often looked to Egypt for its opinions; Constans, when wanting copies of the Greek Scriptures for Rome, had lately sent to Alexandria, and had received the approved text from Athanasius. The two countries held nearly the same opinions and had the same dislike of the Greeks; so when Jerome visited Egypt he found the Church holding, he said, the true Roman faith as taught by the apostles. Under Didymus, who was then the head of the catechetical school, Jerome pursued his studies, having the same religious opinions with the Egyptian, and the same dislike to Arianism. But no dread of heresy stopped Jerome in his search for knowledge and for books. He obtained copies of the whole of Origen's works, and read them with the greatest admiration. It is true that he finds fault with many of his opinions; but no admirer of Origen could speak in higher terms of praise of his virtues and his learning, of the qualities of his head and of his heart, than Jerome uses while he timidly pretends to think that he has done wrong in reading his works.

At this time—the end of the eleventh century after the building of the city—the emperor himself did not refuse to mark on his Roman coins the *happy renewal of the years* by the old Egyptian astrological fable of the return of the phœnix.

From the treatise of Julius Fermicus against the pagan superstitions, it would seem that the sacred animals of the Egyptians were no longer kept in the several cities in which they used to be worshipped, and that many of the old gods had been gradually dropped from the mythology, which was then chiefly confined to the worship of Isis and Osiris. The great week of the year was the feast of Isis, when the priests joined the goddess in her grief for the loss of the good Osiris, who had been killed through jealousy by the wicked Typhon. The priests shaved their heads, beat their breasts, tore the skin off their arms, and opened up the old wounds of former years, in grief for the death of Osiris, and in honour of the widowed Isis. The river Nile was also still worshipped for the blessings which it scatters along its banks, but we hear no more of Amon-Ra, Chem, Horus, Aroëris, and the other gods of the Thebaid, whose worship ceased with the fall of that part of the country.

COIN OF CONSTANTIUS, A. D. 347

But great changes often take place with very little improvement; the fall of idolatry only made way for the rise of magic and astrology. Abydos in Upper Egypt had latterly gained great renown for the temple of Bîsû, whose oracle was much consulted, not only by the Egyptians but by Greek strangers, and by others who sent their questions in writing. Some of these letters on parchment had been taken from the temple by informers, and carried to the emperor, whose ears were never deaf to a charge against the pagans. On this accusation numbers of all ranks were dragged out of Egypt, to be tried and punished in Syria, with torture and forfeiture of goods. Such indeed was the nation's belief in these oracles and prophecies that it gave to the priests a greater power than it was safe to trust them with. By prophesying that a man was to be an emperor, they could make him a traitor, and perhaps raise a village in rebellion. As the devotedness of their followers made it dangerous for the magistrates to punish the mischief-makers, they had no choice but to punish those who consulted them. Without forbidding the divine oracle to answer, they forbade anybody to question it. Parnasius, who had been a prefect of Egypt, a man of spotless character, was banished for thus illegally seeking a knowledge of the future; and Demetrius Cythras, an aged philosopher, was put to the rack on a charge of having sacrificed to the god, and only released because he persisted through his tortures in asserting that he sacrificed in gratitude and not from a wish thus to learn his future fate.

In the falling state of the empire the towns and villages of Egypt found their rulers too weak either to guard them or to tyrannise over them, and they sometimes formed themselves into small societies, and took means for their own defence. The law had so far allowed this as in some cases to grant a corporate constitution to a city. But in other cases a city kept in its pay a courtier or government servant powerful enough to guard it against the extortions of the provincial tax-gatherer, or would put itself under the patronage of a neighbour rich enough and strong enough to guard it. This, however, could not be allowed, even if not used as the means of throwing off the authority of the provincial government; and accordingly at this time we begin to find laws against the new crime of *patronage*. These associations gave a place of refuge to criminals, they stopped the worshipper in his way to the temple, and the tax-gatherer in collecting the tribute. But new laws have little weight when there is no power to enforce them, and the orders from Constantinople were little heeded in Upper Egypt.

But this *patronage* which the emperor wished to put down was weak compared to that of the bishops and clergy, which the law allowed and even upheld, and which was the great check to the tyranny of the civil governor. While the emperor at a distance gave orders through his prefect, the people looked up to the bishop as their head; and hence the power of each was checked by the other. The emperors had not yet made the terrors of religion a tool in the hands of the magistrate; nor had they yet learned from the pontifex and augurs of pagan Rome the secret that civil power is never so strong as when based on that of the Church.

On the death of Constantius, in 361, Julian was at once acknowledged as emperor, and the Roman world was again, but for the last time, governed by a pagan. The Christians had been in power for fifty-five years under Constantine and his sons, during which time the pagans had been made to feel that their enemies had got the upper hand of them. But on the accession of Julian their places were again changed; and the Egyptians among others crowded to Constantinople to complain of injustice done by the Christian prefect and bishop, and to pray for a redress of wrongs. They were, however, sadly disappointed in their emperor; he put them off with an unfeeling joke; he ordered them to meet him at Chalcedon on the other side of the straits of Constantinople, and, instead of following them according to his promise, he gave orders that no vessel should bring an Egyptian from Chalcedon to the capital; and the Egyptians, after wasting their time and money, returned home in despair. But though their complaints were laughed at, they were not overlooked, and the author of their grievances was punished; Artemius, the prefect of Egypt, was summoned to Chalcedon, and not being able to disprove the crimes laid to his charge by the Alexandrians, he paid his life as the forfeit for his misgovernment during the last reign.

While Artemius was on his trial the pagans of Alexandria remained quiet, and in daily fear of his return to power, for after their treatment at Chalcedon they by no means felt sure of what would be the emperor's policy in matters of religion; but they no sooner heard of the death of Artemius than they took it as a sign that they had full leave to revenge themselves on the Christians. The mob rose first against the Bishop George, who had lately been careless or wanton enough publicly to declare his regret that any of their temples should be allowed to stand; and they seized him in the streets and trampled him to death. They next slew Dracontius, the prefect of the Alexandrian mint, whom they accused of overturning a pagan altar within that building. Their anger was then turned against Diodorus, who was employed in building a church on a waste spot of ground that had once been sacred to the worship of Mithra, but had since been given by the Emperor Constantius to the Christians. In clearing the ground, the workmen had turned up a number of human bones that had been buried there in former ages, and these had been brought forward by the Christians in reproach against the pagans as so many proofs of human sacrifices. In his

Christian zeal, Diodorus also had wounded at the same time their pride and superstition by cutting off the single lock from the heads of the young Egyptians. This lock had in the time of Ramses been the mark of youthful royalty; under the Ptolemies the mark of high rank; but was now common to all. Diodorus treated it as an offence against his religion. For this he was attacked and killed, with George and Dracontius. The mob carried the bodies of the three murdered men upon camels to the side of the lake, and there burned them, and threw the ashes into the water, for fear, as they said, that a church should be built over their remains, as had been sometimes done, even at that early date, over the bodies of martyrs.

When the news of this outrage against the laws was brought to the philosophical emperor, he contented himself with threatening by an imperial edict that if the offence were repeated, he would visit it with severe punishment. But in every act of Julian we trace the scholar and the lover of learning. George had employed his wealth in getting together a large library, rich in historians, rhetoricians, and philosophers of all sects; and, on the murder of the bishop, Julian wrote letter after letter to Alexandria, to beg the prefect and his friend Porphyrius to save these books, and send them to him in Cappadocia. He promised freedom to the librarian if he gave them up, and torture if he hid them; and further begged that no books in favour of Christianity should be destroyed, lest other and better books should be lost with them.

A YOUNG EGYPTIAN WEARING THE ROYAL LOCK.

There is too much reason to believe that the friends of Athanasius were not displeased at the murder of the Bishop George and their Arian fellow-Christians; at any rate they made no effort to save them, and the same mob that had put to death George as an enemy to paganism now joined his rival, Athanasius, in a triumphal entry into the city, when, with the other Egyptian bishops, he was allowed to return from banishment. Athanasius could brook no rival to his power; the civil force of the city was completely overpowered by his party, and the Arian clergy were forced to hide themselves, as the only means of saving their lives. But, while thus in danger from their enemies, the Arians proceeded to elect a successor to their murdered bishop, and they chose Lucius to that post of honour, but of danger. Athanasius, however, in reality and openly filled the office of bishop; and he summoned a synod at Alexandria, at which he re-admitted into the church Lucifer and Eusebius, two bishops who had been banished to the Thebaid, and he again decreed that the three persons in the Trinity were of one substance.

Though the Emperor Julian thought that George, the late bishop, had deserved all that he suffered, as having been zealous in favour of Christianity, and forward in putting down paganism and in closing the temples, yet he was still more opposed to Athanasius. That able churchman held his power as a rebel by the help of the Egyptian mob, against the wishes of the Greeks of Alexandria and against the orders of the late emperor; and Julian made an edict, ordering that he should be driven out of the city within twenty-four hours of the command reaching Alexandria. The prefect of Egypt was at first unable, or unwilling, to enforce these orders against the wish of the inhabitants; and Athanasius was not driven into banishment till Julian wrote word that, if the rebellious bishop were to be found in any part of Egypt after a day then named, he would fine the prefect and the officers under him one hundred pounds weight of gold. Thus Athanasius was for the fourth time banished from Alexandria.

Though the Christians were out of favour with the emperor, and never were employed in any office of trust, yet they were too numerous for him to venture on a persecution. But Julian allowed them to be ill-treated by his prefects, and took no notice of their complaints. He made a law, forbidding any Christians being educated in pagan literature, believing that ignorance would stop the spread of their religion. In the churches of Greece, Asia Minor, and Syria, this was felt as a heavy grievance; but it was less thought of in Egypt. Science and learning were less cultivated by the Christians in Alexandria since the overthrow of the Arian party; and a little later, to charge a writer with Græcizing was the same as saying that he wanted orthodoxy.

Julian was a warm friend to learning and philosophy among the pagans. He recalled to Alexandria the physician Zeno, who in the last reign had fled from the Georgian faction, as the Christians were then called. He founded in the same city a college for music, and ordered the Prefect Ecdicius to look out for some young men of skill in that science, particularly from among the pupils of Dioscorus; and he allotted them a maintenance from the treasury, with rewards for the most skilful. At Canopus, a pagan philosopher, Antoninus, the son of Eustathius, taking advantage of the turn in public opinion, and copying the Christian monks of the Thebaid, drew round him a crowd of followers by his self-denial and painful torture of the body. The Alexandrians flocked in crowds to his dwelling; and such was his character for holiness that his death, in the beginning of the reign of Theodosius, was thought by the Egyptians to be the cause of the overthrow of paganism.

But Egyptian paganism, which had slumbered for fifty years under the Christian emperors, was not again to be awaked to its former life. Though the wars between the several cities for the honour of their gods, the bull, the crocodile, or the fish, had never ceased, all reverence for those gods was dead. The sacred animals, in particular the bulls Apis and Mnevis, were again waited upon by their priests as of old; but it was a vain attempt. Not only was the Egyptian religion overthrown, but the Thebaid, the country of that religion, was fallen too low to be raised again. The people of Upper Egypt had lost all heart, not more from the tyranny of the Roman government in the north than from the attacks and settlement of the Arabs in the south. All changes in the country, whether for the better or the worse, were laid to the charge of these latter unwelcome neighbours; and when the inquiring traveller asked to be shown the crocodile, the river-horse, and the other animals for which Egypt had once been noted, he was told with a sigh that they were seldom to be seen in the Delta since the Thebaid had been peopled with the Blemmyes. Falsehood, the usual vice of slaves, had taken a deep hold on the Egyptian character. A denial of their wealth was the means by which they usually tried to save it from the Roman tax-gatherer; and an Egyptian was ashamed of himself as a coward if he could not show a back covered with stripes gained in the attempt to save his money. Peculiarities of character often descend unchanged in a nation for many centuries; and, after fourteen hundred years of the same slavery, the same stripes from the lash of the tax-gatherer still used to be the boast of the Egyptian peasant. Cyrene was already a desert; the only cities of note in Upper Egypt were Koptos, Hermopolis, and Antinoopolis; but Alexandria was still the queen of cities, though the large quarter called the Bruchium had not been rebuilt; and the Serapeum, with its library of seven hundred thousand volumes, was, after the capitol of Rome, the chief building in the world.

This temple of Serapis was situated on a rising ground at the west end of the city, and, though not built like a fortification, was sometimes called the citadel of Alexandria. It was entered by two roads; that on one side was a slope for carriages, and on the other a grand flight of a hundred steps from the street, with each step wider than that below it. At the top of this flight of steps was a portico, in the form of a circular roof, upheld by four columns. Through this was the entrance into the great courtyard, in the middle of which stood the roofless hall or temple, surrounded by columns and porticoes, inside and out. In some of the inner porticoes were the bookcases for the library which made Alexandria

AN EGYPTIAN WATER-CARRIER.

the very temple of science and learning, while other porticoes were dedicated to the service of the ancient religion. The roofs were ornamented with gilding, the capitals of the columns were of copper gilt, and the walls were covered with paintings. In the middle of the inner area stood one lofty column, which could be seen by all the country round, and even from ships some distance out at sea. The great statue of Serapis, which had been made under the Ptolemies, having perhaps marble feet, but for the rest built of wood, clothed with drapery, and glittering with gold and silver, stood in one of the covered chambers, which had a small window so contrived as to let the sun's rays kiss the lips of the statue on the appointed occasions. This was one of the tricks employed in the sacred mysteries, to dazzle the worshipper by the sudden blaze of light which on the proper occasions was let into the dark room. The temple itself, with its fountain, its two obelisks, and its gilt ornaments, has long since been destroyed; and the column in the centre, under the name of Pompey's Pillar,[1] alone remains to mark the spot where it stood, and is one of the few works of Greek art which in size and strength vie with the old Egyptian monuments.

The reign of Julian, instead of raising paganism to its former strength, had only shown that its life was spent; and under Jovian (A. D. 363—364) the Christians were again brought into power. A Christian emperor, however, would have been but little welcome to the Egyptians if, like Constantius, and even Constantine in his latter years, he had leaned to the Arian party; but Jovian soon showed his attachment to the Nicene creed, and he re-appointed Athanasius to the bishopric of Alexandria. But though Athanasius regained his rank,

[1] See Volume X, page 317.

yet the Arian bishop Lucius was not deposed. Each party in Alexandria had its own bishop; those who thought that the Son was of the *same* substance with the Father looked up to Athanasius, while those who gave to Jesus the lower rank of being of a *similar* substance to the Creator obeyed Lucius.

This curious metaphysical proposition was not, however, the only cause of the quarrel which divided Egypt into such angry parties. The creeds were made use of as the watchwords in a political struggle. Blood, language, and geographical boundaries divided the parties; and religious opinions seldom cross these unchanging and inflexible lines.

Every Egyptian believed in the Nicene creed and the incorruptibility of the body of Jesus, and hated the Alexandrian Greeks; while the more refined Greeks were as united in explaining away the Nicene creed by the doctrine of the two natures of Christ, and in despising the ignorant Egyptians. Christianity, which speaks so forcibly to the poor, the unlearned, and the slave, had educated the Egyptian population, had raised them in their own eyes; and, as the popular party gained strength, the Arians lost ground in Alexandria. At the same time the Greeks were falling off in learning and in science, and in all those arts of civilisation which had given them the superiority. Like other great political changes, this may not have been understood at the time; but in less than a hundred years it was found that the Egyptians were no longer the slaves, nor the Greeks the masters.

On the death of Jovian, when Valentinian divided the Roman empire with his brother, he took Italy and the West for his own kingdom, and gave to Valens Egypt and the Eastern provinces, in which Greek was the language of the government. Each emperor adopted the religion of his capital; Valentinian held the Nicene faith, and Valens the Arian faith; and unhappy Egypt was the only part of the empire whose religion differed from that of its rulers. Had the creeds marked the limits of the two empires, Egypt would have belonged to Rome; but, as geographical boundaries and language form yet stronger ties, Egypt was given to Constantinople, or rather to Antioch, the nearer of the two Eastern capitals.

By Valens, Athanasius was forced for the fifth time to fly from Alexandria, to avoid the displeasure which his disobedience again drew down upon him. But his flock again rose in rebellion in favour of their popular bishop; and the emperor was either persuaded or frightened into allowing him to return to his bishopric, where he spent the few remaining years of his life in peace. Athanasius died at an advanced age, leaving a name more famous than that of any one of the emperors under whom he lived. He taught the Christian world that there was a power greater than that of kings, namely the Church. He was often beaten in the struggle, but every victory over him was followed by the defeat of the civil power; he was five times banished, but five times he returned in triumph. The temporal power of the Church was in its infancy; it only rose upon the conversion of Constantine, and it was weak compared to what it became in after ages; but, when the Emperor of Germany did penance barefoot before Pope Hildebrand, and a king of England was whipped at Becket's tomb, we only witness the full-grown strength of the infant power that was being reared by the Bishop of Alexandria. His writings are numerous and wholly controversial, chiefly against the Arians. The Athanasian creed seems to have been so named only because it was thought to contain his opinions, as it is known to be by a later author.

On the death of Athanasius, the Homoousian party chose Peter as his successor in the bishopric, overlooking Lucius, the Arian bishop, whose election had been approved by the emperors Julian, Jovian, and Valens. But as the Egyptian church had lost its great champion, the emperor ventured to re-assert his authority. He sent Peter to prison, and ordered all the churches to be given up to the Arians, threatening with banishment from Egypt whoever disobeyed his edict. The persecution which the Homoousian party throughout Upper Egypt then suffered from the Arians equalled, says the ecclesiastical historian, anything that they had before suffered from the pagans. Every monastery in Egypt was broken open by Lucius at the head of an armed force, and the cruelty of the bishop surpassed that of the soldiers. The breaking open of the monasteries seems to have been for the purpose of making the inmates bear their share in the military service of the state, rather than for any religious reasons. When Constantine embraced Christianity, he immediately recognised all the religious scruples of its professors; and not only bishops and presbyters but all laymen who had entered the monastic orders were freed from the duty of serving in the army. But under the growing dislike of military service, and the difficulty of finding soldiers, when to escape from the army many called themselves Christian monks, this excuse could no longer be listened to, and Valens made a law that monastic vows should not save a man from enlistment. But this law was not easily carried into force in the monasteries on the borders of the desert, which were often well-built and well-guarded fortresses; and on Mount Nitria, in particular, many monks lost their lives in their resistance to the troops that were sent to fetch recruits.

The monastic institutions of Egypt had already reached their full growth. They were acknowledged by the laws of the empire as ecclesiastical corporations, and allowed to hold property; and by a new law of this reign, if a monk or nun died without a will or any known kindred, the property went to the monastery as heir at law. One of the most celebrated of these monasteries was on Tabenna, where Pachomius had gathered round him thirteen hundred followers, who owned him as the founder of their order, and gave him credit for the gift of prophecy. His disciples in the other monasteries of Upper Egypt amounted to six thousand more. Anuph was at the head of another order of monks, and he boasted that he could by prayer obtain from heaven whatever he wished. Hor was at the head of another monastery, where, though wholly unable to read or write, he spent

REMAINS OF CHRISTIAN CHURCH IN THE TEMPLE AT LUXOR.

his life in singing psalms, and, as his followers and perhaps he himself believed, in working miracles. Serapion was at the head of a thousand monks in the Arsinoïte nome, who raised their food by their own labour, and shared it with their poorer neighbours. Near Nitria, a place in the Mareotic nome which gave its name to the nitre springs, there were as many as fifty cells; but those who aimed at greater solitude and severer mortification withdrew farther into the desert, to Scetis in the same nome, a spot already sanctified by the trials and triumphs of St. Anthony. Here, in a monastery surrounded by the sands, by the side of a lake whose waters are salter than the brine of the ocean, with no grass or trees to rest the aching eye, where the dazzling sky is seldom relieved with a cloud, where the breezes are too often laden with dry dust, these monks cultivated a gloomy religion, with hearts painfully attuned to the scenery around them. Here dwelt Moses, who in his youth had been a remarkable sinner, and in his old age became even more remarkable as a saint. It was said that for six years he spent every night in prayer, without once closing his eyes in sleep; and that one night, when his cell was attacked by four robbers, he carried them all off at once on his back to the neighbouring monastery to be punished, because he would himself hurt no man. Benjamin also dwelt at Scetis; he consecrated oil to heal the diseases of those who washed with it, and during the eight months that he was himself dying of a dropsy, he touched for their diseases all who came to the door of his cell to be healed. Hellas carried fire in his bosom without burning his clothes. Elias spent seventy years in solitude on the borders of the Arabian desert near Antinoopolis. Apelles was a blacksmith near Achoris; he was tempted by the devil in the form of a beautiful woman, but he scorched the tempter's face with a red-hot iron. Dorotheus, who though a Theban had settled near Alexandria, mortified his flesh by trying to live without sleep. He never willingly lay down to rest, nor indeed ever slept till the weakness of the body sunk under the efforts of the spirit. Paul, who dwelt at Pherma, repeated three hundred prayers every day, and kept three hundred pebbles in a bag to help him in his reckoning. He was the friend of Anthony, and when dying begged to be wrapt in the cloak given him by that holy monk, who had himself received it as a present from Athanasius. His friends and admirers claimed for Paul the honour of being the first Christian hermit, and they maintained their improbable opinion by asserting that he had been a monk for ninety-seven years, and that he had retired to the desert at the age of sixteen, when the Church was persecuted in the reign of Valerian.

All Egypt believed that the monks were the especial favourites of Heaven, that they worked miracles, and that divine wisdom flowed from their lips without the help or hindrance of human learning. They were all Homoousians, believing that the Son was of one substance with the Father; some as trinitarians holding the opinions of Athanasius; some as Sabellians believing that Jesus was the creator of the world, and that his body therefore was not liable to corruption; some as anthropomorphites believing God was of human form like Jesus; but all warmly attached to the Nicene creed, denying the two natures of Christ, and hating the Arian Greeks of Alexandria and the other cities. Gregory of Nazianzum remarks that Egypt was the most Christ-loving of countries, and adds with true simplicity that, wonderful to say, after having so lately worshipped bulls, goats, and crocodiles, it was now teaching the world the worship of the Trinity in the truest form.

The pagans, who were now no longer able to worship publicly as they chose, took care to proclaim their opinions indirectly in such ways as the law could not reach. In the hippodrome, which was the noisiest of the places where the people met in public, they made a profession of their faith by the choice of which horses they bet on; and Christians and pagans alike showed their zeal for religion by hooting and clapping of hands. Prayers and superstitious ceremonies were used on both sides to add to the horses' speed; and the monk Hilarion, the pupil of Anthony, gained no little credit for sprinkling holy water on the horses of his party, and thus enabling Christianity to outrun paganism in the hippodrome at Gaza.

During these reigns of weakness and misgovernment, it was no doubt a cruel policy rather than humanity that led the tax-gatherers to collect the tribute in kind. More could be squeezed out of a ruined people by taking what they had to give than by requiring it to be paid in copper coin. Hence Valens made a law that no tribute throughout the empire should be taken in money; and he laid a new land-tax upon Egypt, to the amount of a soldier's clothing for every thirty acres.

The Saracens [1] had for some time past been encroaching on the Eastern frontiers of the empire, and had only been kept back by treaties which proved the weakness of the Romans, as the armies of Constantinople were still called, and which encouraged the barbarians in their attacks. On the death of their king, the command over the Saracens fell to their Queen Mævia, who broke the last treaty, laid waste Palestine and Phœnicia with her armies, conquered or gained over the Arabs of Petra, and pressed upon the Egyptians at the head of the Red Sea. On this, Valens renewed the truce, but on terms still more favourable to the invaders. Many of the Saracens were Christians, and by an article of the treaty they were to have a bishop granted them for their church, and for this purpose they sent Moses to Alexandria to be ordained. But the Saracens sided with the Egyptians, in religion as well as policy, against the Arian Greeks. Hence Moses refused to be ordained by Lucius, the patriarch of Alexandria, and chose rather to receive his appointment from some of the Homoousian bishops who were living in banishment in the Thebaid. After this advance of the barbarians the interesting city of Petra, which since the time of Trajan had been in the power or the friendship of Rome or Constantinople, was lost to the civilised world. This rocky fastness, which was

[1] The name *Saraceni* was given by the Greeks and Romans to the nomadic Arabs who lived on the borders of the desert. During the Middle Ages, the Muhammedans, coming from apparently the same localities, were also called Saracens.

ornamented with temples, a triumphal arch, and a theatre, and had been a bishop's see, was henceforth closed against all travellers; it had no place in the map till it was discovered by Burckhardt in our own days without a human being dwelling in it, with oleanders and tamarisks choking up its entrance through the cliff, and with brambles trailing their branches over the rock-hewn temples.

The reign of Theodosius, which extended from 379

TEMPLE COURTYARD, MEDINET ABU.

to 395, is remarkable for the blow then given to paganism. The old religion had been sinking even before Christianity had become the religion of the emperors; it had been discouraged by Constantine, who had closed many of the temples; but Theodosius made a law in the first year of his reign that the whole of the empire should be Christian, and should receive the trinitarian faith. He soon afterwards ordered that Sunday should be kept holy, and forbade all work and law-proceedings on that day; and he sent Cynegius, the prefect of the palace, into Egypt, to see these laws carried into effect in that province.

The wishes of the emperor were ably followed up by Theophilus, Bishop of Alexandria. He cleansed the temple of Mithra, and overthrew the statues in the celebrated temple of Serapis, which seemed the very citadel of paganism. He also exposed to public ridicule the mystic ornaments and statues which a large part of his fellow-citizens still regarded as sacred. It was not, however, to be supposed that this could be peaceably borne by a people so irritable as the Alexandrians. The students in the schools of philosophy put themselves at the head of the mob to stop the work of destruction, and to revenge themselves upon their assailants, and several battles were fought in the streets between the pagans and the Christians, in which both parties lost many lives; but as the Christians were supported by the power of the prefect, the pagans were routed, and many whose rank would have made them objects of punishment were forced to fly from Alexandria.

No sooner had the troops under the command of the prefect put down the pagan opposition than the work of destruction was again carried forward by the zeal of the bishop. The temples were broken open, their ornaments destroyed, and the statues of the gods melted for the use of the Alexandrian church. One statue of an Egyptian god was alone saved from the wreck, and was set up in mockery of those who had worshipped it; and this ridicule of their religion was a cause of greater anger to the pagans than even the destruction of the other statues. The great statue of Serapis, which was made of wood covered with plates of metal, was knocked to pieces by the axes of the soldiers. The head and limbs were broken off, and the wooden trunk was burnt in the amphitheatre amid the shouts and jeers of the bystanders. A conjectured fragment of this statue is now in the British Museum.

In the plunder of the temple of Serapis, the great library of more than seven hundred thousand volumes was wholly broken up and scattered. Orosius, the Spaniard, who visited Alexandria in the next reign, may be trusted when he says that he saw in the temple the empty shelves, which, within the memory of men then living, had been plundered of the books that had formerly been got together after the library of the Bruchium was burnt by Julius Cæsar. In a work of such lawless plunder, carried on by ignorant zealots, many of these monuments of pagan genius and learning must have been wilfully or accidentally destroyed, though the larger number may have been carried off by the Christians for the other public and private libraries of the city. How many other libraries this city of science may have possessed we are not told, but there were no doubt many. Had Alexandria during the next two centuries given birth to poets and orators, their works, the offspring of native genius, might perhaps have been written without the help of libraries; but the labours of the mathematicians and grammarians prove that the city was still well furnished with books, beside those on the Christian controversies.

When the Christians were persecuted by the pagans, none but men of unblemished lives and unusual strength of mind stood to their religion in the day of trial, and suffered the penalties of the law; the weak, the ignorant, and the vicious readily joined in the superstitions required of them, and, embracing the religion of the stronger party, easily escaped punishment. So it was when the pagans of Alexandria were persecuted by Theophilus; the chief sufferers were the men of learning, in whose minds paganism was a pure deism, and who saw nothing but ignorance and superstition on the side of their oppressors; who thought their worship of the Trinity only a new form of polytheism, and jokingly declared that they were not arithmeticians enough to understand it. Olympius, who was the priest of Serapis when the temple was sacked, and as such the head of the pagans of Alexandria, was a man in every respect the opposite of the Bishop Theophilus. He was of a frank, open countenance and agreeable manners; and though his age might have allowed him to speak among his followers in the tone of command, he chose rather in his moral lessons to use the mild persuasion of an equal; and few hearts were so hardened as not to be led into the paths of duty by his exhortations. Whereas the furious monks, says the indignant pagan, were men only in form, but swine in manners. Whoever put on a black coat, and was not ashamed to be seen with dirty linen, gained a tyrannical power over the minds of the mob, from their belief in his holiness; and these men attacked the temples of the gods as a propitiation for their own enormous sins. Thus each party reproached the other, and often unjustly. Among other religious frauds and pretended miracles of which the pagan priests were accused, was that of having an iron statue of Serapis hanging in the air in a chamber of the temple, by means of a loadstone fixed in the ceiling. The natural difficulties shield them from this charge, but other accusations are not so easily rebutted.

After this attack upon the pagans, their religion was no longer openly taught in Alexandria. Some of the more zealous professors withdrew from the capital to Canopus, about ten miles distant, where the ancient priestly learning was still taught, unpersecuted because unnoticed; and there, under the pretence of studying hieroglyphics, a school was opened for teaching magic and other forbidden rites. When the pagan worship ceased throughout Egypt, the temples were very much used as churches, and in some cases received in their ample courtyard a smaller church of Greek architecture, as in that of Medinet Abu. In other cases Christian ornaments were added to the old walls, as in the rock temple of Kneph, opposite to Abû Simbel, where the figure of the Saviour with a glory round his head has been painted on the ceiling. The Christians, in order to remove from before their eyes the memorials of the old superstition, covered up the sculpture on the walls with mud from the Nile and white plaster. This coating we now take away, at a time when the idolatrous figures are no longer dangerous to religion, and we find the sculpture and painting fresh as when covered up fourteen hundred years ago.

It would be unreasonable to suppose that the Egyptians, upon embracing Christianity, at once threw off all of their pagan rites. Among other customs that they still clung to, was that of making mummies of the bodies of the dead. St. Anthony had tried to dissuade the Christian converts from that practice; not because the mummy-cases were covered with pagan inscriptions,

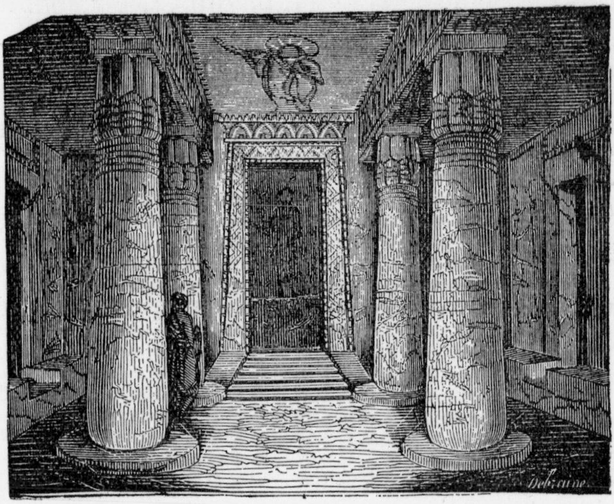

CHRISTIAN PICTURE AT ABÛ SIMBEL.

but he boldly asserted, what a very little reading would have disproved, that every mode of treating a dead body, beside burial, was forbidden in the Bible. St. Augustine, on the other hand, well understanding that the immortality of the soul without the body was little likely to be understood or valued by the ignorant, praises the Egyptians for that very practice, and says that they were the only Christians who really believed in the resurrection from the dead. The tapers burnt before the altars were from the earliest times used to light up the splendours of the Egyptian altars, in the darkness of their temples, and had been burnt in still greater numbers in the yearly festival of the candles. The playful custom of giving away sugared cakes and sweetmeats on the twenty-fifth day of Tybi, our twentieth of January, was then changed to be kept fourteen days earlier, and it still marks the Feast of Epiphany or Twelfth-night. The division of the people into clergy and laity, which was unknown to Greeks and Romans, was introduced into Christianity in the fourth century by the Egyptians. While the rest of Christendom were clothed in woollen, linen, the common dress of the Egyptians, was universally adopted by the clergy as more becoming to the purity of their manners. At the same time the clergy copied the Egyptian priests in the custom of shaving the crown of the head bald.

The new law in favour of trinitarian Christianity was enforced with as great strictness against the Arians as against the pagans. The bishops and priests of that party were everywhere turned out of their churches, which were then given up to the Homoousians. Theodosius summoned a council of one hundred and fifty bishops at Constantinople, to re-enact the Nicene creed; and in the future religious rebellions of the Egyptians they always quoted against the Greeks this council of Constantinople, with that of Nicæa, as the foundation of their faith. By this religious policy, Theodosius did much to delay the fall of the empire. He won the friendship of his Egyptian subjects, as well as of their Saracen neighbours, all of whom, as far as they were Christian, held to the Nicene creed. Egypt became the safest of his provinces; and, when his armies had been recruited with so many barbarians that they could no longer be trusted, these new levies were marched into Egypt under the command of Hormisdas, and an equal number of Egyptians were drafted out of the army of Egypt, and led into Thessaly.

When the season came for the overflow of the Nile,

MANFALOOT, SHOWING THE HEIGHT OF THE NILE IN SUMMER.

in the first summer after the destruction of the temples, the waters happened to rise more slowly than usual; and the Egyptians laid the blame upon the Christian emperor, who had forbidden their sacrificing the usual offerings in honour of the river-god. The alarm for the loss of their crops carried more weight in the religious controversy than any arguments that could be brought against pagan sacrifices; and the anger of the people soon threatened a serious rebellion. Evagrius the prefect, being disturbed for the peace of the country, sent to Constantinople for orders; but the emperor remained firm; he would make no change in the law against paganism, and the fears of the Egyptians and Alexandrians were soon put an end to by a most plenteous overflow.

Since the time of Athanasius, and the overthrow of the Arian party in Alexandria, the learning of that city was wholly in the hands of the pagans, and was chiefly mathematical. Diophantus of Alexandria is the earliest writer on algebra whose works are now remaining to us, and has given his name to the Diophantine problems. Pappus wrote a description of the world, and a commentary on Ptolemy's *Almagest*, beside a work on geometry, published under the name of his *Mathematical Collections*. Theon, a professor in the museum, wrote on the smaller astrolabe—the instrument then used to measure the star orbits—and on the rise of the Nile, a subject always of interest to the mathematicians of Egypt, from its importance to the husbandman. From Theon's astronomical observations we learn that the Alexandrian astronomers still made use of the old Egyptian movable year of three hundred and sixty-five days only, and without a leap-year. Paul the Alexandrian astrologer, on the other hand, uses the Julian year of three hundred and sixty-five days and a quarter, and he dates from the era of Diocletian. His rules for telling the day of the week from the day of the month, and for telling on what day of the week each year began, teach us that our present mode of dividing time was used in Egypt. Horapollo, the grammarian, was also then a teacher in the schools of Alexandria. He wrote in the Koptic language a work in explanation of the old hieroglyphics, which has gained a notice far beyond its deserts, because it is the only work on the subject that has come down to us.

The only Christian writings of this time, that we know of, are the paschal letters of Theophilus, Bishop of Alexandria, which were much praised by Jerome, and by him translated into Latin. They are full of bitter reproaches against Origen and his writings, and they charge him with having treated Jesus more cruelly than Pilate or the Jews had done. John, the famous monk of the Thebaid, was no writer, though believed to have the gift of prophecy. He was said to have foretold the victory of Theodosius over the rebel Maximus; and, when the emperor had got together his troops to march against Eugenius, another rebel who had seized the passes of the Julian Alps, he sent his trusty eunuch Eutropius to fetch the holy Egyptian, or at least to learn from him what would be the event of the war. John refused to go to Europe, but he told the messenger that Theodosius would conquer the rebel, and soon afterwards die; both of which came to pass as might easily have been guessed.

On the death of Theodosius, in 395, the Roman empire was again divided. Arcadius, his elder son, ruled Egypt and the East, while Honorius, the younger, held the West; and the reins of government at once passed from the ablest to the weakest hands. But the change was little felt in Egypt, which continued to be governed by the patriarch Theophilus, without the name but with very nearly the power of a prefect. He was a bold and wicked man, but as his religious opinions were for the

Homoousians as against the Arians, and his political feelings were for the Egyptians as against the Greeks, he rallied to his government the chief strength of the province. As the pagans and Arians of Alexandria were no longer worthy of his enmity, he fanned into a flame a new quarrel which was then breaking out in the Egyptian church. The monks of Upper Egypt, who were mostly ignorant and unlettered men, were anthropomorphites, or believers that God was in outward shape like a man. They quoted from the Jewish Scriptures that he made man in his own image, in support of their opinion. They held that he was of a strictly human form, like Jesus, which to them seemed fully asserted in the Nicene creed. In this opinion they were opposed by those who were better educated, and it suited the policy of Theophilus to side with the more ignorant and larger party. He branded with the name of Origenists those who argued that God was without form, and who quoted the writings of Origen in support of their opinion. This naturally led to a dispute about Origen's orthodoxy; and that admirable writer, who had been praised by all parties for two hundred years, and who had been quoted as authority as much by Athanasius as by the Arians, was declared to be a heretic by a council of bishops. The writings of Origen were accordingly forbidden to be read, because they contradicted the anthropomorphite opinions.

The quarrel between the Origenists and the anthropomorphites did not end in words. A proposition in theology, or a doubt in metaphysics, was no better cause of civil war than the old quarrels about the bull Apis or the crocodile; but a change of religion had not changed the national character. The patriarch, finding his party the stronger, attacked the enemy in their own monasteries; he marched to Mount Nitria at the head of a strong body of soldiers, and, enrolling under his banners the anthropomorphite monks, attacked Dioscorus and the Origenists, set fire to their monasteries, and laid waste the place.

Theophilus next quarrelled with Peter, the chief of the Alexandrian presbyters, whom he accused of admitting to the sacraments of the church a woman who had not renounced the Manichean heresy; and he then quarrelled with Isidorus, who had the charge of the poor of the church, because he bore witness that Peter had the orders of Theophilus himself for what he did.

In this century there was a general digging up of the bodies of the most celebrated Christians of former ages, to heal the diseases and strengthen the faith of the living; and Constantinople, which as the capital of the empire had been ornamented by the spoils of its subject provinces, had latterly been enriching its churches with the remains of numerous Christian saints. The tombs of Egypt, crowded with mummies that had lain there for centuries, could of course furnish relics more easily than most countries, and in this reign Constantinople received from Alexandria a quantity of bones which were supposed to be those of the martyrs slain in the pagan persecutions. The archbishop John Chrysostom received them gratefully, and, though himself smarting under the reproach that he was not orthodox enough for the superstitious Egyptians, he thanks God that Egypt, which sent forth its grain to feed its hungry neighbours, could also send the bodies of so many martyrs to sanctify their churches.

We have traced the fall of the Greek party in Alexandria, in the victories over the Arians during the religious quarrels of the last hundred years; and in the laws we now read the city's loss of wealth and power. The corporation of Alexandria was no longer able to bear the expense of cleansing the river and keeping open the canals; and four hundred *solidi*—about twelve hundred dollars—were each year set apart from the custom-house duties of the city for that useful work.

The arrival of new settlers in Alexandria had been very much checked by the less prosperous state of the country since the reign of Diocletian. We still find, however, that many of the men of note were not born in Egypt. Paulus, the physician, was a native of Ægina. He has left a work on diseases and their remedies. The chief man of learning was Synesius, a platonic philosopher whom the patriarch Theophilus persuaded to join the Christians. As a platonist he naturally leaned towards many of the doctrines of the popular religion, but he could not believe in a resurrection; and it was not till after Theophilus had ordained him Bishop of Ptolemais near Cyrene that he acknowledged the truth of that doctrine. Nor would he then put away or disown his wife, as the custom of the Church required; indeed, he accepted the bishopric very unwillingly. He was as fond of playful sport as he was of books, and very much disliked business. He has left a volume of writings, which has saved the names of two prefects of Cyrene; the one Anysius, under whose good discipline even the barbarians of Hungary behaved like Roman legionaries, and the other Pæonius, who cultivated science in this barren spot. To encourage Pæonius in his praiseworthy studies he made him a present of an astrolabe, to measure the distances of the stars and planets, an instrument which was constructed under the guidance of Hypatia.

Trade and industry were checked by the unsettled state of the country, and misery and famine were spreading over the land. The African tribes of Mazices and Auxoriani, leaving the desert in hope of plunder, overran the province of Libya, and laid waste a large part of the Delta. The barbarians and the sands of the desert were alike encroaching on the cultivated fields. Nature seemed changed. The valley of the Nile was growing narrower. Even within the valley the retreating waters left behind them harvests less rich, and fever more putrid. The quarries were no longer worth working for their building stone. The mines yielded no more gold.

On the death of Arcadius, his son Theodosius was only eight years old, but he was quietly acknowledged as Emperor of the East in 408, and he left the government of Egypt, as heretofore, very much in the hands of the patriarch. In the fifth year of his reign Theophilus died; and, as might be supposed, a successor was not appointed without a struggle for the double honour of Bishop of

Alexandria and Governor of Egypt. The remains of the Greek and Arian party proposed Timotheus, an archdeacon in the church; but the Egyptian party were united in favour of Cyril, a young man of learning and talent, who had the advantage of being the nephew of the late bishop. Whatever were the forms by which the

QUARRIES AT TOORAH ON THE NILE.

election should have been governed, it was in reality settled by a battle between the two parties in the streets; and though Abundantius, the military prefect, gave the weight of his name, if not the strength of his cohort, to the party of Timotheus, yet his rival conquered, and Cyril was carried into the cathedral with a pomp more like a pagan triumph than the modest ordination of a bishop.

Cyril was not less tyrannical in his bishopric than his uncle had been before him. His first care was to put a stop to all heresy in Alexandria, and his second to banish the Jews. The theatre was the spot in which the riots between Jews and Christians usually began, and the Sabbath was the time, as being the day on which the Jews chiefly crowded in to see the dancing. On one occasion the quarrel in the theatre ran so high that the prefect with his cohort was scarcely able to keep them from blows; and the Christians reproached the Jews with plotting to burn down the churches. But the Christians were themselves guilty of the very crimes of which they accused their enemies. The next morning, as soon as it was light, Cyril headed the mob in their attacks upon the Jewish synagogues; they broke them open and plundered them, and in one day drove every Jew out of the city. No Jew had been allowed to live in Alexandria or any other city without paying a poll-tax, for leave to worship his God according to the manner of his forefathers; but religious zeal is stronger than the love of money; the Jews were driven out, and the tax lost to the city.

Orestes, the prefect of Alexandria, had before wished to check the power of the bishop; and he in vain tried to save the Jews from oppression, and the state from the loss of so many good citizens. But it was useless to quarrel with the patriarch, who was supported by the religious zeal of the whole population. The monks of Mount Nitria and of the neighbourhood burned with a holy zeal to fight for Cyril, as they had before fought

Street and Mosque of Mahdjiar

for Theophilus; and when they heard that a jealousy had sprung up between the civil and ecclesiastical authorities, more than five hundred of them marched into Alexandria to avenge the affronted bishop. They met the prefect Orestes as he was passing through the streets in his open chariot, and began reproaching him with being a pagan and a Greek. Orestes answered that he was a Christian, and he had been baptised at Constantinople. But this only cleared him of the lesser charge, he was certainly a Greek; and one of these Egyptian monks taking up a stone threw it at his head, and the blow covered his face with blood. They then fled from the guards and people who came up to help the wounded prefect; but Ammonius, who threw the stone, was taken and put to death with torture. The grateful bishop buried him in the church with much pomp; he declared him to be a martyr and a saint, and gave him the name of St. Thaumasius. But the Christians were ashamed of the new martyr: and the bishop, who could not withstand the ridicule, soon afterwards withdrew from him the title.

Bad as was this behaviour of the bishop and his friends, the most disgraceful tale still remains to be told. The beautiful and learned Hypatia, the daughter of Theon the mathematician, was at that time the ornament of Alexandria and the pride of the pagans. She taught philosophy publicly in the platonic school which had been founded by Ammonius, and which boasted of Plotinus as its pupil. She was as modest as she was graceful, eloquent, and learned; and though, being a pagan, she belonged to neither of the rival Christian parties, yet, as she had more hearers among the Greek friends of the prefect than among the ignorant followers of the bishop, she became an object of jealousy with the Homoousian party. A body of these Christians, says the orthodox historian, attacked this admirable woman in the street; they dragged her from her chariot, and hurried her off into the church named Cæsar's temple, and there stripped her and murdered her with some broken tiles. She had written commentaries on the mathematical works of Diophantus, and on the conic sections of Apollonius. The story of her life has been related in the nineteenth century by Charles Kingsley in the novel which bears her name.

Arianism took refuge from the Egyptians within the camps of the Greek soldiers. One church was dedicated to the honour of St. George, the late bishop, within the lofty towers of the citadel of Babylon, which was the strongest fortress in Egypt; and a second in the city of Ptolemais, where a garrison was stationed to collect the toll of the Thebaid. St. George became a favourite saint with the Greeks in Egypt, and in those spots where the Greek soldiers were masters of the churches this Arian and unpopular bishop was often painted on the walls riding triumphantly on horseback and slaying the dragon of Athanasian error. On the other hand, in Alexandria, where his rival's politics and opinions held the upper hand, the monastery of St. Athanasius was built in the most public spot in the city, probably that formerly held by the Soma or royal burial-place; and in Thebes a cathedral church was dedicated to St. Athanasius within the great courtyard of Medinet-Abu, where the small and paltry Greek columns are in strange contrast to the grand architecture of Ramses III. which surrounds them.

In former reigns the Alexandrians had been in the habit of sending embassies to Constantinople to complain of tyranny or misgovernment, and to beg for a redress of grievances, when they thought that justice could be there obtained when it was refused in Alexandria. But this practice was stopped by Theodosius, who made a law that the Alexandrians should never send an embassy to Constantinople, unless it were agreed to by a decree of the town council, and had the approbation of the prefect. The weak and idle emperor would allow no appeal from the tyranny of his own governor.

We may pass over the banishment of John Chrysostom, Bishop of Constantinople, as having less to do with the history of Egypt, though, as in the cases of Arius and Nestorius, the chief mover of the attack upon him was a bishop of Alexandria, who accused him of heresy, because he did not come up to the Egyptian standard of orthodoxy. But among the bishops who were deposed with Chrysostom was Palladius of Galatia, who was sent a prisoner to Syênê. As soon as he was released from his bonds, instead of being cast down by his misfortunes, he proposed to take advantage of the place of his banishment, and he set forward on his travels through Ethiopia for India, in search of the wisdom of the Brahmins. He arrived in safety at Adule, the port on the Red Sea in latitude 15°, now known as Zula, where he made acquaintance with Moses, the bishop of that city, and persuaded him to join him in his distant and difficult voyage.

From Adule the two set sail in one of the vessels employed in the Indian trade; but they were unable to accomplish their purpose, and Palladius returned to Egypt worn out with heat and fatigue, having scarcely touched the shores of India. On his return through Thebes he met with a traveller who had lately returned from the same journey, and who consoled him under his disappointment by recounting his own failure in the same undertaking. His new friend had himself been a merchant in the Indian trade, but had given up business because he was not successful in it; and, having taken a priest as his companion, had set out on the same voyage in search of Eastern wisdom. They had sailed to Adule on the Abyssinian shore, and then travelled to Auxum, the capital of that country. From that coast they set sail for the Indian ocean, and reached a coast which they thought was Taprobane or Ceylon. But there they were taken prisoners, and, after spending six years in slavery, and learning but little of the philosophy that they were in search of, were glad to take the first opportunity of escaping and returning to Egypt. Palladius had travelled in Egypt before he was sent there into banishment, and he had spent many years in examining the monasteries of the Thebaid and their rules, and he has left a history of the lives of many of those holy men and woman, addressed to his friend Lausus.

When Nestorius was deposed from the bishopric of Constantinople for refusing to use the words "Mother of God" as the title of Jesus' mother, and for falling short in other points of what was then thought orthodoxy, he was banished to Hibe in the Great Oasis. While he was living there, the Great Oasis was overrun by the Blemmyes, the Roman garrison was defeated, and those that resisted were put to the sword. The Blemmyes pillaged the place and then withdrew; and, being themselves at war with the Mazices, another tribe of Arabs, they kindly sent their prisoners to the Thebaid, lest they should fall into the hands of the latter. Nestorius then went to Panopolis to show himself to the governor, lest he should be accused of running away from his place of banishment, and soon afterwards he died of the sufferings brought on by these forced and painful journeys through the desert.

About the same time Egypt was visited by Cassianus, a monk of Gaul, in order to study the monastic institutions of the Thebaid. In his work on that subject he has described at length the way of life and the severe rules of the Egyptian monks, and has recommended them to the imitation of his countrymen. But the natives of Italy and the West do not seem to have been contented with copying the Theban monks at a distance. Such was the fame of the Egyptian monasteries that many zealots from Italy flocked there, to place themselves under the severe discipline of those holy men. As these Latin monks did not understand either Koptic or Greek, they found some difficulty in regulating their lives with the wished-for exactness; and the rules of Pachomius, of

Theodorus, and of Oresiesis, the most celebrated of the founders, were actually sent to Jerome at Rome, to be by him translated into Latin for the use of these settlers in the Thebaid. These Latin monks made St. Peter a popular saint in some parts of Egypt; and in the temple of Asseboua, in Nubia, when the Christians plastered over the figure of one of the old gods, they painted in its place the Apostle Peter holding the key in his hand. They did not alter the rest of the sculpture; so that Ramses II. is there now seen presenting his offering to the Christian saint. The mixed group gives us proof of the nation's decline in art rather than of its improvement in religion.

RAMSES II. AND ST. PETER.

Among the monks of Egypt there were also some men of learning and industry, who in their cells in the desert had made at least three translations of the New Testament into the three dialects of the Koptic language; namely, the Sahidic of Upper Egypt, the Bashmuric of the Bashmour province of the eastern half of the Delta, and the Koptic proper of Memphis and the western half of the Delta. To these were afterwards added the Acts of the council of Nicæa, the lives of the saints and martyrs, the writings of many of the Christian fathers, the rituals of the Koptic church, and various treatises on religion.

Other monks were as busy in making copies of the Greek manuscripts of the Old and New Testament; and, as each copy must have needed the painful labour of months, and often years, their industry and zeal must have been great. Most of these manuscripts were on papyrus, or on a manufactured papyrus which might be called paper, and have long since been lost; but the three most ancient copies on parchment which are the pride of the Vatican, the Paris library, and the British Museum, are the work of the Alexandrian penmen.

Copies of the Bible were also made in Alexandria for sale in western Europe; and all our oldest manuscripts show their origin by the Egyptian form of spelling in some of the words. The Beza manuscript at Cambridge, and the Clermont manuscript at Paris, which have Greek on one side of the page and Latin on the other, were written in Alexandria. The Latin is that more ancient version which was in use before the time of Jerome, and which he corrected, to form what is now called the Latin Vulgate. This old version was made by changing each Greek word into its corresponding Latin word, with very little regard to the different characters of the two languages. It was no doubt made by an Alexandrian Greek, who had a very slight knowledge of Latin.

Already the papyrus on which books were written was, for the most part, a manufactured article and might claim the name of paper. In the time of Pliny in the first century the sheets had been made in the old way; the slips of the plant laid one across the other had been held together by their own sticky sap without the help of glue. In the reign of Aurelian, in the third century, if not earlier, glue had been largely used in the manufacture; and it is probable that at this time, in the fifth century, the manufactured article almost deserved the name of paper. But this manufactured papyrus was much weaker and less lasting than that made after the old and more simple fashion. No books written upon it remain to us. At a later period, the stronger fibre of flax was used in the manufacture, but the date of this improvement is also unknown, because at first the paper so made, like that made from the papyrus fibre, was also too weak to last. It was doubtless an Alexandrian improvement. Flax was an Egyptian plant; paper-making was an Egyptian trade; and Theophilus, a Roman writer on manufactures, when speaking of paper made from flax, clearly points to its Alexandrian origin, by giving it the name of Greek parchment. Between the papyrus of the third century, and the strong paper of the eleventh century, no books remain to us but those written on parchment.

The monks of Mount Sinai suffered much during these reigns of weakness from the marauding attacks of the Arabs. These men had no strong monastery; but hundreds of them lived apart in single cells in the side of the mountains round the valley of Feiran, at the foot of Mount Serbal, and they had nothing to protect them but their poverty. They were not protected by Egypt, and they made treaties with the neighbouring Arabs, like an independent republic, of which the town of Feiran was the capital. The Arabs, from the Jordan to the Red

Sea, made robbery the employment of their lives, and they added much to the voluntary sufferings of the monks. Nilus, a monk who had left his family in Egypt, to spend his life in prayer and study on the spot where Moses was appointed the legislator of Israel, describes these attacks upon his brethren, and he boasts over the Israelites that, notwithstanding their sufferings, the monks spent their whole lives cheerfully in those very deserts which God's chosen people could not even pass through without murmuring. Nilus has left some letters and exhortations. It was then, probably, that the numerous inscriptions were made on the rocks at the foot of Mount Serbal, and on the path towards its sacred peak, which have given to one spot the name of Mokatteb, or *the valley of writing.* A few of these inscriptions are in the Greek language.

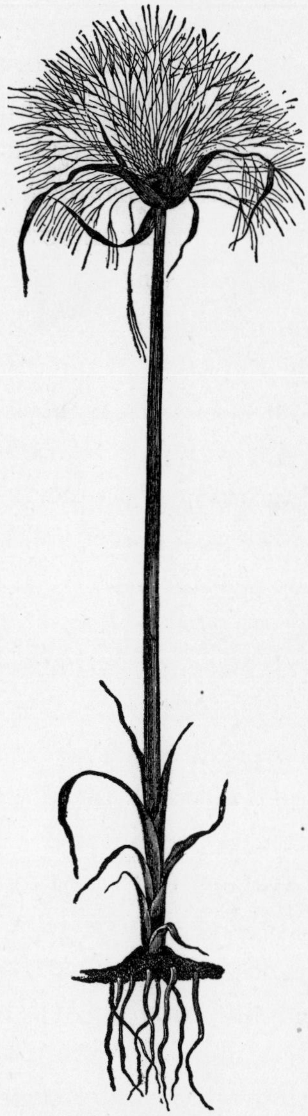

THE PAPYRUS PLANT.

The Egyptian physicians had of old always formed a part of

the priesthood, and they seem to have done much the same after the spread of Christianity. We find some monks named *Parabalani*, who owned the Bishop of Alexandria as their head, and who united the offices of physician and nurse in waiting on the sick and dying. As they professed poverty they were maintained by the state and had other privileges; and hence it was a place much sought after, and even by the wealthy. But to lessen this abuse it was ordered by an imperial rescript that none but poor people who had been rate-payers should be *Parabalani;* and their number was limited, first to five hundred, but afterwards, at the request of the bishop, to six hundred. A second charitable institution in Alexandria had the care of strangers and the poor, and was also managed by one of the priests.

Alexandria was fast sinking in wealth and population, and several new laws were now made to lessen its difficulties. One was to add a hundred and ten bushels of grain to the daily alimony of the city, the supply on which the riotous citizens were fed in idleness. By a second and a third law the five chief men in the corporation, and every man that had filled a civic office for thirty years, were freed from all bodily punishment, and only to be fined when convicted of a crime. Theodosius built a large church in Alexandria, which was called after his name; and the provincial judges were told in a letter to the prefect that, if they wished to earn the emperor's praise, they must not only restore those buildings which were falling through age and neglect but must also build new ones.

Though the pagan philosophy had been much discouraged at Alexandria by the destruction of the temples and the cessation of the sacrifices, yet the philosophers were still allowed to teach in the schools. Syrianus was at the head of the Platonists, and he wrote largely on the Orphic, Pythagorean, and Platonic doctrines. In his Commentary on Aristotle's Metaphysics he aims at showing how a Pythagorean or a Platonist would successfully answer Aristotle's objections. He seems to look upon the writings of Plotinus, Porphyry, and Iamblichus as the true fountains of Platonic wisdom, quite as much as the works of the great philosopher who gave his name to the sect. Syrianus afterwards removed to Athens, to take charge of the Platonic school in that city, and Athens became the chief seat of Alexandrian Platonism.

Olympiodorus was at the same time undertaking the task of forming a Peripatetic school in Alexandria, in opposition to the new Platonism, and he has left some of the fruits of his labour in his Commentaries on Aristotle. But the Peripatetic philosophy was no longer attractive to the pagans, though after the fall of the catechetical school it had a strong following of Christian disciples. Olympiodorus also wrote a history, but it has long since been lost, with other works of a second-rate merit. He was a native of the Thebaid, and travelled over his country. He described the Great Oasis as still a highly cultivated spot, where the husbandman watered his fields every third day in summer, and every fifth day in winter, from wells of two and three hundred feet in depth, and thereby raised two crops of barley, and often three of millet, in a year. Olympiodorus also travelled beyond Syênê into Nubia, with some danger from the Blemmyes, but he was not able to see the emerald mines, which were worked on Mount Smaragdus in the Arabian desert between Koptos and Berenicê, and which seem to have been the chief object of his journey.

Proclus came to Alexandria about the end of this reign, and studied many years under Olympiodorus, but not to the neglect of the platonic philosophy, of which he afterwards became such a distinguished ornament and support. The other Alexandrians under whom Proclus studied were Hero, the mathematician, a devout and religious pagan, Leonas, the rhetorician, who introduced him to all the chief men of learning, and Orion, the grammarian, who boasted of his descent from the race of Theban priests. Thus the pagans still held up their heads in the schools. Nor were the ceremonies of their religion, though unlawful, wholly stopped. In the twenty-eighth year of this reign, when the people were assembled in a theatre at Alexandria to celebrate the midnight festival of the Nile, a sacrifice which had been forbidden by Constantine and the council of Nicæa, the building fell beneath the weight of the crowd, and upwards of five hundred persons were killed by the fall.

It will be of some interest to review here the machinery of officers and deputies, civil as well as military, by which Egypt was governed under the successors of Constantine. The whole of the Eastern empire was placed under two prefects, the pretorian prefect of the East and the pretorian prefect of Illyricum, who, living at

ARABS RESTING IN THE DESERT.

Constantinople, like modern secretaries of state, made edicts for the government of the provinces and heard the appeals. Under the prefect of the East were fifteen consular provinces, together with Egypt, which was not any longer under one prefect. There was no consular governor in Egypt between the prefect at Constantinople and the six prefects of the smaller provinces. These provinces were Upper Libya or Cyrene, Lower Libya or the Oasis, the Thebaid, Ægyptiaca or the western part of the Delta, Augustanica or the eastern part of the Delta, and the Heptanomis, now named Arcadia, after the late emperor. Each of these was under an Augustal prefect, attended by a *Princeps*, a *Cornicularius*, an *Adjutor*, and others, and was assisted in civil matters by a *Commentariensis*, a corresponding secretary, a secretary *ab actis*, with a crowd of *numerarii* or clerks.

The military government was under a count with two dukes, with a number of legions, cohorts, troops, and wedges of cavalry, stationed in about fifty cities, which, if they had looked as well in the field as they do upon paper, would have made Theodosius II. as powerful as Augustus. But the number of Greek and Roman troops was small. The rest were barbarians who held their own lives at small price, and the lives of the unhappy Egyptians at still less. The Greeks were only a part of the fifth Macedonian legion, and Trajan's second legion, which were stationed at Memphis, at Parembole, and at Apollinopolis; while from the names of the other cohorts we learn that they were Franks, Portuguese,

Germans, Quadri, Spaniards, Britons, Moors, Vandals, Gauls, Sarmati, Assyrians, Galatians, Africans, Numidians, and others of less known and more remote places. Egypt itself furnished the Egyptian legion, part of which was in Mesopotamia, Diocletian's third legion of Thebans, the first Maximinian legion of Thebans which was stationed in Thrace, Constantine's second Flavian legion of Thebans, Valens' second Felix legion of Thebans, and the Julian Alexandrian legion, stationed in Thrace. Beside these, there were several bodies of native militia, from Abydos, Syênê, and other cities, which were not formed into legions. The Egyptian cavalry were a first and second Egyptian troop, several bodies of native archers mounted, three troops on dromedaries, and a body of Diocletian's third legion promoted to the cavalry. These Egyptian troops were chiefly Arab settlers in the Thebaid, for the Kopts had long since lost the use of arms. The Kopts were weak enough to be trampled on; but the Arabs were worth bribing by admission into the legions. The taxes of the province were collected by a number of counts of the sacred largesses, who were under the orders of an officer of the same title at Constantinople, and were helped by a body of counts of the exports and imports, prefects of the treasury and of the mints, with an army of clerks of all titles and all ranks. From this government the Alexandrians were exempt, living under their own military prefect and corporation, and, instead of paying any taxes beyond the custom-house duties at the port, they received a bounty in grain out of the taxes of Egypt.

Soon after this we find the political division of Egypt slightly altered. It is then divided into eight governments; the Upper Thebaid with eleven cities under a duke; the Lower Thebaid with ten cities, including the Great Oasis and part of the Heptanomis, under a general; Upper Libya or Cyrene under a general; Lower Libya or Paraetonium under a general; Arcadia, or the remainder of the Heptanomis, under a general; Ægyptiaca, or the western half of the Delta, under an Augustalian prefect; the first Augustan government, or the rest of the Delta, under a *Corrector;* and the second Augustan government, from Bubastis to the Red Sea, under a general. We also meet with several military stations named after the late emperors: a Maximianopolis and a Dioclesianopolis in the Upper Thebaid; a Theodosianopolis in the Lower Thebaid, and a second Theodosianopolis in Arcadia. But it is not easy to determine what villages were meant by these high-sounding names, which were perhaps only used in official documents.

The empire of the East was gradually sinking in power during this long and quiet reign of Theodosius II.; but the empire of the West was being hurried to its fall by the revolt of the barbarians in every one of its widespread provinces. Henceforth in the weakness of the two countries Egypt and Rome are wholly separated. After having influenced one another in politics, in literature, and in religion for seven centuries, they were now as little known to one another as they were before the day when Fabius arrived at Alexandria on an embassy from the senate to Ptolemy Philadelphus.

Theological and political quarrels, under the name of the Homoousian and Arian controversy, had nearly separated Egypt from the rest of the empire during the reigns of Constantius and Valens, but they had been healed by the wisdom of the first Theodosius, who governed Egypt by means of a popular bishop; and the policy which he so wisely began was continued by his successors through weakness. But in the reign of Marcian (450—457) the old quarrel again broke out, and, though it was under a new name, it again took the form of a religious controversy. Cyril, the Bishop of Alexandria, died in the last reign; and as he had succeeded his uncle, so on his death the bishopric fell to Dioscorus, a relation of his own, a man of equal religious violence and of less learning, who differed from him only in the points of doctrine about which he should quarrel with his fellow-Christians. About the same time Eutyches, a priest of Constantinople, had been condemned by his superiors and expelled from the Church for denying the two natures of Christ, and for maintaining that he was truly God, and in no respect a man. This was the opinion of the Egyptian church, and therefore Dioscorus, the Bishop of Alexandria, who had no right whatever to meddle in the quarrels at Constantinople, yet, acting on the forgotten rule that each bishop's power extended over all Christendom, undertook of his own authority to absolve Eutyches from his excommunication, and in return to excommunicate the Bishop of Constantinople who had condemned him. To settle this quarrel, a general council was summoned at Chalcedon; and there six hundred and thirty-two bishops met and condemned the faith of Eutyches, and further explained the Nicene creed, to which Eutyches and the Egyptians always appealed. They excommunicated Eutyches and his patron Dioscorus, who were banished by the emperor; and they elected Proterius to the then vacant bishopric of Alexandria.

In thus condemning the faith of Eutyches, the Greeks were excommunicating the whole of Egypt. The Egyptian belief in the one nature of Christ, which soon afterwards took the name of the Jacobite faith from one of its popular supporters, might perhaps be distinguished by the microscopic eye of the controversialist from the faith of Eutyches; but they equally fell under the condemnation of the council of Chalcedon. Egypt was no longer divided in its religious opinions. There had been a party who, though Egyptian in blood, held the Arian and half-Arian opinions of the Greeks, but that party had ceased to exist. Their religion had pulled one way and their political feelings another; the latter were found the stronger, as being more closely rooted to the soil; and their religious opinions had by this time fitted themselves to the geographical boundaries of the country. Hence the decrees of the council of Chalcedon were rejected by the whole of Egypt; and the quarrel between the Chalcedonian and Jacobite party, like the former quarrel between the Athanasians and the Arians, was little more than another name for the unwillingness of the Egyptians to be governed by Constantinople.

Proterius, the new bishop, entered Alexandria supported by the prefect Florus at the head of the troops.

But this was the signal for a revolt of the Egyptians, who overpowered the cohort with darts and stones; and the magistrates were driven to save their lives in the celebrated temple of Serapis. But they found no safety there; the mob surrounded the building and set fire to it, and burned alive the Greek magistrates and friends of the new bishop; and the city remained in the power of the rebellious Egyptians. When the news of this rising reached Constantinople the emperor sent to Egypt a further force of two thousand men, who stormed Alexandria and sacked it like a conquered city, and established Proterius in the bishopric. As a punishment upon the city for its rebellion, the prefect stopped for some time the public games and the allowance of grain to the citizens, and only restored them after the return to peace and good order.

In the weak state of the empire, the Blemmyes, and Nubades, or Nobatæ, had latterly been renewing their inroads upon Upper Egypt; they had overpowered the Romans, as the Greek and barbarian troops of Constantinople were always called, and had carried off a large booty and a number of prisoners. Maximinus, the imperial general, then led his forces against them; he defeated them, and made them beg for peace. The barbarians then proposed, as the terms of their surrender, never to enter Egypt while Maximinus commanded the troops in the Thebaid; but the conqueror was not contented with such an unsatisfactory submission, and would make no treaty with them till they had released the Roman prisoners without ransom, paid for the booty that they had taken, and given a number of the nobles as hostages. On this Maximinus agreed to a truce of a hundred years.

The people now called the Nubians, living on both sides of the cataract of Syênê, declared themselves of the true Egyptian race by their religious practices. They had an old custom of going each year to the temple of Isis on the isle of Elephantine, and of carrying away one of the statues with them and returning it to the temple when they had consulted it. But as they were now being driven out of the province, they bargained with Maximinus for permission to visit the temple each year without hindrance from the Roman guards. The treaty was written on papyrus and nailed up in this temple. But friendship in the desert, says the proverb, is as weak and wavering as the shade of the acacia tree; this truce was no sooner agreed upon than Maximinus fell ill and died; and the Nubades at once broke the treaty, regained by force their hostages, who had not yet been carried out of the Thebaid, and overran the province as they had done before their defeat.

ISIS AS THE DOG STAR.

By this success of the Nubians, Christianity was largely driven out of Upper Egypt; and about seventy years after the law of Thedosius I., by which paganism was supposed to be crushed, the religion of Isis and Serapis was again openly professed in the Thebaid, where it had perhaps always been cultivated in secret. A certain master of the robes in one of the Egyptian temples came at this time to the temple of Isis in the island of Philæ, and his votive inscription there declares that he was the son of Pachomius, a prophet, and successor by direct descent from a yet more famous Pachomius, a prophet, who we may easily believe was the Christian prophet who gathered together so many followers in the island of Tabenna, near Thebes, and there founded an order of Christian monks. These Christians now all returned to their paganism. Nearly all the remains of Christian architecture which we meet with in the Thebaid were built during the hundred and sixty years between the defeat of the Nubians by Diocletian, and their victories in the reign of Marcian.

The Nubians were far more civilised than their neighbours, the Blemmyes, whom they were usually able to drive back into their native deserts. We find an inscription in bad Greek, in the great temple at Talmis, now the village of Kalabshe, which was probably written about this time. A conqueror of the name of Silco there declares that he is king of the Nubians and all the Ethiopians; that in the upper part of his kingdom he is called Mars, and in the lower part Lion; that he is as great as any king of his day; that he has defeated the Blemmyes in battle again and again; and that he has made himself master of the country between Talmis and Primis. While such were the neighbours and inhabitants of the Thebaid, the fields were only half-tilled, and the desert was encroaching on the paths of man. The sand was filling up the temples, covering the overthrown statues, and blocking up the doors to the tombs; but it was at the same time saving, to be dug out in after ages, those records which the living no longer valued.

On the death of the Emperor Marcian, the Alexandrians, taking advantage of the absence of the military prefect Dionysius, who was then fighting against the Nubades in Upper Egypt, renewed their attack upon the Bishop Proterius, and deposed him from his office. To fill his place they made choice of a monk named Timotheus Ælurus, who held the Jacobite faith, and, having among them two deposed bishops, they got them to ordain him Bishop of Alexandria, and then led him by force of arms into the great church which had formerly been called Cæsar's temple. Upon hearing of the rebellion, the prefect returned in haste to Alexandria; but his approach was only the signal for greater violence, and the enraged people murdered Proterius in the baptistery, and hung up his body at the Tetrapylon in mockery. This was not a rebellion of the mob. Timotheus was supported by the men of chief rank in the city; the *Honorati* who had borne state offices, the *Politici* who had borne civic offices, and the *Navicularii*, or contractors for the freight of the Egyptian tribute, were all opposed to the emperor's claim to appoint the officer whose duties were much more those of prefect of the city than patriarch of Egypt. With such an opposition as this, the emperor would do nothing without the greatest caution, for he was in danger of losing Egypt altogether. But so much were the minds of all men then engrossed in ecclesiastical matters that this political struggle wholly took the form of a dispute in controversial divinity, and the emperor wrote a letter to the chief bishops in Christendom to ask their advice in his difficulty. These theologians were too busily engaged in their controversies to take any notice of the danger of Egypt's revolting from the empire and joining the Persians; so they strongly advised Leo not to depart from the decrees of the council of Chalcedon, or to acknowledge as Bishop of Alexandria a man who denied the two natures of Christ. Accordingly, the emperor again risked breaking the slender ties by which he held Egypt; he banished the popular bishop, and forced the Alexandrians to receive in his place one who held the Chalcedonian faith.

On the death of Leo, he was succeeded by his grandson, Leo the Younger, who died in 473, after a reign of one year, and was succeeded by his father Zeno, the son-in-law of the elder Leo. Zeno gave himself up at once to debauchery and vice, while the empire was harassed on all sides by the barbarians, and the provinces were roused into rebellion by the cruelty of the prefects. The rebels at last found a head in Basilicus, the brother-in-law of Leo. He declared himself of the Jacobite faith, which was the faith of the barbarian enemies, of the barbarian troops, and of the barbarian allies of the empire, and, proclaiming himself emperor, made himself master of Constantinople without a battle, and drove Zeno into banishment in the third year of his reign.

The first step of Basilicus was to recall from banishment Timotheus Ælurus, the late Bishop of Alexandria, and to restore him to the bishopric (A. D. 477). He then addressed to him and the other recalled bishops a circular letter, in which he repeals the decrees of the council of Chalcedon, and re-establishes the Nicene creed, declaring that Jesus was of one substance with the Father, and that Mary was the mother of God. The march of Timotheus to the seat of his own government, from Constantinople whither he had been summoned, was more like that of a conqueror than of a preacher of peace. He deposed some bishops and restored others, and, as the decrees of the council of Chalcedon were the particular objects of his hatred, he restored to the city of Ephesus the patriarchal power which that synod had taken away from it. Basilicus reigned for about two years, when he was defeated and put to death by Zeno, who regained the throne.

As soon as Zeno was again master of the empire, he re-established the creed of the council of Chalcedon, and drove away the Jacobite bishops from their bishoprics. Death, however, removed Timotheus Ælurus before the emperor's orders were put in force in Alexandria, and the Egyptians then chose Peter Mongus as his successor, in direct opposition to the orders from Constantinople. But the emperor was resolved not to be beaten; the bishopric of Alexandria was so much a civil office that to have given up the appointment to the Egyptians would have been to allow the people to govern themselves; so he banished Peter, and recalled to the head of the Church Timotheus Salophaciolus, who had been living at Canopus ever since his loss of the bishopric.

But, as the patriarch of Alexandria enjoyed the ecclesiastical revenues, and was still in appearance a teacher of religion, the Alexandrians, in recollection of the former rights of the Church, still claimed the appointment. They sent John, a priest of their own faith and dean of the church of John the Baptist, as their ambassador to Constantinople, not to remonstrate against the late acts of the emperor, but to beg that on future occasions the Alexandrians might be allowed the old privilege of choosing their own bishop. The Emperor Zeno seems to have seen through the ambassador's earnestness, and he first bound him by an oath not to accept the bishopric if he should even be himself chosen to it, and he then sent him back with the promise that the Alexandrians should be allowed to choose their own patriarch on the next vacancy. But unfortunately John's ambition was too strong for his oath, and on the death of Timotheus, which happened soon afterwards, he spent a large sum of money in bribes among the clergy and chief men of the city, and thereby got himself chosen patriarch. On this, the emperor seems to have thought only of punishing John, and he at once gave up the struggle with the Egyptians. Believing that, of the two patriarchs who had been chosen by the people, Peter Mongus, who was living in banishment, would be found more dutiful than John, who was on the episcopal throne, he banished John and recalled Peter; and the latter agreed to the terms of an imperial edict which Zeno then put forth, to heal the disputes in the Egyptian church, and to recall the province to obedience. This celebrated peace-making edict, usually called the Henoticon, is addressed to the clergy and laity of Alexandria, Egypt, Libya, and the

Pentapolis, and is an agreement between the emperor and the bishops who countersigned it, that neither party should ever mention the decrees of the council of Chalcedon, which were the great stumbling-block with the Egyptians. But in all other points the Henoticon is little

STREET SPRINKLER AT ALEXANDRIA.

short of a surrender to the people of the right to choose their own creed; it styles Mary the mother of God, and allows that the decrees of the council of Nicæa and Constantinople contain all that is important of the true faith. John, when banished by Zeno, like many of the former deposed bishops, fled to Rome for comfort and for help. There he met with the usual support; and Felix, Bishop of Rome, wrote to Constantinople, remonstrating with Zeno for dismissing the patriarch. But this was only a small part of the emperor's want of success in his attempt at peace-making; for the crafty Peter, who had gained the bishopric by subscribing to the peace-making edict, was no sooner safely seated on his episcopal throne than he denounced the council of Chalcedon and its decrees as heretical, and drove out of their monasteries all those who still adhered to that faith. Nephalius, one of these monks, wrote to the emperor at Constantinople in complaint, and Zeno sent Cosmas to the bishop to threaten him with his imperial displeasure, and to try to re-establish peace in the Church. But the arguments of Cosmas were wholly unsuccessful; and Zeno then sent an increase of force to Arsenius, the military prefect, who settled the quarrel for the time by sending back the most rebellious of the Alexandrians as prisoners to Constantinople.

Soon after this dispute Peter Mongus died, and fortunately he was succeeded in the bishopric by a peacemaker. Athanasius, the new bishop, very unlike his great predecessor of the same name, did his best to heal the angry disputes in the Church, and to reconcile the Egyptians to the imperial government.

Hierocles, the Alexandrian, was at this time teaching philosophy in his native city, where his zeal and eloquence in favour of Platonism drew upon him the anger of the Christians and the notice of the government.

He was sent to Constantinople to be punished for not believing in Christianity, for it does not appear that, like the former Hierocles, he ever wrote against it. There he bore a public scourging from his Christian torturers, with a courage equal to that formerly shown by their forefathers when tortured by his. When some of the blood from his shoulders flew into his hand, he held it out in scorn to the judge, saying with Ulysses, "Cyclops, since human flesh has been thy food, now taste this wine." After his punishment he was banished, but was soon allowed to return to Alexandria, and there he again taught openly as before. Paganism never wears so fair a dress as in the writings of Hierocles; his commentary on the Golden Verses of the Pythagoreans is full of the loftiest and purest morality, and not less agreeable are the fragments that remain of his writings on our duties, and his beautiful chapter on the pleasures of a married life. In the Facetiæ of Hierocles we have one of the earliest jest-books that has been saved from the wreck of time. It is a curious proof of the fallen state of learning; the Sophists had long since made themselves ridiculous; books alone will not make a man of sense; and in the jokes of Hierocles the blunderer is always called a man of learning.

Ætius, the Alexandrian physician, has left a large work containing a full account of the state of Egyptian medicine at this time. He describes the diseases and their remedies, quoting the recipes of numerous authors, from the King Nechepsus, Galen, Hippocrates, and Dioscorides, down to Archbishop Cyril. He is not wholly free from superstition, as when making use of a green jasper set in a ring; but he observes that the patients recovered as soon when the stone was plain as when a dragon was engraved upon it according to the recommendation of Nechepsus. In Nile water he finds every virtue, and does not forget dark paint for the ladies' eyebrows, and Cleopatra-wash for the face.

Anastasius, the next emperor, succeeding in 491, followed the wise policy which Zeno had entered upon in the latter years of his reign, and he strictly adhered to the terms of the peace-making edict. The four patriarchs of Alexandria who were chosen during this reign, John, a second John, Dioscorus, and Timotheus, were all of the Jacobite faith; and the Egyptians readily believed that the emperor was of the same opinion. When called upon by the quarrelling theologians, he would neither reject nor receive the decrees of the council of Chalcedon, and by this wise conduct he governed Egypt without any religious rebellion during a long reign.

The election of Dioscorus, however, the third patriarch of this reign, was not brought about peaceably. He was the cousin of a former patriarch, Timotheus Ælurus, which, if we view the bishopric as a civil office, might be a reason for the emperor's wishing him to have the appointment. But it was no good reason with the Alexandrians, who declared that he had not been chosen according to the canons of the apostles; and the magistrates of the city were forced to employ the troops to lead him in safety to his throne. After the first ceremony, he went, as was usual at an installation, to St. Mark's

Church, and there the clergy robed him in the patriarchal state robes. The grand procession then moved through the streets to the church of St. John, where the new bishop went through the communion service. But the city was much disturbed during the whole day, and in the riot Theodosius, the son of Calliopus, a man of Augustalian rank, was killed by the mob. The Alexandrians treated the affair as murder, and punished with death those who were thought guilty; but the emperor looked upon it as a rebellion of the citizens, and the bishop was obliged to go on an embassy to Constantinople to appease his just anger.

Anastasius, who had deserved the obedience of the Egyptians by his moderation, pardoned their ingratitude when they offended; but he was the last Byzantine emperor who governed Egypt with wisdom, and the last who failed to enforce the decrees of the council of Chalcedon. It may well be doubted whether any wise conduct on the part of the rulers could have healed the quarrel between the two countries, and made the Egyptians forget the wrongs that they had suffered from the Greeks.

In the tenth year of the reign of Anastasius, A. D. 501, the Persians, after overrunning a large part of Syria and defeating the Roman generals, passed Pelusium and entered Egypt. The army of Kobades laid waste the whole of the Delta up to the very walls of Alexandria. Eustatius, the military prefect, led out his forces against the invaders and fought many battles with doubtful success; but as the capital was safe the Persians were at last obliged to retire, leaving the people ruined as much by the loss of a harvest as by the sword. Alexandria suffered severely from famine and the diseases which followed in its train; and history has gratefully recorded the name of Urbib, a Christian Jew of great wealth, who relieved the starving poor of that city with his bounty. Three hundred persons were crushed to death in the church of Arcadius on Easter Sunday in the press of the crowd to receive his alms. As war brought on disease and famine, they also brought on rebellion. The people of Alexandria, in want of grain and oil, rose against the magistrates, and many lives were lost in the attempt to quell the riots.

In the early part of this history we have seen ambitious bishops quickly disposed of by banishment to the Great Oasis; and again, as the country became more desolate, criminals were sufficiently separated from the rest of the empire by being sent to Thebes. Alexandria was then the last place in the world in which a pretender to the throne would be allowed to live. But Egypt was now ruined; and Anastasius began his reign by banishing, to the fallen Alexandria, Longinus, the brother of the late king, and he had him ordained a presbyter, to mark him as unfit for the throne.

Julianus, who was during a part of this reign the prefect of Egypt, was also a poet, and he has left us a number of short epigrams that form part of the volume of Greek Anthology which was published at Constantinople soon after this time. Christodorus of Thebes was another poet who joined with Julianus in praising the Emperor Anastasius. He also removed to Constantinople, the seat of patronage; and the fifth book of the Greek Anthology contains his epigrams on the winners in the horse-race in that city and on the statues which stood around the public gymnasium. The poet's song, like the traveller's tale, often related the wonders of the river Nile. The overflowing waters first manured the fields, and then watered the crops, and lastly carried the

ILLUSTRATIONS FROM COPY OF DIOSCORIDES.

grain to market; and one writer in the Anthology, to describe the country life in Egypt, tells the story of a sailor, who, to avoid the dangers of the ocean, turned husbandman, and was then shipwrecked in his own meadows.

The book-writers at this time sometimes illuminated their more valuable parchments with gold and silver letters and sometimes employed painters to ornament them with small paintings. The beautiful copy of the work of Dioscorides on Plants in the library at Vienna was made in this reign for the Princess Juliana of Constantinople. In one painting the figure of science or invention is holding up a plant, while on one side of her is the painter drawing it on his canvas, and on the other side is the author describing it in his book. Other paintings are of the plants and animals mentioned in the book. A copy of the Book of Genesis, also in the library at Vienna, is of the same class and date. A large part of it is written in gold and silver; and it has eighty-eight small paintings of various historical subjects. In these the story is well told, though the drawing and perspective are bad and the figures crowded. But these Alexandrian paintings are better than those made in Rome or Constantinople at this time.

With the spread of Christianity theatrical representations had been gradually going out of use. The Greek tragedies, as we see in the works of Æschylus, Sophocles, and Euripides, those models of pure taste in poetry, are founded on the pagan mythology; and in many of them the gods are made to walk and talk upon the stage. Hence they of necessity fell under the ban of the clergy. As the Christians became more powerful the several cities of the empire had one by one discontinued these popular spectacles, and horse-races usually took their place. But the Alexandrians were the last people to give up a favourite amusement; and by the end of this reign Alexandria was the only city in the empire where tragic and comic actors and Eastern dancers were to be seen in the theatre.

The tower or lighthouse on the island of Pharos, the work of days more prosperous than these, had latterly been sadly neglected with the other buildings of the country. For more than seven hundred years, the pilot on approaching this flat shore after dark had pointed out to his shipmate what seemed a star on the horizon, and comforted him with the promise of a safe entrance into the haven, and told him of Alexander's tower. But the waves breaking against its foot had long since carried away the outworks, and laid bare the foundations; the wall was undermined and its fall seemed close at hand. The care of Anastasius, however, surrounded it again with piles and buttresses; and this monument of wisdom and science, which deserved to last for ever, was for a little while longer saved from ruin. An epigram in the Anthology informs us that Ammonius was the name of the builder who performed this good work, and to him and to Neptune the grateful sailors then raised their hands in prayer and praise.

In 518 Justin I. succeeded Anastasius on the throne of Constantinople, and in the task of defending the empire against the Persians. And this task became every year more difficult, as the Greek population of his Egyptian and Asiatic provinces fell off in numbers. For some years after the division of the empire under the sons of Constantine, Antioch in Syria had been the capital from which Alexandria received the emperor's commands. The two cities became very closely united; and now that the Greeks were deserting Antioch, a part of the Syrian church began to adopt the more superstitious creed of

Egypt. Severus, Bishop of Antioch, was successful in persuading a large party in the Syrian church to deny the humanity of Christ, and to style Mary the mother of God. But the chief power in Antioch rested with the opposite party. They answered his arguments by threats of violence, and he had to leave the city for safety. He fled to Alexandria, and with him began the friendship between the two churches which lasted for several centuries. In Alexandria he was received with the honour due to his religious zeal. But though in Antioch his opinions had been too Egyptian for the Syrians, in Alexandria they were too Syrian for the Egyptians. The Egyptians, who said that Jesus had been crucified and died only in appearance, always denied that his body was liable to corruption. Severus, however, argued that it was liable to corruption before the resurrection; and this led him into a new controversy, in which Timotheus, the Alexandrian bishop, took part against his own more superstitious flock, and sided with his friend, the Bishop of Antioch. Severus has left us, in the Syriac language, the baptismal service as performed in Egypt. The priest breathes three times into the basin to make the water holy, he makes three crosses on the child's forehead, he adjures the demons of wickedness to quit him, he again makes three crosses on his forehead with oil, he again blows three times into the water in the form of a cross, he anoints his whole body with oil, and then plunges him in the water. Many other natives of Syria soon followed Severus to Alexandria; so many indeed that as Greek literature decayed in that city, Syriac literature rose. Many Syrians also came to study the religious life in the monasteries of Egypt, and after some time the books in the library of the monastery at Mount Nitria were found to be half Arabic and half Syriac.

Justin, the new emperor, again lighted up in Alexandria the flames of discord which had been allowed to slumber since the publication of Zeno's peace-making edict. But in the choice of the bishop he was not able to command without a struggle. In the second year of his reign, on the death of Timotheus, the two parties again found themselves nearly equal in strength; and Alexandria was for several years kept almost in a state of civil war between those who thought that the body of Jesus had been liable to corruption, and those who thought it incorruptible. The former chose Gaianas, whom his adversaries called a Manichean; and the latter Theodosius, a Jacobite, who had the support of the prefect; and each of these in his turn was able to drive his rival out of Alexandria.

Those Persian forces which in the last reign overran the Delta were chiefly Arabs from the opposite coast of the Red Sea. To make an end of these attacks, and to engage their attention in another quarter, was the natural wish of the statesmen of Constantinople; and for this purpose Anastasius had sent an embassy to the Homeritæ on the southern coast of Arabia, to persuade them to attack their northern neighbours. The Homeritæ held the strip of coast now called Hadramout. They were enriched, though hardly civilised, by being the channel along which much of the Eastern trade passed from India to the Nile, to avoid the difficult navigation of the ocean. They were Jewish Arabs, who had little in common with the Arabs of Yemen, but had frequent intercourse with Abyssinia and the merchants of the Red Sea. Part of the trade of Solomon and the Tyrians was probably to their coast. To this distant and little tribe the Emperor of Constantinople now sent a second pressing embassy. Julianus, the ambassador, went up the Nile from Alexandria, and then crossed the Red Sea, or Indian Sea as it was also called, to Arabia. He was favourably received by the Homeritæ. Arethas, the king, gave him an audience in grand barbaric state. He was standing in a chariot drawn by four elephants; he wore no clothing but a cloth of gold around his loins; his arms were laden with costly armlets and bracelets; he held a shield and two spears in his hands, and his nobles stood around him armed, and singing to his honour. When the ambassador delivered the emperor's letter, Arethas kissed the seal, and then kissed Julianus himself. He accepted the gifts which Justin had sent, and promised to move his forces northward against the Persians as requested, and also to keep the route open for the trade to Alexandria.

Justinian, the successor of Justin in 527, settled the quarrel between the two Alexandrian bishops by summoning them both to Constantinople, and then sending them into banishment. But this had no effect in healing the divisions in the Egyptian church; and for the next half-century the two parties ranged themselves, in their theological or rather political quarrel, under the names of their former bishops, and called themselves Gaianites and Theodosians. Nor did the measures of Justinian tend to lessen the breach between Egypt and Constantinople. He appointed Paul to the bishopric, and required the Egyptians to receive the decrees of the council of Chalcedon.

After two years Paul was displaced either by the emperor or by his flock; and Zoilus was then seated on the episcopal throne by the help of the imperial forces. He maintained his dangerous post for about six years, when the Alexandrians rose in open rebellion, overpowered the troops, and forced him to seek safety in flight; and the Jacobite party then turned out all the bishops who held the Greek faith.

When Justinian heard that the Jacobites were masters of Egypt he appointed Apollinarius to the joint office of prefect and patriarch of Alexandria, and sent him with a large force to take possession of his bishopric. Apollinarius marched into Alexandria in full military dress at the head of his troops; but when he entered the church he laid aside his arms, and putting on the patriarchal robes began to celebrate the rites of his religion. The Alexandrians were by no means overawed by the force with which he had entered the city; they pelted him with a shower of stones from every corner of the church, and he was forced to withdraw from the building in order to save his life. But three days afterwards the bells were rung through the city, and the people were summoned to meet in the church on the following Sunday, to hear the emperor's letter read. When Sunday came the whole city flocked to hear and to disobey Justinian's orders. Apollinarius began his address by threatening his hearers that, if they continued obstinate in their opinions, their children should be made orphans and their widows given up to the soldiery; and he was as before stopped with a shower of stones. But this time he was prepared for the attack; this Christian bishop had placed his troops in ambush round the church, and on a signal given they rushed out on his unarmed flock, and by his orders the crowds within and without the church were put to rout by the sword, the soldiers waded up to their knees in blood, and the city and whole country yielded its obedience for the time to bishops who held the Greek faith.

Henceforth the Melchite or royalist patriarchs, who were appointed by the emperor and had the authority of civil prefects, and were supported by the power of the military prefect, are scarcely mentioned by the historian of the Koptic church. They were too much engaged in civil affairs to act the part of ministers of religion. They collected their revenues principally in grain, and carried on a large export trade, transporting their stores to those parts of Europe where they would bring the best price. On one occasion we hear of a small fleet belonging to the church of Alexandria, consisting of thirteen ships of about thirty tons burden each, and bearing ten thousand bushels of grain, being overtaken by a storm on the coast of Italy. The princely income of the later patriarchs, raised from the churches of all Egypt under the name of the offerings of the pious, sometimes amounted to two thousand pounds of gold, or four hundred thousand dollars. But while these Melchite or royalist bishops were enjoying the ecclesiastical revenues, and administering the civil affairs of the diocese and of the great monasteries, there was a second bishop who held the Jacobite faith, and who, having been elected by the people according to the ancient forms of the Church, equally bore the title of patriarch, and administered in his more humble path to the spiritual wants of his flock. The Jacobite bishop was always a monk. At his ordination he was declared to be elected by the popular voice, by the bishops, priests, deacons, monks, and all the people of Lower Egypt; and prayers were offered up through the intercession of the Mother of God, and of the glorious Apostle Mark. The two churches no longer used the same prayer-book. The Melchite church continued to use the old liturgy, which, as it had been read in Alexandria from time immemorial, was called the liturgy of St. Mark, altered however to declare that the Son was of the same substance with the Father. But the Koptic church made use of the newer liturgies by their own champions, Bishop Cyril, Basil of Cæsarea, and Gregory Nazianzen. These three liturgies were all in the Koptic language, and more clearly denied the two natures of Christ. Of the two churches the Koptic had less learning, more bigotry, and opinions more removed from the teachings of the New Testament; but then the Koptic bishop alone had any moral power to lead the minds of his flock towards piety and religion. Had the emperors been at all times either humane or politic enough to employ bishops of the same religion as the people, they would perhaps have kept the good-will of their subjects; but as it was, the Koptic church, smarting under its insults, and forgetting the greater evils of a foreign conquest, would sometimes look with longing eyes to the condition of their neighbours, their brethren in faith, the Arabic subjects of Persia.

The Christianity of the Egyptians was mostly superstition; and as it spread over the land it embraced the whole nation within its pale, not so much by purifying the pagan opinions as by lowering itself to their level, and fitting itself to their corporeal notions of the Creator. This was in a large measure induced by the custom of using the old temples for Christian churches; the form of worship was in part guided by the form of the building, and even the old traditions were engrafted on the new religion. Thus the traveller Antonius, after visiting the remarkable places in the Holy Land, came to Egypt to search for the chariots of the Egyptians who pursued Moses, petrified into rocks at the bottom of the Red Sea, and for the footsteps left in the sands by the infant Jesus while he dwelt in Egypt with his parents. At Memphis he enquired why one of the doors in the great temple of Phtah, then used as a church, was always closed, and he was told that it had been rudely shut against the infant Jesus five hundred years before, and mortal strength had never since been able to open it.

The records of the empire declared that the first Cæsars had kept six hundred and forty-five thousand men under arms to guard Italy, Africa, Spain, and Egypt, a number perhaps much larger than the truth; but Justinian could with difficulty maintain one hundred and fifty thousand ill-disciplined troops, a force far from large enough to hold even those provinces that remained to him. During the latter half of his reign the eastern frontier of this falling empire was sorely harassed by the Persians under their king Chosroes. They overran Syria, defeated the army of the empire in a pitched battle, and then took Antioch. By these defeats the military roads were stopped; Egypt was cut off from the rest of the empire and could be reached from the capital only by sea. Hence the emperor was driven to a change in his religious policy. He gave over the persecution of the Jacobite opinions, and even went so far in one of his decrees as to call the body of Jesus incorruptible, as he thought that these were the only means of keeping the allegiance of his subjects or the friendship of his Arab neighbours, all of whom, as far as they were Christians, held the Jacobite view of the Nicene creed, and denied the two natures of Christ.

As the forces of Constantinople were driven back by the victorious armies of the Persians, the emperors had lost, among other fortresses, the capital of Arabia Nabatæa, that curious rocky fastness that well deserved the name of Petra, and which had been garrisoned by Romans from the reign of Trajan till that of Valens. On this loss it became necessary to fortify a new frontier post on the Egyptian side of the Elanitic Gulf. Justinian then built the fortified monastery near Mount Sinai, to guard the only pass by which Egypt could be entered without the help of a fleet; and when it was found to be commanded by one of the higher points of the mountain he beheaded the engineer who built it, and remedied the fault, as far as it could be done, by a small fortress on the higher ground. This monastery was held by the Egyptians, and maintained out of the Egyptian taxes. When the Egyptians were formerly masters of their own country, before the Persian and Greek conquests, they were governed by a race of priests, and the temples were their

FORTRESS NEAR MOUNT SINAI.

only fortresses. The temples of Thebes were the citadels of the capital, and the temples of Elephantine guarded the frontier. So now, when the military prefect is too weak to make himself obeyed, the emperor tries to govern through means of the Christian priesthood; and when it is necessary for the Egyptians to defend their own frontier, he builds a monastery and garrisons it with monks.

Part of the Egyptian trade to the East was carried on through the islands of Ceylon and Socotra; but it was chiefly in the hands of uneducated Arabs of Ethiopia, who were little able to communicate to the world much knowledge of the countries from which they brought their highly valued goods. At Ceylon they met with traders from beyond the Ganges and from China, of whom they bought the silk which Europeans had formerly thought a product of Arabia. At Ceylon was a Christian church, with a priest and a deacon, frequented by the Christians from Persia, while the natives of the place were pagans. The coins there used were Roman, borne thither by the course of trade, which during so many centuries carried the gold and silver eastward. The trade was lately turned more strongly into this channel because a war had sprung up between the two tribes of Jewish Arabs, the Hexumitæ of Abyssinia on the coast of the Red Sea near Adule, and the Homeritæ who dwelt in Arabia on the opposite coast, at the southern end of the Red Sea. The Homeritæ had quarrelled with the Alexandrian merchants in the Indian trade, and had killed some of them as they were passing their mountains from India to the country of the Hexumitæ.

Immediately after these murders the Hexumitæ found the trade injured, and they took up arms to keep the passage open for the merchants. Hadad their king crossed the Red Sea and conquered his enemies; he put to death Damianus, the King of the Homeritæ, and made a new treaty with the Emperor of Constantinople. The Hexumitæ promised to become Christians. They sent to Alexandria to beg for a priest to baptise them, and to ordain their preachers; and Justinian sent John, a man of piety and high character, the dean of the church of St. John, who returned with the ambassadors and became bishop of the Hexumitæ.

It was possibly this conquest of the Homeritæ by Hadad, King of the Hexumitæ, which was recorded on the monument of Adule, at the foot of the inscription set up eight centuries earlier by Ptolemy Euergetes. The monument is a throne of white marble. The conqueror, whose name had been broken away before the inscription was copied, there boasts that he crossed over the Red Sea and made the Arabians and Sabæans pay him tribute. On his own continent he defeated the tribes to the north of him, and opened the passage from his own country to Egypt; he also marched eastward, and conquered the tribes on the African incense coast; and lastly, he crossed the Astaborus to the snowy mountains in which that branch of the Nile rises, and conquered the tribes between that stream and the Astapus. This valuable inscription, which tells us of snowy mountains within the tropics, was copied by Cosmas, a merchant of Alexandria, who passed through Adule on his way to India.

Former emperors, Anastasius and Justin, had sent several embassies to these nations at the southern end of the Red Sea; to the Homeritæ, to persuade them to attack the Persian forces in Arabia, and to the Hexumitæ, for the encouragement of trade. Justinian also sent an embassy to the Homeritæ under Abram; and, as he was successful in his object, he entrusted a second embassy to Abram's son. Nonnosus landed at Adule on the Abyssinian coast, and then travelled inward for fifteen days to Auxum, the capital. This country was then called

Ethiopia; it had gained the name which before belonged to the valley of the Nile between Egypt and Meroë. On his way to Auxum, he saw troops of wild elephants, to the number, as he supposed, of five thousand. After delivering his message to Elesbaas, then King of Auxum, he crossed the Red Sea to Caisus, King of the Homeritæ, a grandson of that Arethas to whom Justin had sent his embassy. Notwithstanding the natural difficulties of the journey, and those arising from the tribes through which he had to pass, Nonnosus performed his task successfully, and on his return home wrote a history of his embassies.

The advantage gained to the Hexumitæ by their invasion of the Homeritæ was soon lost, probably as soon as their forces were withdrawn. The trade through the country of the Homeritæ was again stopped; and such was the difficulty of navigation from the incense coast of Africa to the mouths of the Indus, that the loss was severely felt at Auxum. Elesbaas therefore undertook to repeat the punishment which had been before inflicted on his less civilised neighbours, and again to open the trade to the merchants from the Nile. It was while he was preparing his forces for this invasion that Cosmas, the Alexandrian traveller, passed through Adule; and he copied for the King of Auxum the inscription above spoken of, which recorded the victories of his predecessor over the enemies he was himself preparing to attack.

The invasion by Elesbaas, or Elesthæus as he is also named, was immediately successful. The Homeritæ were conquered, their ruler was overthrown; and, to secure their future obedience, the conqueror set over these Jewish Arabs an Abyssinian Christian for their king. Esimaphæus was chosen for that post; and his first duty was to convert his new subjects to Christianity. Political reasons as well as religious zeal would urge him to this undertaking, to make the conquered bear the badge of the conqueror. For this purpose he engaged the assistance of Gregentius, a bishop, who was to employ his learning and eloquence in the cause. Accordingly, in the palace of Threlletum, in the presence of their new king, a public dispute was held between the Christian bishop and Herban, a learned Jew. Gregentius has left us an account of the controversy, in which he was wholly successful, being helped, perhaps, by the threats and promises of the king. The arguments used were not quite the same as they would be now. The bishop explained the Trinity as the Holy Spirit proceeding from the Mind or Father, and resting on the Word or Son, which was then the orthodox view of this mysterious doctrine. On the other hand, the Jew quoted the Old Testament to show that the Lord their God was one Lord. It is related that suddenly the Jews present were struck blind. Their sight, however, was restored to them on the bishop's praying for them; and they were then all thereby converted and baptised on the spot. The king stood godfather to Herban, and rewarded him with a high office under his government.

Esimaphæus did not long remain King of the Homeritæ. A rebellion soon broke out against him, and he was deposed. Elesbaas, King of Auxum, again sent an army to recall the Homeritæ to their obedience, but this time the army joined in the revolt; and Elesbaas then made peace with the enemy, in hopes of thus gaining the advantages which he was unable to grasp by force of arms. From a Greek inscription on a monument at Auxum we learn the name of Æizanas, another king of

PYRAMID OF MEDUM.

that country, who also called himself, either truly or boastfully, king of the opposite coast. He set up the monument to record his victories over the Bougætæ, a people who dwelt between Auxum and Egypt, and he styles himself the invincible Mars, king of kings, King of the Hexumitæ, of the Ethiopians, of the Sabæans, and of the Homeritæ. These kings of the Hexumitæ ornamented the city of Auxum with several beautiful and lofty obelisks, each made of a single block of granite like those in Egypt.

Egypt in its mismanaged state seemed to be of little value to the empire save as a means of enriching the prefect and the tax-gatherers; it yielded very little tribute to Constantinople beyond the supply of grain, and that by no means regularly. To remedy these abuses Justinian made a new law for the government of the province, with a view of bringing about a thorough reform. By this edict the districts of Menelaites and Mareotis, to the west of Alexandria, were separated from the rest of Egypt, and they were given to the prefect of Libya, whose seat of government was at Paraetonium, because his province was too poor to pay the troops required to guard it. The several governments of Upper Egypt, of Lower Egypt, of Alexandria, and of the troops were then given to one prefect. The two cohorts, the Augustalian and the Ducal, into which the two Roman legions had gradually dwindled, were henceforth to be united under the name of the Augustalian Cohort, which was to contain six hundred men, who were to secure the obedience and put down any rebellion of the Egyptian and barbarian soldiers. The somewhat high pay and privileges of this favoured troop were to be increased; and, to secure its loyalty and to keep out Egyptians, nobody was to be admitted into it till his fitness had been inquired into by the emperor's examiners. The first duty of the cohort was to collect the supply of grain for Constantinople and to see it put on board the ships; and as for the supply which was promised to the Alexandrians, the magistrates were to collect it at their own risk, and by means of their own cohort. The grain for Constantinople was required to be in that city before the end of August, or within four months after the harvest, and the supply for Alexandria not more than a month later. The prefect was made answerable for the full collection, and whatever was wanting of that quantity was to be levied on his property and his heirs, at the rate of one *solidus* for three *artabæ* of grain, or about three dollars for fifteen bushels; while in order to help the collection, the export of grain from Egypt was forbidden from every port but Alexandria, except in small quantities. The grain required for Alexandria and Constantinople, to be distributed as a free gift among the idle citizens, was eight hundred thousand *artabæ*, or four millions of bushels, and the cost of collecting it was fixed at eighty thousand *solidi*, or about three hundred thousand dollars. The prefect was ordered to assist the collectors at the head of his cohort, and if he gave credit for the taxes which he was to collect he was to bear the loss himself. If the archbishop interfered, to give credit and screen an unhappy Egyptian, then he was to bear the loss, and if his property was not enough the property of the Church was to make it good; but if any other bishop gave credit, not only was his property to bear the loss, but he was himself to be deposed from his bishopric; and lastly, if any riot or rebellion should arise to cause the loss of the Egyptian tribute, the tribunes of the Augustalian Cohort were to be punished with forfeiture of all property, and the cohort was to be removed to a station beyond the Danube.

Such was the new law which Justinian, the great Roman lawgiver, proposed for the future government of Egypt. The Egyptians were treated as slaves, whose duty was to raise grain for the use of their masters at Constantinople, and their taskmasters at Alexandria. They did not even receive from the government the usual benefit of protection from their enemies, and they felt bound to the emperor by no tie either of love or interest. The imperial orders were very little obeyed beyond those places where the troops were encamped; the Arabs were each year pressing closer upon the valley of the Nile, and helping the sands of the desert to defeat the labours of the disheartened husbandmen; and the Greek language, which had hitherto followed and marked the route of commerce from Alexandria to Syênê, and to the island of Socotra, was now but seldom heard in Upper Egypt. The Alexandrians were sorely harassed by Hæphæstus, a lawyer, who had risen by court favour to the chief post in the city. He made monopolies in his own favour of all the necessaries of life, and secured his ill-gotten gains by ready loans of part of it to Justinian. His zeal for the emperor was at the cost of the Alexandrians, and to save the public granaries he lessened the supply of grain which the citizens looked for as a right. The city was sinking fast; and the citizens could ill bear this loss, for its population, though lessened, was still too large for the fallen state of Egypt.

The grain of the merchants was shipped from Alexandria to the chief ports of Europe, between Constantinople in the east and Cornwall in the west. Britain had been left by the Romans, as too remote for them to hold in their weakened condition; and the native Britons were then struggling against their Saxon invaders, as in a distant corner of the world, beyond the knowledge of the historian. But to that remote country the Alexandrian merchants sailed every year with grain to purchase tin, enlightening the natives, while they only meant to enrich themselves. Under the most favourable circumstances they sometimes performed the voyage in twenty days. The wheat was sold in Cornwall at the price of a bushel for a piece of silver, perhaps worth about twenty cents, or for the same weight of tin, as the tin and the silver were nearly of equal worth. This was the longest of the ancient voyages, being longer than that from the Red Sea to the island of Ceylon in the Indian Ocean; and it had been regularly performed for at least eight centuries without ever teaching the British to venture so far from their native shores.

The suffering and riotous citizens made Alexandria a very unpleasant place of abode for the prefect and magistrates. They therefore built palaces and baths for their own use, at the public cost, at Taposiris, about a day's journey to the west of the city, at a spot yet marked by the remains of thirty-six marble columns, and a lofty tower, once perhaps a lighthouse. At the same time it became necessary to fortify the public granaries against the rebellious mob. The grain was brought from the Nile by barges on a canal to the village of Chæreum, and thence to a part of Alexandria named Phialæ, or *The Basins*, where the public granaries stood. In all riots and rebellions this place had been a natural point of attack; and often had the starving mob broken open these buildings, and seized the grain that was on its way to Constantinople. But Justinian surrounded them with a strong wall against such attacks for the future, and at the same time he rebuilt the aqueduct that had been destroyed in one of the sieges of the city.

In civil suits at law an appeal had always been allowed from the prefect of the province to the emperor, or rather to the prefect of the East at Constantinople; but as this was of course expensive, it was found necessary to forbid it when the sum of money in dispute was small. Justinian forbade all Egyptian appeals for sums less than ten pounds weight of gold, or about two thousand five hundred dollars; for smaller sums the judgment of the prefect was to be final, lest the expense should swallow up the amount in dispute.

In this reign the Alexandrians, for the first time within the records of history, felt the shock of an earthquake. Their naturalists had very fairly supposed that the loose alluvial nature of the soil of the Delta was the reason why earthquakes were unknown in Lower Egypt, and believed that it would always save them from a misfortune which often overthrew cities in other countries. Pliny thought that Egypt had been always free from earthquakes. But this shock was felt by everybody in the city; and Agathias, the Byzantine historian, who, after reading law in the university of Beirut, was finishing his studies at Alexandria, says that it was strong enough to make the inhabitants all run into the street for fear the houses should fall upon them.

The reign of Justinian is remarkable for another blow then given to paganism throughout the empire, or at least through those parts of the empire where the emperor's laws were obeyed. Under Justinian the pagan schools were again and from that time forward closed. Isidorus the platonist and Salustius the Cynic were among the learned men of greatest note who then withdrew from Alexandria. Isidorus had been chosen by Marinus as his successor in the platonic chair at Athens, to fill the high post of the platonic successor; but he had left the Athenian school to Zenodotus, a pupil of Proclus, and had removed to Alexandria. Salustius the Cynic was a Syrian, who had removed with Isidorus from Athens to Alexandria. He was virtuous in his morals though jocular in his manners, and as ready in his witty attacks upon the speculative opinions of his brother philosophers as upon the vices of the Alexandrians. These learned men, with Damascius and others from Athens, were kindly received by the Persians, who soon afterwards, when they made a treaty of peace with Justinian, generously bargained that these men, the last teachers of

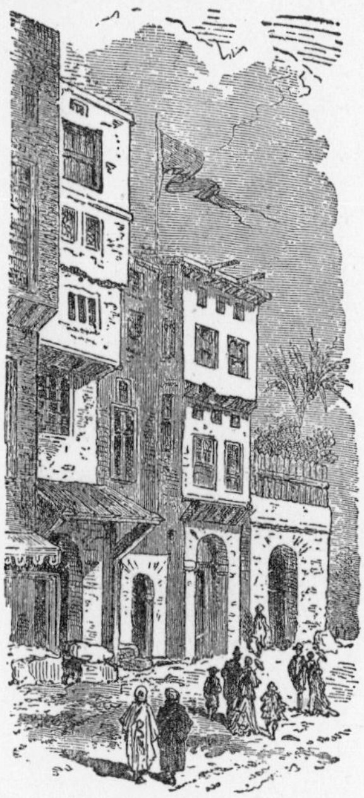

A MODERN HOUSE IN THE DELTA AT ROSETTA.

paganism, should be allowed to return home, and pass the rest of their days in quiet.

After the flight of the pagan philosophers, but little learning was left in Alexandria. One of the most remarkable men in this age of ignorance was Cosmas, an Alexandrian merchant, who wished that the world should not only be enriched but enlightened by his travels. After making many voyages through Ethiopia to India for the sake of gain, he gave up trade and became a monk and an author. When he writes as a traveller about the Christian churches of India and Ceylon, and the inscriptions which he copied at Adule in Abyssinia, everything that he tells us is valuable; but when he reasons as a monk, the case is sadly changed. He is of the dogmatical school which forbids all inquiry as heretical. He fights the battle which has been so often fought before and since, and is even still fought so resolutely, the battle of religious ignorance against scientific knowledge. He sets the words of the Bible against the results of science; he denies that the world is a sphere, and quotes the Old Testament against the pagan astronomers, to show that it is a plane, covered by the firmament as by a roof, above which he places the kingdom of heaven. His work is named *Christian Topography*, and he is himself usually called Cosmas Indicopleustes, from the country which he visited.

During the latter years of the government of Apollinarius, such was his unpopularity as a spiritual bishop that both the rival parties, the Gaianites and the Theodosians, had been building places of worship for themselves, and the more zealous Jacobites had quietly left the churches to Apollinarius and the Royalists. But on the death of an archdeacon they again came to blows with the bishop; and a monk had his beard torn off his chin by the Gaianites in the streets of Alexandria. The emperor was obliged to interfere, and he sent the Abbot Photinus to Egypt to put down this rebellion, and heal the quarrel in the Church. Apollinarius died soon afterwards, and Justinian then appointed John to the joint office of prefect of the city and patriarch of the Church. The new archbishop was accused of being a Manichean; but this seems to mean nothing but that he was too much of the Egyptian party, and that, though he was the imperial patriarch, and not acknowledged by the Koptic church, yet his opinions were disliked by the Greeks. On his death, which happened in about three years, they chose Peter, who held the Jacobite or Egyptian opinions, and whose name is not mentioned in the Greek lists of the patriarchs. Peter's death occurred in the same year as that of the emperor.

Under Justinian we again find some small traces of a national coinage in Egypt. Ever since the reign of Diocletian, the old Egyptian coinage had been stopped, and the Alexandrians had used money of the same weight, and with the same Latin inscriptions, as the rest of the empire. But under Justinian, though the inscriptions on the coins are still Latin, they have the name of the city in Greek letters. Like the coins of Constantinople, they have a cross, the emblem of Christianity; but while the other coins of the empire have the Greek numeral letters,

E, I, K, Λ, or M, to denote the value, meaning 5, 10, 20, 30, or 40, the coins of Alexandria have the letters I B for 12, showing that they were on a different system of weights from those of Constantinople. On these the head of the emperor is in profile. But later in his reign the style was changed, the coins were made larger, and the head of the emperor had a front face. On these larger coins the numeral letters are Λ Γ for 33. We thus learn that the Alexandrians at this time paid and received money rather by weight than by tale, and avoided all

COINS OF JUSTINIAN.

depreciation of the currency. As the early coins marked 12 had become lighter by wear, those which were meant to be of about three times their value were marked 33.

During the period from 566 to 602 Justin II. reigned twelve years, Tiberius reigned four years, and Mauricius, his son-in-law, twenty; and under these sovereigns the empire gained a little rest from its enemies by a rebellion among the Persians, which at last overthrew their king Chosroes. He fled to Mauricius for help, and was by him restored to his throne, after which the two kingdoms remained at peace to the end of his reign.

The Emperor Mauricius was murdered by Phocas, who, in 602, succeeded him on the throne of Constantinople. No sooner did the news of his death reach

Persia than Chosroes, the son of Hormuz, who had married Maria, the daughter of Mauricius, declared the treaty with the Romans at an end, and moved his forces against the new emperor, the murderer of his father-in-law. During the whole of his reign Constantinople was kept in a state of alarm and almost of siege by the Persians; and the crimes and misfortunes of Phocas alike prepared his subjects for a revolt. In the seventh year Alexandria rebelled in favour of the young Heraclius, son of the late prefect of Cyrene; and the patriarch of Egypt was slain in the struggle. Soon afterwards Heraclius entered the port of Constantinople with his fleet, and Phocas was put to death after an unfortunate reign of eight years, in which he had lost every province of the empire.

During the first three years of the reign of Heraclius, Theodorus was Bishop of Alexandria; but upon his death the wishes of the Alexandrians so strongly pointed to John, the son of the prefect of Cyprus, that the emperor, yielding to their request, appointed him to the bishopric. Alexandria was not a place in which a good man could enjoy the pleasures of power without feeling the weight of its duties. It was then suffering under all those evils which usually befall the capital of a sinking state. It had lost much of its trade, and its poorer citizens no longer received a free supply of grain. The unsettled state of the country was starving the larger cities, and the population of Alexandria was suffering from want of employment. The civil magistrates had removed their palace to a distance. But the new bishop seemed formed for these unfortunate times, and, though appointed by the emperor, he was in every respect worthy of the free choice of the citizens. He was foremost in every work of benevolence and charity. The five years of his government were spent in lightening the sufferings of the people, and he gained the truly Christian name of John the Almsgiver. Beside his private acts of kindness he established throughout the city hospitals for the sick and almshouses for the poor and for strangers, and as many as seven lying-in hospitals for poor women. John was not less active in outrooting all that he thought heresy.

The first years of the reign of Heraclius are chiefly marked by the successes of the Persians. While Chosroes, their king, was himself attacking Constantinople, one general was besieging Jerusalem and a second overrunning Lower Egypt. Crowds fled before the invading army to Alexandria as a place of safety, and the famine increased as the province of the prefect grew narrower and the population more crowded. To add to the distress the Nile rose to a less height than usual; the seasons seemed to assist the enemy in the destruction of Egypt. The patriarch John, who had been sending money, grain, and Egyptian workmen to assist in the pious work of rebuilding the church of Jerusalem which the Persians had destroyed, immediately found all his means needed, and far from enough, for the poor of Alexandria. On his appointment to the bishopric he found in its treasury eight thousand pounds of gold; he had in the course of five years received ten thousand more from the offerings of the pious, as his princely ecclesiastical revenue was named; but this large sum of four million dollars had all been spent in deeds of generosity or charity, and the bishop had no resource but borrowing to relieve the misery with which he was surrounded. In the fifth year the unbelievers were masters of Jerusalem, and in the eighth they entered Alexandria, and soon held all the Delta; and in that year the grain which had hitherto been given to the citizens of Constantinople was sold to them at a small price, and before the end of the year the supply from Egypt was wholly stopped.

When the Persians entered Egypt, the patrician Nicetas, having no forces with which he could withstand their advance, and knowing that no succour was to be looked for from Constantinople, and finding that the Alexandrians were unwilling to support him, fled with the patriarch John the Almsgiver to Cyprus, and left the province to the enemy. As John denied that the Son of God had suffered on the cross, his opinions would seem not to have been very unlike those of the Egyptians; but as he was appointed to the bishopric by the emperor, though at the request of the people, he is not counted among the patriarchs of the Koptic church; and one of the first acts of the Persians was to appoint Benjamin, a Jacobite priest, who already performed the spiritual office of Bishop of Alexandria, to the public exercise of that duty, and to the enjoyment of the civil dignity and revenues.

The troops with which Chosroes conquered and held Egypt were no doubt in part Syrians and Arabs, people with whom the fellahs or labouring class of Egyptians were closely allied in blood and feelings. Hence arose the readiness with which the whole country yielded when the Roman forces were defeated. But hence also arose the weakness of the Persians, and their speedy loss of this conquest when the Arabs rebelled. Their rule, however, in Egypt was not quite unmarked in the history of these dark ages.

At this time Thomas, a Syrian bishop, came to Alexandria to correct the Syriac version of the New Testament, which had been made about a century before by Philoxenus. He compared the Gospels, Acts, and Epistles with the Greek manuscripts in the monastery of St. Anthony in the capital; and we still possess the fruits of his learned labour, in which he altered the ancient text to make it agree with the newer Alexandrian manuscripts. From his copy the Philoxenian version is now printed. A Syriac manuscript of the New Testament written by Alexandrian penmen in the sixth year of Heraclius, is now to be seen in the library of the Augustan friars in Rome. At the same time another Syrian scholar, Paul of Tela, in Mesopotamia, was busy in the Alexandrian monastery of St. Zacchæus in translating the Old Testament into Syriac, from the Septuagint Greek; and he closes his labours with begging the reader to pray for the soul of his friend Thomas. Such was now the reputation of the Alexandrian edition of the Bible, that these scholars preferred it both to the original Hebrew of the Old and to the earlier manuscripts of the New Testament. Among other works of this time were the medical writings of Aaron the physician of

Alexandria, formerly written in Syriac, and afterwards much valued by the Arabs. The Syrian monks in numbers settled in the monastery of Mount Nitria; and in that secluded spot there remained a colony of these monks for several centuries, kept up by the occasional arrival of newcomers from the churches on the eastern side of the Euphrates.

For ten years the Egyptians were governed by the Persians, and had a patriarch of their own religion and of their own choice; and the building of the Persian palace in Alexandria proves how quietly they lived under their new masters. But Heraclius was not idle under his misfortunes. The Persians had been weakened by the great revolt of the Arabs, who had formed their chief strength on the side of Constantinople and Egypt; and Heraclius, leading his forces bravely against Chosroes, drove him back from Syria and became in his turn the invader, and he then recovered Egypt. The Jacobite patriarch Benjamin fled with the Persians; and Heraclius appointed George to the bishopric, which was declared to have been empty since John the Almsgiver fled to Cyprus.

The revolt of the Arabs, which overthrew the power of the Persians in their western provinces and for a time restored Egypt to Constantinople, was the foundation of the mighty empire of the caliphs; and the Hegira, or flight of Muhammed, from which the Arabic historians count their lunar years, took place in 622, the twelfth year of Heraclius. The vigour of the Arab arms rapidly broke the Persian yoke, and the Moslems then overran every province in the neighbourhood. This was soon felt by the Romans, who found the Arabs, even in the third year of their freedom, a more formidable enemy than the Persians whom they had overthrown; and, after a short struggle of only two years, Heraclius was forced to pay a tribute to the Moslems for their forbearance in not conquering Egypt. For eight years he was willing to purchase an inglorious peace by paying tribute to the caliph; but when his treasure failed him and the payment was discontinued, the Arabs marched against the nearest provinces of the empire, offering to the inhabitants their choice of either paying tribute or receiving the Muhammedan religion; and they then began on their western frontier that rapid career of conquest which they had already begun on the eastern frontier against their late masters, the Persians.

ORNAMENT FROM THE PORCH OF THE SULTAN HASSAN.

CHAPTER III

EGYPT DURING THE MUHAMMEDAN PERIOD

The Rise of Muhammedanism: The Arabic Conquest of Egypt: The Ommayad and Abbasid Dynasties.

ORNAMENT FROM THE MOSQUE OF BERKUK.

THE course of history now follows the somewhat uneventful period which introduced Arabian rule into the valley of the Nile. It is only necessary to remind the reader of the striking incidents in the life of Muhammed. He was born at Mecca, in Arabia, in July, 571, and spent his earliest years in the desert. At the age of twelve he travelled with a caravan to Syria, and probably on this occasion first came into contact with the Jews and Christians. After a few youthful adventures, his poetic and religious feelings were awakened by study. He gave himself up to profound meditation upon both the Jewish and Christian ideals, and subsequently beholding the archangel Gabriel in a vision, he proclaimed himself as a prophet of God. After preaching his doctrine for three years, and gaining a few converts (the first of whom was his wife, Khadija), the people of Mecca rose against him and he was forced to flee from the city in 614. New visions and subsequent conversions of influential Arabs strengthened his cause, especially in Medina, whither Muhammed was forced to flee a second time from Mecca in 622, this second flight being known as the Hegira, from which dates the Muhammedan era. In the next year, at Medina, he built his first mosque and married Ayesha, and in 624 was compelled to defend his pretensions by an appeal to arms. He was at first successful, and thereupon appointed Friday as a day of public worship, and, being embittered against the Jews, ordered that the attitude of prayer should no longer be towards Jerusalem, but towards his birthplace, Mecca. In 625 the Muhammedans were defeated by the Meccans, but one tribe after another submitted to him, and after a series of victories Muhammed prepared, in 629, for further conquests in Syria, but he died in 632 before they could be accomplished. His successors were known as caliphs, but from the very first his disciples quarrelled about the leadership, some affirming the rights of Ali, who had married Muhammed's daughter, Fatima, and others supporting the claims of Abu Bekr, his father-in-law. There was also a religious quarrel concerning certain oral traditions relating to the Koran, or the Muhammedan sacred scriptures. Those who accepted the tradition were known as Sunnites, and those who rejected it as Shiites, the latter being the supporters of Ali, both sects, however, being known as Moslems or Islamites.

COIN OF ALI.

Omar, a Sunnite, obtained the leadership in 634, and proceeded to carry out the prophet's ambitious schemes of conquest. He subdued successively Syria, Palestine, and Phœnicia, and in 639 directed operations against Egypt. The general in charge of this expedition was Amr, who led four thousand men against Pelusium, which surrendered after a siege of thirty days. This easy victory was crowned by the capture of Alexandria. Amr entered the city on December 22, 640, and he seems to have been surprised at his own success. He immediately wrote to the caliph a letter in which he says:

"I have conquered the town of the West, and I cannot recount all it contains within its walls. It contains four thousand baths and twelve thousand venders of green vegetables, four thousand Jews who pay tribute, and four thousand musicians and mountebanks."

Amr was anxious to conciliate and gain the affection of the new subjects he had added to the caliph's empire, and during his short stay in Alexandria received them with kindness and personally heard and attended to their demands. It is commonly believed that in this period the Alexandrian Library was dismantled; but, as we have already seen, the books had been destroyed by the zeal of contending Christians. The story that attributes the destruction of this world-famous institution to the Arabian conquerors is so much a part of history, and has been so generally accepted as correct, that the traditional version should be given here.

Among the inhabitants of Alexandria whom Amr had so well received, says the monkish chronicler, was one John the Grammarian, a learned Greek, disciple of the Jacobite sect, who had been imprisoned by its persecutors. Since his disgrace, he had given himself up entirely to study, and was one of the most assiduous readers in the famous library. With the change of masters he believed the rich treasure would be speedily dispersed, and he wished to obtain a portion of it himself. So, profiting by the special kindness Amr had shown him, and the pleasure he appeared to take in his conversation, he ventured to ask for the gift of several of the philosophic books whose removal would put an end to his learned researches.

COIN OF OMAR.

At first Amr granted this request without hesitation, but in his gratitude John the Grammarian expatiated so unwisely on the extreme rarity of the manuscripts and their inestimable value, that Amr, on reflection, feared he had overstepped his power in granting the learned man's request. "I will refer the matter to the caliph," he said, and thereupon wrote immediately to

Omar and asked the caliph for his commands concerning the disposition of the whole of the precious contents of the library.

The caliph's answer came quickly. "If," he wrote, "the books contain only what is in the book of God (the Koran), it is enough for us, and these books are useless. If they contain anything contrary to the holy book, they are pernicious. In any case, burn them."

Amr wished to organise his new government, and, having left a sufficient garrison in Alexandria, he gave orders to the rest of his army to leave the camp in the town and to occupy the interior of Egypt. "Where shall we pitch our new camp?" the soldiers asked each other, and the answer came from all parts, "Round the general's tent." The army, in fact, did camp on the banks of the Nile, in the vicinity of the modern Cairo, where Amr had ordered his tent to be left; and round this tent, which had become the centre of reunion, the soldiers built temporary huts which were soon changed into solid, permanent habitations. Spacious houses were built for the leaders, and palaces for the generals, and this collection of buildings soon became an important military town, with strongly marked Muhammedan characteristics. It was called Fostât (tent) in memory of the event, otherwise unimportant, which was the origin of its creation. Amr determined to make his new town the capital of Egypt; whilst still preserving the name of Fostât, he added that of Misr,—a title always borne by the capital of Egypt, and which Memphis had hitherto preserved in spite of the rivalry of Alexandria.

Fostât was then surrounded by fortifications, and Amr took up his residence there, forming various establishments and giving himself up entirely to the organisation of the vast province whose government the caliph had entrusted to him. The personal tax, which was the only one, had been determined in a fixed manner by the treaty of submission he had concluded with the Kopts; and an unimportant ground rent on landed property was added in favour of the holy towns of Mecca and Medina, as well as to defray some expenses of local administration.

Egypt was entirely divided into provincial districts, all of which had their own governor and administrators taken from among the Kopts themselves. The lands which had belonged to the imperial government of Constantinople, and those of the Greeks who had abandoned Egypt or been killed in the war against the Mussulmans, were either declared to be the property of the new government or given out again as fiefs or rewards to the chief officers of the army. All these lands were leased to the Koptic farmers, and the respective rights of the new proprietors or tenant farmers and of the peasant proprietors were determined by decisive and invariable rules. Thus the agricultural population enjoyed under the Mussulmans a security and ease which replaced the tyrannical annoyances and arbitrary exactions of the Christian agents of the treasury of Constantinople; for, in fact, little by little, there had disappeared under these Greek agents the sound principles of the old administration that had been established by the wise kings of

OLD CAIRO (FOSTÂT).

ancient Egypt, and which the Ptolemies had scrupulously preserved, as did also the first governors under the Cæsars.

After all these improvements in the internal administration, the governor turned his attention to the question of justice, which until that moment had been subject to the decision of financial agents, or of the soldiers of the Greek government. Amr now created permanent and regular tribunals composed of honourable, independent, and enlightened men, who enjoyed public respect and esteem. To Amr dates back the first of those *divans*, chosen from the élite of the population, as sureties of the fairness of the *cadis*, which received appeals from first judgments to confirm them, or, in the case of wrongful decisions, to alter them. The decrees of the Arab judges had force only for those Mussulmans who formed a part of the occupying army. Whenever a Koptic inhabitant was a party in an action, the Koptic authorities had the right to intervene, and the parties were judged by their equals in race and religion.

One striking act of justice succeeded in winning for Amr the hearts of all. Despite the terror inspired by the religious persecutions which Heraclius had carried on with so much energy, one man, the Koptic patriarch Benjamin, had bravely kept his faith intact. He belonged to the Jacobite sect and abandoned none of its dogmas, and in their intolerance the all-powerful Melchites did not hesitate to choose him as their chief victim. Benjamin was dispossessed of his patriarchal throne, his liberty and life were threatened, and he only succeeded in saving both by taking flight. He lived thus forgotten in the various refuges that the desert monasteries afforded him, while Heraclius replaced him by an ardent supporter of the opinions favoured at court. The whole of Egypt was then divided into two churches separated from each other by an implacable hatred. At the head of the Melchites was the new patriarch, who was followed by a few priests and a small number of partisans who were more attached to him by fear than by faith. The Jacobites, on the other hand, comprised the immense majority of the population, who looked upon the patriarch as an intruder chosen by the emperor. The church still acknowledged as its real head Benjamin, the patriarch who had been for thirteen years a wanderer, and whose return was ardently desired. This wish found public expression as soon as the downfall of the imperial power in Egypt permitted its free manifestation. Amr listened to the supplications that were addressed to him, and, turning out the usurper in his turn, recalled Benjamin from his long exile and replaced him on the patriarchal throne.

But even here Amr's protection of the Koptic religion did not end. He opened the door of his Mussulman town, and allowed them to live in Fostât and to build churches there in the midst of the Mussulman soldiers, even when Islamism was still without a temple in the city, or a consecrated place worthy of the religion of the conquerors.

Amr at length resolved to build in his new capital a magnificent mosque in imitation of the one at Mecca.

Designs were speedily drawn up, the location of the new temple being, according to Arab authors, that of an ancient pyre consecrated by the Persians, and which had been in ruins since the time of the Ptolemies. The monuments of Memphis had often been pillaged by

A MODERN KOPT.

Greek and Roman emperors, and now they were once again despoiled to furnish the mosque of Amr with the beautiful colonnades of marble and porphyry which adorn the walls, and on which, the Arab historians assure us, the whole Koran was written in letters of gold.

Omar died in 644, and under his successor, Othman, the Arabian conquests were extended in Northern Africa. Othman dying in 656, the claims of Ali were warmly supported, but not universally recognised, many looking to Muawia as an acceptable candidate for the caliphate. This was especially the view of the Syrian Muhammedans, and in 661 Muawia I. was elected caliph. He promptly transferred the capital from Medina to Damascus, and became in fact the founder of a dynasty known as the Ommayads, the new caliph being a descendant of the famous Arabian chieftain Ommayad. Egypt acknowledged the new authority and remained quiet and submissive. It furnished Abd el-Malik, who became caliph in 685, not only with rich subsidies and abundant provisions, but also with part of his troops.

The attachment of the Egyptians to their new masters was chiefly owing to the gentleness and wisdom of Abd el-Aziz ibn Merwan, who administered the country after Amr was put to death in 689. He visited all the provinces of Egypt, and, arriving at Alexandria, he ordered the building of a bridge over the canal, recognising the importance of this communication between the town and country.

Benefiting by the religious liberty that Mussulman sovereignship had secured them, the Kopts no longer attended to the quarrels of their masters. They only occupied themselves in maintaining the quiet peacefulness they had obtained by regular payment of their taxes, and by supplying men and commodities when occasion demanded it. During the reign of Abd el-Malik in Egypt the only remarkable event there was the election, in 688, of the Jacobite Isaac as patriarch of Alexandria. The Koptic clergy give him no other claim to historical remembrance than the formulating of a decree

MOSQUE OF AMR.

ordaining "that the patriarch can only be inaugurated on a Sunday."

Isaac was succeeded by Simon the Syrian, whom the Koptic church looks upon as a saint, and for whom is claimed the power of reviving the dead. He nevertheless died from the effects of poison given him at the altar by some jealous rival. Arab historians relate how deputies came to Simon from India to ask for a bishop and some priests. The patriarch refused to comply with this request, but Abd el-Aziz, thinking that this relation with India might prove politically useful, gave the order to other and more docile priests.

The patriarchal seat was empty for three years after the death of Simon. The Kopts next appointed a patriarch named Alexander, who held the office for a little over twenty years. The Koptic writers who recount the history of this patriarch mention their discontent with the governor Abd el-Aziz. The monks and other members of the clergy had grown very numerous in Egypt and claimed to be exempt from taxation. Abd el-Aziz, whose yearly tax was fixed, thought it unjust that the poorest classes of the people should be made to pay while the priests, the bishop, and the patriarch, all possessing abundance, should be privileged by exemption. He therefore had a census made of all the monks and put on them a tax of one dinar (about $2.53), while he exacted from the patriarch an annual payment of three thousand dinars, or about $7,600. This act of justice was the cause of many complaints among the clergy, but they were soon suppressed and were without result.

After more than twenty years of a prosperous government of Egypt, Abd el-Aziz ibn Merwan died at Fostât in the year 708 (A. H. 86) at the very time when, with many fresh plans for the future, he had completed the building of a large and magnificent palace called ed-Dar el-mudahaba (the golden house), and a quarter of the town called Suk el-hammam (the pigeon market). The Caliph Abd el-Malik felt deeply the loss of this brother, whose qualities he highly appreciated and whom he had appointed as his successor.

COIN OF ABU BEKR.

He now named as his heir to the caliphate Walid, his eldest son, and replaced Abd el-Aziz in the government of Egypt with his second son, Abd Allah ibn Abd el-Malik. The Kopts hoped to obtain from the new governor the repeal of the act that exacted yearly tribute from the clergy, but Abd Allah did not think it fair to grant this unjust discrimination against the poorer classes of the Egyptians. Those monks who have written the history of the patriarchs have therefore painted Abd Allah in even blacker colours than they did his predecessor. For the rest, Abd Allah only held the reins of government in Egypt until the death of his father, which occurred a few months later.

COIN OF OTHMAN.

Suleiman succeeded his brother Walid I. The new caliph vigorously put into execution all the plans his brother had formed for the propagation of the religion of the Prophet. In the first year of his reign he conquered Tabaristan and Georgia, and sent his brother

Maslama to lay fresh siege to Constantinople. On his accession to the throne Suleiman placed the government of Egypt in the hands of Assama ibn Yazid, with the title of agent-general of finances.

The Koptic clerical historians, according to their usual habit, portray this governor as still worse than his predecessors, but in this case the Mussulman authorities are in agreement in accusing him of the most iniquitous extortions and most barbarous massacres. The gravest reproach they bring against him is that, calling all the monks together, he told them that not only did he intend to maintain the old regulations of Abd el-Aziz, by which they had to pay an annual tax of one dinar ($2.53), but also that they would be obliged to receive yearly from his agents an iron ring bearing their name and the date of the financial transaction, for which ring they were to make personal contribution. He forced the wearing of this ring continually, and the hand found without this strange form of receipt was to be cut off. Several monks who endeavoured to evade this strict order were pitilessly mutilated, while a number of them, rebelling against the payment of the tax, retired into convents, thinking they could safely defraud the treasury. Assama, however, sent his soldiers to search these retreats, and all the monks found without rings were beheaded or put to death by the bastinado.

COIN OF MALIK.

Careful about all that related to the Egyptian revenues, Assama commanded the keeping up of the various Nilometers, which still served to regulate the assessment of the ground tax. In the year 718 he learned that the Nilometer established at Helwan, a little below Fostât, had fallen in, and hastened to report the fact

CITADEL OF CAIRO (FOSTÂT).

to the caliph. By the orders of this prince the ruined Nilometer was abandoned, and a new one built at the meridional point of the island now called Rhodha, just between Fostât and Gizeh. But of all the financial transactions of Assama, the one that vexed most the inhabitants of Egypt, and which brought down on him the most violent and implacable hatred, was the ordinance by which all ascending or descending the Nile were obliged to provide themselves with a passport bearing a tax. This exorbitant claim was carried out with an abusive and arbitrary sternness. A poor widow, the Oriental writers say, was travelling up the Nile with her son, having with her a correct passport, the payment of which had taken nearly all she possessed. The young man, while stretched along the boat to drink of the river's water, was seized by a crocodile and swallowed, together with the passport he carried in his breast. The treasury officers insisted that the wretched widow should take a fresh one; and to obtain payment for it she sold all she had, even to the very clothes she wore. Such intolerable exactions and excesses ended by thoroughly rousing the indignant Egyptians. The malcontents assembled, and a general revolt would have been the result but for the news of the death of the Caliph Suleiman (717), which gave birth to the hope that justice might be obtained from his successor.

The next caliph was Omar II., a grandson of Merwan I., who had been nominated as his successor by Suleiman. In his reign the Muhammedans were repulsed from Constantinople, and the political movement began which finally established the Abbasid dynasty at Baghdad. Omar dying in the year 720, Yazid II., a son of Abd el-Malik, succeeded to the caliphate, and reigned for four years, history being for the most part silent as to the general condition of Egypt under these two caliphs. It is recorded that in the year 720, one of Yazid's brothers, by name Muhammed ibn Abd el-Malik, ruled over Egypt. The Kopts complained of his rule, and declared that during the whole reign of Yazid ibn Abd el-Malik the Christians were persecuted, crosses overthrown, and churches destroyed.

Yazid was succeeded, in 724 A. D., by his brother Hisham, surnamed Abu'l-Walid, the fourth son of Abd el-Malik to occupy the throne of Islam, who, having been appointed by his brother as his successor, took possession of the throne on the very day of his death. Muhammed was replaced in Egypt by his cousin, Hassan ibn Yusuf, who only held office for three years, resigning voluntarily in the year 730 A. D., or 108 of the Hegira. The Caliph Hisham replaced him by Hafs ibn Walid, who was deposed a year later, and in the year 109 of the Hegira the caliph appointed in his place Abd el-Malik ibn Rifa, who had already governed Egypt during the caliphate of Walid I. Hisham made many changes in the governorship of Egypt, and amid a succession of rulers appointed Handhala to the post. He had already been governor of Egypt under Yazid II. He administered the province for another six years, and, according to the Christian historians of the East, pursued the same course of intolerance and tyranny that he had adopted when he governed Egypt for the first time under Yazid.

A CROCODILE USED AS A TALISMAN.

The Caliph Hisham enjoined Handhala to be gentle with his subjects and to treat the Christians with kindness, but far from conforming with these wise and kindly intentions, he overwhelmed them with vexations and tyrannous acts. He doubled the taxes by a general census, subjecting not only men but also their animals to an impost. The receipts for the new duty had to be stamped with the impression of a lion, and every Christian found without one of these documents was deprived of one of his hands.

In the year 746 (A. H. 124), on being informed of these abuses, the caliph deprived him of the government of Egypt, and, giving him the administration of Mauritania, appointed as his successor Hafs ibn Walid, who, according to some accounts, had previously governed Egypt for sixteen years, and who had left pleasanter recollections behind him. Hafs, however, now only held office for a year.

Nothing of political importance happened in Egypt under the long reign of Hisham, the only events noticed by the Christian historians being those which relate solely to their ecclesiastical history. The 108th year of the Hegira saw the death of Alexander, the forty-third Koptic Patriarch of Alexandria. Since the conquest of Egypt by Omar, for a period of about twenty-four years, the patriarchate had been in the hands of the Jacobites; all the bishops in Egypt belonged to that sect, and they had established Jacobite bishops even in Nubia, which they had converted to their religion. The orthodox Christians elected Kosmas as their patriarch. At that time the heretics had taken possession of all the churches in Egypt, and the patriarch only retained that of Mar-Saba, or the Holy Sabbath. Kosmas, by his solicitations, obtained from Hisham an order to his financial administrator in Egypt, Abd Allah ibn es-Sakari, to see that all the churches were returned to the sect to which they belonged.

After occupying the patriarchal throne for only fifteen months, Kosmas died. In the 109th year of the Hegira (A. D. 727—28) Kosmas was succeeded by the patriarch Theodore. He occupied the seat for eleven years. His patriarchate was a period of peace and quiet for the church of Alexandria, and caused a temporary cessation of the quarrels between the Melchites and the Jacobites. A vacancy of six years followed his death until, in the year 127 of the Hegira (749 A. D.), Ibn Khalil was promoted to the office of patriarch, and held his seat for twenty-three years.

Walid II. succeeded to the caliphate in the year 749. One of his first acts was to take the government of Egypt from Hafs, in spite of the kindness of his rule, the wisdom and moderation of which had gained for him the affection of all the provinces which he governed. He was replaced by Isa ibn Abi Atta, who soon created a universal discontent, as his administrative measures were oppressive.

In the year 750 the Ommayads were supplanted by the Abbasids, who transferred the capital from Damascus to Baghdad. The first Abbasid caliph was Abu'l-Abbas, who claimed descent from Abbas, the uncle of Muhammed. The caliph Merwan II., the last of the Ommayads, in his flight from his enemies came to Egypt and sent troops from Fostât to hold Alexandria. He was now pursued to his death by the Abbasid general Salih ibn Ali, who took possession of Fostât for the new dynasty in 750. The change from the Ommayad to the Abbasid caliphs was effected with little difficulty, and Egypt continued to be a province of the caliphate and was ruled by governors who were mostly Arabs or members of the Abbasid family.

Abu'l-Abbas, after being inaugurated, began his rule by recalling all the provincial governors, whom he replaced by his kinsmen and partisans. He entrusted the government of Egypt to his paternal uncle, Salih ibn Ali, who had obtained the province for him. Salih, however, did not rule in person, but was represented by Abu Aun Abd el-Malik ibn Yazid, whom he appointed vice-governor. The duties of patriarch of Alexandria were then performed by Michel, commonly called Khail by the Kopts. This patriarch was of the Jacobite sect and the forty-fifth successor of St. Mark: he held the office about three years. He in turn was succeeded by the patriarch Myna, a native of Semennud (the ancient Sebennytus).

In the year 754 Abu'l-Abbas died at the age of thirty-two, after reigning four years, eight months, and twenty-six days, the Arabian historians being always very precise in recording the duration of the reign of the caliphs. He was the first of the caliphs to appoint a vizier, the Ommayad caliphs employing only secretaries during their administration. The successor of Abu'l-

Abbas was his brother Abu Jafar, surnamed El-Mansur. Three years after his accession he took the government of Egypt from his uncle, and in less than seven years Egypt passed successively through the hands of six different governors. These changes were instigated by the mistrustful disposition of the caliph, who saw in every man a traitor and conspirator, dismissing on the slightest provocation his most devoted adherents, some of whom were even put to death by his orders. His last choice, Yazid ibn Hatim, governed Egypt for eight years, and the caliph bestowed the title of Prince of Egypt (Emir Misri) upon him, which title was also borne by his successors.

These continual changes in the government of Egypt had not furthered the prosperity and well-being of the inhabitants. Each ruler, certain of speedy dismissal, busied himself with his personal affairs to the detriment of the country, anxious only to amass by every possible means sufficient money to compensate him for his inevitable deposition. Moreover, each governor increased the taxation levied by his predecessor. Such was the greed and rapacity of these governors that every industry was continually subjected to increased taxation; the working bricklayer, the vender of vegetables, the camel-driver, the gravedigger, all callings, even that of mendicant, were taxed, and the lower classes were reduced to eating dog's flesh and human remains. At the moment when Egypt, unable to support such oppression longer, was on the verge of insurrection, the welcome tidings of the death of El-Mansur arrived.

Muhammed el-Mahdi, son of El-Mansur, succeeded his father and was the third caliph of the house of Abbas. He was at Baghdad when his father expired near Mecca, but, despite his absence, was immediately proclaimed caliph. El-Mahdi betrayed in his deeds that same fickleness which had signalised the caliphate of his father, El-Mansur. He appointed a different governor of Egypt nearly every year. These many changes resulted probably from the political views held by the caliph, or perhaps he already perceived the tendency shown by each of his provinces to separate itself from the centre of Islamism. Perhaps also he already foresaw those divisions which destroyed the empire about half a century later. Thus his prudence sought, in allowing but a short period of power to each governor, to prevent their strengthening themselves sufficiently in their provinces to become independent.

Egypt remained calm and subdued under these constant changes of government. Syria and the neighbouring provinces followed suit, and the Caliph el-Mahdi profited by this peaceful state of things to attack the Emperor of the Greeks. His second son, Harun, undertook the continuation of this war, and the young prince displayed such talent and bravery that he gained brilliant victories, and returned to Baghdad after having captured several cities from the Greeks, overthrown their generals, and forced Constantinople to pay an annual tribute of seventy thousand dinars (about $180,000). The Caliph el-Mahdi rewarded Harun by solemnly naming him the future successor of his eldest son, Musa el-Hadi, whom he had just definitely declared his heir to the throne. Shortly after this decision, el-Mahdi died, in the year 785, having reigned ten years and two months.

Musa el-Hadi, his eldest son, succeeded him, being the fourth caliph of the race of Abbasids. On ascending the throne, he withdrew the government of Egypt from Fadl ibn Salih, appointing in his place Ali ibn Suleiman, also a descendant of Abbas. El-Hadi plotted against the claims of Harun to the succession, but he died before his plans had matured, and Harun became caliph in the year 786.

DOOR OF AN ARABIAN HOUSE.

The reign of Harun er-Rashid was the most brilliant epoch of the empire of Islamism, and his glory penetrated from the far East to the western countries of Europe, where his name is still celebrated. Harun seems to have been as reluctant as his father and grandfather were before him to leave a province too long in the hands of a governor, and he even surpassed them in his precautionary measures. In the year 171 of the Hegira, he recalled Ali ibn Suleiman, and gave the government of Egypt to Musa ibn Isa, a descendant of the Caliph Ali.

Thereafter the governors were changed on an average of once a year, and their financial duties were separately administered. Musa ibn Isa, however, held the appointment of Governor of Egypt on three separate occasions, and of his third period Said ibn Batrik tells the following anecdote:

"While Obaid Allah ibn el-Mahdi was ruling in Egypt," he relates, "he sent a beautiful young Koptic slave to his brother, the caliph, as a gift. The Egyptian odalisk so charmed the caliph that he fell violently in love with her. Suddenly, however, the favourite was laid prostrate by a malady which the court physicians could neither cure nor even diagnose. The girl insisted that, being Egyptian, only an Egyptian physician could cure her. The caliph instantly ordered his brother to send post haste the most skilful doctor in Egypt. This proved to be the Melchite patriarch, for in those days Koptic priests practised medicine and cultivated other sciences. The patriarch set out for Baghdad, restored the favourite to health, and in reward received from the caliph an imperial diploma, which restored to the orthodox Christians or Melchites all those privileges of which they had been deprived by the Jacobite heretics since their union with the conqueror Amr ibn el-Asi."

If this story be true, one cannot but perceive the plot skilfully laid and carried out by the powerful clergy, to whom any means, even the sending of a concubine to the caliph, seemed legitimate to procure the restoration of their supremacy and the humiliation of their adversaries.

The year 204 of the Hegira was memorable for the death of the Iman Muhammed ibn Idris, surnamed esh-Shafi. This celebrated doctor was the founder of one of the four orthodox sects which recognised the Moslem religion, and whose followers take the name "Shafites" from their chief. The Iman esh-Shafi died at Fostât when but forty-three years old. His dogmas are more especially followed in Egypt, where his sect is still represented and presided over by one of the four Imans at the head of the famous Mosque Jam el-Azar, or mosque of flowers.

A VEILED BEAUTY.

The distance of Egypt from Baghdad, the caliph's capital, was the cause of the neglect of many of his commands, and upon more than one occasion was his authority slighted. Thus it happened that for more than five years the government of Egypt was in the hands of Abd Allah ibn es-Sari, whom the soldiers elected, but whose appointment was never confirmed by the caliph. Abd Allah ibn Tahir, the son of the successful general, had, in the year A. H. 210, settled at Belbeys in Egypt. With a large number of partisans, he assumed almost regal privileges. In 211 A. H. he proceeded to Fostât and there dismissed Abd Allah ibn es-Sari and replaced him by Ayad ibn Ibrahim, whom he also dismissed the following year, giving the governorship to Isa ibn Yazid, surnamed el-Jalud. In the year 213, the Caliph el-Mamun ordered Abd Allah ibn Tahir to retire, and confided the government of Egypt and also that of Syria to his own brother el-Mutasim, third son of the Caliph Harun er-Rashid.

In the year 218 of the Hegira (A. D. 833), Muhammed el-Mutasim succeeded his brother el-Mamun. He was the first caliph who brought the name of God into his surname. On ascending the throne, he assumed the title el-Mutasim b'Illah, that is "strengthened by God," and his example was followed by all his successors.

From the commencement of this reign, el-Mutasim b'Illah was forced to defend himself against insurgents and aspirants to the caliphate. In the year 219 of the Hegira, Kindi, the Governor of Egypt, died, and the caliph named his son, Mudhaffar ibn Kindi, as his successor. Mudhaffar ibn Kindi, dying the following year, was succeeded by Musa, son of Abu'l-Abbas, surnamed esh-Shirbani by some writers, esh-Shami (the Syrian) by others. In the year 224 Musa was recalled and his place taken by Malik, surnamed by some el-Hindi (the Indian), by others ibn el-Kindi. A year later the caliph dismissed Malik, and sent Ashas to Egypt in his place. This was the last governor appointed by el-Mutasim b'Illah, for the caliph died of fever in the year 227 of the Hegira.

Oriental historians have noticed that the numeral eight affected this caliph in a singular manner. Between himself and Abbas, the head of his house, there were eight generations; he was born in the month of Shaban, the eighth month of the Mussulman year; he was the eighth Abbasidian caliph, and ascended the throne in the year 218, aged thirty-eight years and eight months; he reigned eight years, eight months, and eight days, and died in the forty-eighth year of his age, leaving eight sons and eight daughters. He fought in eight battles,

TOMB OF A SHEIKH.

and on his death eight million dinars and eighty thousand dirhems were discovered in his private treasury. It is this singular coincidence which gave him the name Mutamma.

But a sadder fatality exercised its influence over the Caliph Mutamma, for from him dates the beginning of the decadence of his dynasty, and to him its first cause may be ascribed. The fact is, Mutasim was uneducated, without ability, and lacking in moral principles; he was unable even to write. Endowed with remarkable strength and muscles of iron, he was able, so Arab historians relate, to lift and carry exceptionally heavy weights; to this strength was added indomitable courage and love of warfare, fine weapons, horses, and warriors. This taste led him, even before the death of his father, to organise a picked corps, for which he selected the finest, handsomest, and strongest of the young Turkish slaves taken in war, or sent as tribute to the caliph.

The vast nation, sometimes called Turks, sometimes Tatars, was distributed, according to all Oriental geographers, over all the countries of Northern Asia, from the river Jihun or Oxus to Kathay or China. That the Turks and the Arabs, both bent upon a persistent policy of conquest, should come into more or less hostile contact was inevitable. The struggle was a long one, and during the numerous engagements many prisoners were taken on both sides. Those Turks who fell into the hands of the Arabs were sent to the different provinces of their domain, where they became slaves of the chief emirs and of the caliphs themselves, where, finding favour in the eyes of the caliphs, they were soon transferred to their personal retinue. The distrust which the caliphs felt for the emirs of their court, whose claims they were only able to appease by making vassals of them, caused them to commit the grave error of confiding in these alien slaves, who, barbaric and illiterate as they were, now living in the midst of princes, soon acquired a knowledge of Muhammedanism, the sciences, and, above all, the politics of the country.

It was not long before they were able to fill the most responsible positions, and, given their freedom by the caliphs, were employed by the government according to their abilities. Not only were they given the chief positions at court, but the government of the principal provinces was entrusted to them. They repaid these favours later by the blackest ingratitude, especially when the formation of a Turkish guard brought a number of their own countrymen under their influence. Ever anxious to augment his own body-guard, and finding the number of Turks he annually received as tribute insufficient, el-Mutasim purchased a great many for the purpose of training them for that particular service. But these youths speedily abused the confidence shown them by the caliph, who, perceiving that their insolence was daily growing more insupportable to the inhabitants of Baghdad, resolved to leave the capital, rebuild the ancient city of Samarrah and again make it the seat of the empire.

At this time the captain of the caliph's guard was one Tulun, a freedman, whom fate would seem to have reduced to servitude for the purpose of showing that a slave might found a dynasty destined to rule over Egypt and Syria. Tulun belonged to the Toghus-ghur, one of the twenty-four tribes composing the population of Turkestan. His family dwelt near Lake Lop, in Little Bukhara. He was taken prisoner in battle by Nuh ibn Assad es-Samami, then in command at Bukhara. This prince, who was subject to the Caliph Mamun, paid an annual tribute of slaves, Turkish horses, and other valuables. In the year 815 A. D., Tulun was among the slaves sent as tribute to the caliph, who, attracted by his bearing, enrolled him in his own body-guard.

Before long he had so gained the caliph's confidence that Mamun gave him his freedom and the command of the guard, at the same time appointing him Emir es-sitri, prince of the veil or curtain. This post, which was a mark of the greatest esteem, comprised the charge of the personal safety of the sovereign, by continually keeping watch without the curtain or rich drapery which hung before the private apartments, and admitting no one without a special order. Tulun spent twenty years at the court of el-Mamun and of his successor, Mutasim, and became the father of several children, one of which, Ahmed ibn Tulun,[1] known later as Abu l'Abbas, was the founder of the Tulunide dynasty in Egypt and Syria.

Before Ahmed ibn Tulun had reached an age to take part in political affairs, two caliphs succeeded Mutasim b'Illah. The first was his son Harun abu Jafar, who, upon his accession, assumed the surname el-Wathik b'Illah (trusting in God). Wathik carried on the tra-

[1] Ahmed ibn Tulun was, according to some historians, born at Baghdad in the year 220 of the Hegira, in the third year of the reign of el-Mutasim b' Illah. Others claim Samarrah as his birthplace. His mother, a young Turkish slave, was named Kassimeh, or some say, Hachimeh. Some historians have denied that Ahmed was the son of Tulun, one of them, Suyuti, in a manuscript belonging to Marcel, quotes Abu Asakar in confirmation of this assertion, who pretends he was told by an old Egyptian that Ahmed was the son of a Turk named Mahdi and of Kassimeh, the slave of Tulun. Suyuti adds that Tulun adopted the child on account of his good qualities, but this statement is unsupported and seems contradicted by subsequent events.

ditional policy of continually changing the governors of the provinces, and, dying in the year 847, was succeeded by his half-brother Mutawakkil. In the following year the new caliph confided the government of Egypt to Anbasa, but dismissed him a few months later in favour of his own son el-Muntasir ibn el-Mutawakkil, whom two years afterwards the caliph named as his successor to the throne. El-Muntasir was to be immediately succeeded by his two younger brothers, el-Mutazz b'Illah and el-Mujib b'Illah.

Mutawakkil then proceeded to divide his kingdom, giving Africa and all his Eastern possessions, from the frontier of Egypt to the eastern boundary of his states, to his eldest son. His second son, el-Mutazz, received Khorassan, Tabaristan, Persia, Armenia, and Aderbaijan as his portion, and to el-Mujib, his third son, he gave Damascus, Hemessa, the basin of the Jordan, and Palestine.

These measures, by which the caliph hoped to satisfy the ambitions of his sons, did not have the desired effect. Despite the immense concessions he had received, el-Muntasir, anxious to commence his rule over the whole of the Islam empire, secretly conspired against his father and meditated taking his life. Finding that in Egypt he was too far from the scene of his intrigues, he deputed the government of that country to Yazid ibn Abd Allah, and returned to his father's court to encourage the malcontents and weave fresh plots. His evil schemes soon began to bear fruit, for, in the year 244 of the Hegira, his agents stirred up the Turkish soldiery at Damascus to insurrection on the ground of deferred payment. Whereupon the caliph paid them the arrears, and left Damascus to retire to Samarrah.

THE MOSQUE OF IBN TULUN, CAIRO.

At length, in the year 861 (A. H. 247), Mutawakkil discovered the scarcely concealed treachery of his son, and reproved him publicly. Some days later the caliph was murdered at night by the captain of his Turkish Guard, and Muntasir, who is commonly supposed to have instigated the crime, was immediately proclaimed as his successor in the government.

The most important event in Egypt during the reign of Mutawakkil was the falling in of the Nilometer at Fostât. This disaster was the result of an earthquake of considerable violence, which was felt throughout Syria. The caliph ordered the reconstruction of the Nilometer, which was accomplished the same year, and the Nilometer of the Island of Rhodha was then called Magaz el-jedid, or the New Nilometer.

After reigning scarcely a year, Muntasir himself succumbed, most probably to poison, and his cousin Ahmed was elected to the caliphate by the Turkish soldiery, with the title of Mustain. During his brief reign the Moslems were defeated by the Byzantines at Awasia, and in 866 the Turkish soldiers revolted against the caliph and elected his brother Mutazz in his place. Mustain was, however, allowed to retire to Ma'szit. He was permitted to take an attendant with him, and his choice fell upon Ahmed, the son of Tulun, already mentioned. Ahmed served the dethroned prince truly, and had no part in the subsequent murder of this unhappy man.

In the meantime the mother of Ahmed had married the influential General Baik-Bey, and when the latter was given the rulership of Egypt in the year 868 A. D. (254 A. H.), he sent his stepson as proxy, according to the custom of the time. On the 23d Ramadhan 254 (15th September, 868), Ahmed ibn Tulun arrived at Fostât. He encountered great difficulties, and discovered that at Alexandria and also in other districts there were independent emirs, who were not directly under the ruler. Soon after his arrival an insurrection broke out in Upper Egypt. Ahmed showed himself born to the place; he crushed the uprising and also suppressed a second revolt that was threatening. By degrees he cleverly undermined the power of his colleagues, and made his own position in Fostât secure.

When Muaffik was nominated commander-in-chief of the West by his brother Mustamid (elected caliph in 870), Ahmed managed to secure the good-will of the vizier of the caliph and thus to obtain the command in Egypt. He kept the regent in Baghdad in a state of complacency, occasionally sending him tribute; but, as wars with the Sinds began to trouble the caliphate, he did not think it worth while to trouble himself further about Baghdad, and decided to keep his money for himself. Muaffik was not the man to stand this, and prepared to attack Ahmed, but the disastrous results of the last war had not yet passed away. When the army intended for Egypt was camping in Mesopotamia, there was not enough money to pay the troops, and the undertaking had to be deferred.

Ahmed had a free hand over the enormous produce of Egypt. The compulsory labour of the industrious Kopt brought in a yearly income of four million gold dinars ($10,120,000), and yet these people felt themselves better off than formerly on account of the greater order and peace that existed under his energetic government. It cannot be denied that Ahmed in the course of years became much more extravagant and luxurious, but he used his large means in some measure for the betterment of the country. He gave large sums not only for the erection of palaces and barracks, but also for hospitals and educational advancement. To this day is to

SANCTUARY OF THE MOSQUE OF IBN TULUN.

be seen the mosque of Ibn Tulun, built by him in the newer part of Fostât,—a district which was later annexed to the town of Cairo.

The numerous wars in which Muaffik was involved gave Ahmed the opportunity of extending his power beyond the boundaries of Egypt. The ruler of the caliphate of Damascus died in the year 897, and soon after Ahmed marched into Syria, and, with the exception of Antioch, which had to be taken by force, the whole country fell into the hands of the mighty emir. The commanders of isolated districts did not feel themselves encouraged to offer any resistance, for they had no feeling of faithfulness for the government, nor had they any hope of assistance from Baghdad.

The triumphant march of Tulun was hindered in the year 879 by bad news from Fostât. One of his sons, El-Abbas, had quarrelled with his father, and had marched to Barca, with troops which he led afterwards to disaster, and had taken with him money to the amount of 1,000,000 dinars ($2,530,000). He thought himself safe from his enraged father there, but the latter quickly returned to Fostât, and the news of the ample preparations which he was hastening for the subjection of his rebel son caused El-Abbas to place himself still farther out of his reach. He suddenly attacked the state of Ibrahim II. (the Aghlabite), and caused serious trouble with his soldiery in the eastern districts of Tripolis. The neighbouring Berbers gave Ibrahim their assistance, and Abbas was defeated and retreated to Barca in 880. He remained there some time until an army sent by Ahmed annihilated his troops and he himself was taken prisoner.

The rebellion of his son was the turning-point in Ahmed's career: Lulu, his general in Mesopotamia, deserted him for Muaffik, and an endeavour to conquer

Mecca was frustrated by the unexpected resistance of numbers of newly arrived pilgrims. Ahmed now caused the report to be spread that Muaffik was a conspirator against the representatives of the Prophet, thus depriving him of his dignity. The emir had also besieged in vain at Tarsus his former general Jasman, who had become presumptuous on account of his victory over the Byzantines. He would eventually have made up for this

THE MOSQUE OF IBN TULUN.

defeat, but an illness overcame him while encamped before Tarsus. He obeyed his doctor's orders as little as the caliph's, and his malady, aggravated by improper diet, caused his death in his fifty-first year at Fostât in 884, whither he had withdrawn. He left seventeen sons,—enough to assure a dynasty of a hundred years.

Khumarawaih, who inherited the kingdom, had not many of his father's characteristics. He was a good-natured, pleasure-loving young man, barely twenty years old, and with a marked distaste for war. He did, however, notwithstanding his peace-loving proclivities, fight the caliph's forces near Damascus, and defeat them, never having seen a battle before. The emir fled from the scene in a panic.

When Muatadid became caliph in 892, he offered his daughter Katr en-Neda (Dewdrop) in marriage to the caliph's son. The Arabic historians relate that Khumarawaih was fearful of assassination, and had his couch guarded by a trained lion, but he was finally put to death (A. H. 282), according to some accounts by women, and according to others by his eunuchs. The death of Khumarawaih was the virtual downfall of the Tulunid dynasty.

The officers of the army then at first made Gaish Abu'l-Asakir (one of Khumarawaih's sons) emir; but, when this fourteen-year-old boy seemed incapable of anything but stupid jokes, they put his brother Harun on the throne. Every commanding officer, however, did as he liked. Rajib, the commander of the army of defence, declared himself on the side of the caliph, and the Syrian emirs gave themselves up to his general, Muhammed ibn Suleiman, without any resistance. At the close of the year he was before Fostât, and at the same time a fleet appeared at Damietta. A quarrel arose amongst Harun's body-guard, in which the unlucky prince was killed (904). His uncle Shaiban, a worthy son of Ahmed, made a last stand, but was obliged to give in to the superior force.

Muhammed behaved with his Turks in the most outrageous way in Fostât: the plundering was unrestrained, and that part of Fostât which Ahmed had built was almost entirely destroyed. The adherents of the reigning family were grossly maltreated, many of them killed, and others sent to Baghdad. The governors changed in rapid succession; disorder, want, and wretchedness existed throughout the entire country west of the caliph's kingdom. At this period the provinces of the empire had already fallen into the hands of the numerous minor princes, who, presuming on the caliph's weakness, had declared themselves independent sovereigns. Nothing remained to the Abbasids but Baghdad, a few neighbouring provinces, and Egypt.

Under the Caliphs Muktadir, Kahir, and Rahdi, Egypt had an almost constant change of governors. One of them, Abu Bekr Muhammed, ultimately became the founder of a new dynasty,—the Ikshidite,—destined to rule over Egypt and Syria. Abu Bekr Muhammed was the son of Takadj, then governor of Damascus. His father had been chief emir at the court of the Tulunid princes, and, after the fall of this dynasty, remained in Egypt, where he occupied a post under the government. Intrigues, however, drove him to Syria, whither his partisans followed him. He first entered the army of the caliph, and, capturing the town of Ramleh, was given the governorship of Damascus as reward. His son Abu Bekr Muhammed did not go to Egypt to fulfil the duties with which he had been invested, and only retained the title for one month. He was subsequently reinstated, and this time repaired thither. But Ahmed ibn Kighlagh, who was then governing Egypt, refused to retire and was only defeated after several engagements, when he and his followers proceeded to Barca in Africa.

In the year 328 of the Hegira, the caliph Radhi bestowed the honour of Emir el-Umara (Prince of Princes) upon Muhammed ibn Raik. This officer, discontented with the government of Palestine, led an army into Syria and expelled Badra, the lieutenant of Muhammed el-Ikshid. The latter left Egypt at once, entrusting the government of that country to his brother, el-Hassan, and brought his forces to Faramah, where the troops of Muhammed ibn Raik were already stationed. Thanks to the mediation of several emirs, matters were concluded peacefully, and Muhammed el-Ikhshid returned to Fostât. Upon his arrival, however, he learnt that Muhammed ibn Raik had again left Damascus and was preparing to march upon Egypt.

This intelligence obliged Muhammed el-Ikshid to return at once to Syria. He encountered the advance-guard of the enemy and promptly led the attack; his right wing was scattered, but the centre, commanded by himself, remained firm, and Muhammed ibn Raik retreated towards Damascus. Husain, brother of el-Ikshid, lost his life in the combat. Despite the enmity between them, Muhammed ibn Raik sent his own son to el-Ikshid, charged with messages of condolence for the loss he had sustained and bearing proposals of peace. Muhammed el-Ikshid received the son of his enemy with much respect, and invested him with a mantle of honour. He then consented to cede Damascus, in consideration of an annual tribute of 140,000 pieces of gold, and the restoration of all that portion of Palestine between Ramleh and the frontiers of Egypt. After having concluded all the arrangements relative to this treaty, Muhammed el-Ikshid returned to Egypt in the year 329 of the Hegira.

The Caliph Rahdi died in the same year (940 A. D.). He was thirty years of age, and had reigned six years, ten months, and ten days. His brother, Abu Ishak Ibrahim, succeeded him, and was henceforth known by the name of Muttaki. A year later Muhammed el-Ikshid was acknowledged Prince of Egypt by the new caliph. Shortly after, he learnt that his former enemy, Muhammed ibn Raik had been killed by the Hamdanites; he thereupon seized the opportunity to recover those provinces he had granted him, and, marching into Syria, captured Damascus and all the possessions he had relinquished upon the conclusion of their treaty. Feeling now that his position was secure, he caused his son Kasim to be recognised by the emirs and the entire army as his successor.

COIN OF ABU BEKR.

The year 332 of the Hegira was a disastrous one in Baghdad. The office of Prince of Princes, bestowed according to the caprice of the Turkish officers upon any of their leaders, was now become a position superior even to that of caliph. It was held at this time by a Turk named Turun, who so oppressed the caliph Muttaki that the latter was forced to fly from his capital and retire to Mosul. He then besought help from the Hamdanites, who immediately rallied their forces and, accompanied by the caliph, marched upon Baghdad. They were, however, completely routed by Turun and obliged to retreat. Muttaki showed his gratitude to the two princes by conferring a mantle of honour upon them, which, for some time past, had been the only gift that Islam sovereigns had been able to bestow.

Leaving Mosul, the caliph proceeded to Rakkah, and there was invited by Turun to return to Baghdad. Seeing that his adherents, the Hamdanites, were greatly discouraged by their recent reverses, Muttaki resolved to accept the offer. When Muhammed el-Ikshid heard this, he hastened to Rakkah and offered the caliph refuge in Egypt. But the caliph refused, agreeing, however, as Muhammed el-Ikshid promised to supply him with the necessary funds, not to return to Baghdad and place himself in the power of Turun. In spite of his promise, when Turun, fearing that the caliph had found powerful friends, came to him, and, casting himself before Muttaki, paid him all the homage due to an Islam sovereign, he allowed himself to be overruled, and accompanied Turun back to Baghdad. Hardly had the unfortunate caliph set foot in his capital when he was murdered, after reigning four years and eleven months. Turun now proclaimed Abd Allah Abu'l Kasim, son of Muttaki, caliph, who, after a short and uneventful reign, was succeeded by his uncle, Abu'l Kasim el-Fadhl, who was the last of the Abbasid caliphs whom Egypt acknowledged as suzerains.

After Muttaki's return to Baghdad, Muhammed el-Ikshid remained for some time in Damascus, and then set out for Egypt. His return was signalised by the war with Saif ed-Dowlah, Prince of Hamdan. The campaign was of varying success. After a disastrous battle, in which the Egyptians lost four thousand men as prisoners, Muhammed el-Ikshid left Egypt with a numerous army and arrived at Maarrah. Saif ed-Dowlah determined to decide the war with one desperate effort, and first secured the safety of his treasure, his baggage, and his harem by sending them to Mesopotamia. Then he marched upon el-Ikshid, who had taken his position at Kinesrin.

Muhammed divided his forces into two corps, placing in the vanguard all those who carried lances; he himself was in the rear with ten thousand picked men. Saif ed-Dowlah charged the vanguard and routed it, but the rear stood firm; this resistance saved el-Ikshid from total defeat. The two armies separated after a somewhat indecisive engagement, and Saif ed-Dowlah, who could claim no advantage save the capture of his adversaries' baggage, went on to Maubej, where he destroyed the bridge, and, entering Mesopotamia, proceeded towards Rakkah; but Muhammed el-Ikshid was already stationed there, and the hostile armies, separated only by the Euphrates, faced one another for several days.

Negotiations were then opened, and peace was concluded. The conditions were that Hemessa, Aleppo, and Mesopotamia should belong to Saif ed-Dowlah, and all the country from Hemessa to the frontiers of Egypt remain in the possession of Muhammed el-Ikshid. A trench was dug between Djouchna and Lebouah, in those places where there were no natural boundaries, to mark the separation of the two states. To ratify this solemn peace, Saif ed-Dowlah married the daughter of Muhammed el-Ikshid; then each prince returned to his own province. The treaty was, however, almost immediately set aside by the Hamdanites, and el-Ikshid, forced to retrace his steps, defeated them in several engagements and seized the town of Aleppo.

Thus we see that the year 334 of the Hegira (A. D. 946) was full of important events, to which was soon added the death of Muhammed el-Ikshid. He died at Damascus, in the last month of the year (Dhu'l-Kada), aged sixty, and had reigned eleven years, three months, and two days. He was buried at Jerusalem. Muhammed el-Ikshid was a man possessing many excellent talents, and chiefly renowned as an admirable soldier. Brave, without being rash, quick to calculate his chances, he was able always to seize the advantage. On the other hand, however, he was so distrustful and timid in the privacy of his palace that he organised a guard of eight thousand armed slaves, one thousand of whom kept constant watch. He never spent the entire night in the same apartment or tent, and no one was ever permitted to know the place where he slept.

We are told that this prince could muster four hundred thousand men; although historians do not definitely specify the boundaries of his empire, which, of course, varied from time to time, we may nevertheless believe that his kingdom, as that of his predecessors, the Tulunites, extended over Egypt, Palestine, Syria, and Mesopotamia, as far as the Euphrates, and even included a large portion of Arabia. The Christians of the East charge him with supporting his immense army at their expense, and persecuting and taxing them to such an extent that they were forced to sell many possessions belonging to their Church before they could pay the required sums.

But, if we may credit a contemporary historian more worthy of belief, these expenses were covered by the treasure Muhammed el-Ikshid himself discovered. In fact, el-Massudi, who died at Cairo in the year 346 of the Hegira, relates that el-Ikshid, knowing much treasure to be buried there, was greatly interested in the excavation of the subterraneous tombs of the ancient Egyptian kings. "The prince," he adds, "was fortunate enough to come across a portion of those tombs, consisting of vast rooms magnificently decorated. There he found marvellously wrought figures of old and young men, women, and children, having eyes of precious stones and faces of gold and silver."

Muhammed el-Ikshid was succeeded by his son, Abu'l Kasim Muhammed, surnamed Ungur. The prince being only an infant, Kafur, the favourite minister of the late caliph, was appointed regent. This Kafur was a black slave purchased by el-Ikshid for the trifling sum of twenty pieces of gold. He was intelligent, zealous, and faithful, and soon won the confidence of his master. Nobility of race in the East appertains only to the descendants of the Prophet, but merit, which may be found in prince and subject alike, often secures the highest positions, and even the throne itself for those of the humblest origin. Such was the fate of Kafur. He showed taste for the sciences, and encouraged scholars; he loaded the poets with benefits, and they sang his praises without measure so long as he continued his favours, but satirised him with equal vigour as soon as his munificence diminished. Invested with supreme authority, Kafur served the young prince with a devotion and fidelity worthy of the highest praise. His first step was to dismiss Abu Bekr Muhammed, the receiver of the Egyptian tributes, against whom he had received well-merited complaints. In his place he appointed a native of Mardin, also called Muhammed, of whose honesty and kindliness he was well aware. He then took his pupil to Egypt, which country they reached in the month of Safar in the year 335 of the Hegira.

Saif ed-Dowlah, hearing of the death of Muhammed el-Ikshid, and the departure of Ungur, deemed this a favourable opportunity to despoil his brother-in-law; he therefore marched upon Damascus, which he captured; but the faithful Kafur promptly arrived upon the scene with a powerful army, and, routing Saif ed-Dowlah, who had advanced as far as Ramleh, drove him back to Rakkah, and relieved Damascus. The remainder of the reign of Ungur passed peacefully, thanks to the watchfulness and wise government of Kafur.

In the year 345 of the Hegira, the King of Nubia invaded the Egyptian territories, advancing to Syênê, which he pillaged and laid waste. Kafur at once despatched his forces overland and along the Nile, and simultaneously ordered a detachment embarking from the Red Sea to proceed along the southern coast, attack the enemy in the rear and completely cut off their retreat. The Nubians, thus surprised on all sides, were defeated and forced to retreat, leaving the fortress of Rym, now known as Ibrim, and situated fifty miles from Syênê,

MOSQUE TOMB NEAR SYENE.

in the hands of the Egyptians. No other events of note took place during the lifetime of Ungur, who, having reigned fourteen years and ten days, died in the year 349 of the Hegira, leaving his brother Ali, surnamed Abu'l-Hasan, as his successor.

The reign of Abu'l-Hasan Ali, the second son of Muhammed el-Ikshid, lasted but five years. His name, as that of his brother Ungur (Abu Hurr), is but little known in history. Kafur was also regent during the reign of Abu'l-Hasan Ali.

In the year 352 of the Hegira, Egypt was stricken with a disastrous famine. The rise of the Nile, which the previous year had been but fifteen cubits, was this year even less, and suddenly the waters fell without irrigating the country. Egypt and the dependent provinces were thus afflicted for nine consecutive years. During this time, whilst the people were agitated by fear for the future, a rupture took place between Abu'l-Hasan Ali and Kafur. This internal disturbance was soon followed by war; and in the year 354 the Greeks of Constantinople, led by the Emperor Nicepherous Phocas, advanced into Syria. They took Aleppo, then in the possession of the Hamdanites, and, encountering Saif ed-Dowlah, overthrew him also. The governor of Damascus, Dalim el-Ukazly, and ten thousand men came to the rescue of the Hamdanites, but Phocas beat a retreat on hearing of his approach.

Abu'l-Hasan Ali died in the year 355 of the Hegira. The regent Kafur then ascended the throne, assuming the surname el-Ikshid. He acknowledged the paramount authority of the Abbasid caliph, Muti, and that potentate recognised his supreme power in the kingdom of Egypt. During the reign of Kafur, which only lasted two years and four months, the greater portion of Said was seized by the Fatimites, already masters of Fayum and Alexandria, and the conquerors were on the point of encroaching still farther, when Kafur died in the year 357 A. H. Ahmed, surnamed Abu'l Fawaris, the son of

Abu'l-Hasan Ali, and consequently grandson of Muhammed el-Ikshid, succeeded Kafur.

The prince was only eleven years old, and therefore incapable of properly controlling Egypt, Syria, and his other domains. Husain, one of his relatives, invaded Syria, but in his turn driven back by the Karmates, returned to Egypt and strove to depose Ahmed. These divisions in the reigning family severed the ties which united the provinces of the Egyptian kingdom. To terminate the disturbances, the emirs resolved to seek the protection of the Fatimites. The latter, anxious to secure the long-coveted prize, gladly rendered assistance, and Husain was forced to return to Syria, where he took possession of Damascus, and the unfortunate Ahmed lost the throne of Egypt.

With him perished the Ikshid dynasty, which, more ephemeral even than that of the Tulunid, flourished only thirty-four years and twenty-four days.

The period upon which this history is now about to enter is of more than usual interest, for it leads immediately to the centuries during which the Arabic forces came into contact with the forces of Western Europe. The town and the coast of Mauritania were then ruled by the Fatimites, a dynasty independent of the Abbasid caliphs of Baghdad. The Fatimites belonged to the tribes of Koramah, who dwelt in the mountains situated near the town of Fez in the extreme west of Africa. In the year 269 of the Hegira, they began to extend their sway in the western regions of Africa, pursuing their conquests farther east. The Fatimite caliph Obaid Allah and his son Abu'l Kasim cherished designs not only upon Egypt, but even aimed at the destruction of the Abbasid caliphate, these plans being so far successful as to leave the Fatimites in secure possession of Alexandria, and more or less in power in Fayum.

The Fatimite caliphs had lofty and pretentious claims to the allegiance of the Moslem world. They traced their descent from Fatima, a daughter of the Prophet, whom Muhammed himself regarded as one of the four perfect women. At the age of fifteen she married Ali, of whom she was the only wife, and the partisans of Ali, as we have seen, disputed with Omar the right to the leadership of Islam upon the Prophet's death. Critics are not wanting who dispute the family origin of Obaid Allah, but his claim appears to have been unhesitatingly admitted by his own immediate followers. The Fatimite successes in the Mediterranean gave them a substantial basis of political power, and doubtless this outward and material success was more important to them than their claim to both a physical and mythical descent from the founder of their religion.

Some accounts trace the descent of Obaid from Abd Allah ibn Maimun el-Kaddah, the founder of the Ismailian sect, of which the Carmathians were a branch. The Ismailians may be best regarded as one of the several sects of Shiites, who originally were simply the partisans of Ali against Omar, but by degrees they became identified as the upholders of the Koran against the validity of the oral tradition, and when, later, the whole of Persia espoused the cause of Ali, the Shiite belief became tinged with all kinds of mysticism. The Ismailians believed, for instance, in the coming of a Messiah, to whom they gave the name Mahdi, and who would one day appear on earth to establish the reign of justice, and revenge the wrongs done to the family of Ali. The Ismailians regarded Obaid himself as the Mahdi, and they also believed in incarnations of the "universal soul," which in former ages had appeared as the Hebrew Prophets, but which to the Muhammedan manifested itself as imans. The iman is properly the leader of public worship, but it is not so much an office as a seership with mystical attributes. The Muhammedan imans so far have numbered eleven, the twelfth, and greatest (El-Mahdi), being yet to come. The Ismailians also introduced mysticism into the interpretation of the Koran, and even taught that its moral precepts were not to be taken in a literal sense. Thus the Fatimite caliphs founded their authority upon a combination of political power and superstition.

Abu'l Kasim, who ruled at Alexandria, was succeeded in 945 by his son, El-Mansur. Under his reign the Fatimites were attacked by Abu Yazid, a Berber, who gathered around him the Sunnites, and the revolutionaries succeeded in taking the Fatimite capital Kairwan. El-Mansur, however, soon defeated Abu Yazid in a decisive battle and rebuilt a new city, Mansuria, on the site of the modern Cairo, to commemorate the event. Dying in 953, he was succeeded by Muiz ad-Din.

Muiz came to the throne just at the time when dissensions as to the succession were undermining the Ikshid dynasty. Seizing the opportunity in the year 969, Muiz equipped a large and well-armed force, with a formidable body of cavalry, the whole under the command of Abu'l-Husain Gohar el-Kaid, a native of Greece and a slave of his father El-Mansur. This general, on his arrival near Alexandria, received a deputation from the inhabitants of Fostât charged to negotiate a treaty. Their overtures were favourably entertained, and the conquest of the country seemed probable without bloodshed. But while the conditions were being ratified, the Ikshidites prevailed on the people to revoke their offer, and the ambassadors, on their return, were themselves compelled to seek safety in flight.

Gohar el-Kaid incurred no delay in pushing his troops forward. He forced the passage of the Nile a few miles south of El-Gizeh at the head of his troops, and the Ikshidites suffered a disastrous defeat. To the honour of the African general, it is related that the inhabitants of Fostât were pardoned and the city was peaceably occupied. The submission of the rest of Egypt to Muiz was secured by this victory. In the year 359 A. H. Syria was also added to his domains, but shortly after was overrun by the Carmathians. The troops of Muiz met with several reverses, Damascus was taken, and those lawless freebooters, joined by the Ikshidites, advanced to Ain Shems. In the meanwhile, Gohar had fortified Cairo (the new capital which he had founded immediately north of Fostât) and taken every precaution to repel the invaders; a bloody battle was fought in the year 361 before the city walls, without any decisive result. Later, however, Gohar obtained a victory over the enemy which proved to be a decisive one.

Muiz subsequently removed his court to his new kingdom. In Ramadhan 362, he entered Cairo, bringing with him the bodies of his three predecessors and vast treasure. Muiz reigned about two years in Egypt, dying in the year 365 A. H. He is described as a warlike and ambitious prince, but, notwithstanding, he was especially distinguished for justice and was fond of learning. He showed great favour to the Christians, especially to Severus, Bishop of El-Ashmunein, and the patriarch Ephrem; and under his orders, and with his assistance, the church of the Mu'allakah, in Old Misr, was rebuilt. He executed many useful works (among others rendering navigable the Tanitic branch of the Nile, which is still called the canal of Muiz), and occupied himself in embellishing Cairo. Gohar, when he founded that city, built the great mosque named El-Azhar, the university of Egypt, which to this day is crowded with students from all parts of the Moslem world.

Aziz Abu-Mansur Nizar, on coming to the throne of his father, immediately despatched an expedition against the Turkish chief El-Eftekeen, who had taken Damascus a short time previously. Gohar again commanded the army, and pressed the siege of that city so vigorously that the enemy called to their aid the Carmathians. Before this united army he was forced to retire slowly to Ascalon, where he prepared to stand a siege; but, being reduced to great straits, he purchased his liberty with a large sum of money. On his return from this disastrous campaign, Aziz took command in person, and, meeting the enemy at Ramleh, was victorious after a bloody battle; while El-Eftekeen, being betrayed into his hands, was with Arab magnanimity received with honour and confidence, and ended his days in Egypt in affluence. Aziz followed his father's example of liberality. It is even said that he appointed a Jew his vizier in Syria, and a Christian to the same post in Egypt. These acts, however, nearly cost him his life, and a popular tumult obliged him to disgrace both these officers. After a reign of twenty-one years of great internal prosperity, he died (A. H. 386) in a bath at Bilbeis, while preparing an expedition against the Greeks who were ravaging his possessions in Syria. Aziz was distinguished for moderation and mildness, but his son and successor rendered himself notorious for very opposite qualities.

Hakim Abu Ali Mansur commenced his reign, according to Moslem historians, with much wisdom, but afterwards acquired a reputation for impiety, cruelty, and unreasoning extravagance, by which he has been rendered odious to posterity. He is said to have had at the same time "courage and boldness, cowardice and timorousness, a love for learning and vindictiveness towards the learned, an inclination to righteousness and a disposition to slay the righteous." He also arrogated to himself divinity, and commanded his subjects to rise at the mention of his name in the congregational prayers, an edict which was obeyed even in the holy cities, Mecca and Medina. He is most famous in connection with the Druses, a sect which he founded and which still holds him in veneration and believes in his future return to the earth. He had made himself obnoxious to all classes of his subjects when, in the year 397 A. H., he nearly lost his throne by foreign invasion.

MOSQUE OF HAKIM.

Hisham, surnamed Abu-Rekweh, a descendant of the house of Ommaya in Spain, took the province of Barca with a considerable force and subdued Upper Egypt. The caliph, aware of his danger, immediately collected his troops from every quarter of the kingdom, and marched against the invaders, whom, after severe fighting, he defeated and put to flight. Hisham himself was taken prisoner, paraded in Cairo with every aggravation of cruelty, and put to death. Hakim having thus by vigorous measures averted this danger, Egypt continued to groan under his tyranny until the year 411 A. H., when he fell by domestic treachery. His sister Sitt el-Mulk had, in common with the rest of his subjects, incurred his displeasure; and, being fearful for her life, she secretly and by night concerted measures with the emir Saif ed-Dowlah, chief of the guard, who very readily agreed to her plans. Ten slaves, bribed by five hundred dinars each ($1,260), having received their instructions, went forth on the appointed day to the desert tract southward of Cairo, where Hakim, unattended, was in the habit of riding, and waylaid him near the village of Helwan, where they put him to death.

Within a week Hakim's son Ali had been raised to the caliphate with the title of Dhahir, at the command of Sitt el-Mulk. As Dhahir was only eighteen years old, and in no way educated for the government, Sitt el-Mulk took the reins of government, and was soon looked upon as the instigator of Hakim's death. This suspicion was strengthened by the fact that his sister had the heir to the throne—who was at that time governor of Aleppo—murdered, and also the chief who had conspired with her in assassinating Hakim. She survived her brother for about four years, but the actual ruler was the Vizier Ali el-Jarjar.

Dhahir's reign offers many points of interest. Peace and contentment reigned in the interior, and Syria continued to be the chief point of interest to the Egyptian politics. Both Lulu and his son Mansur, who received princely titles from Hakim, recognised the suzerainty of the Fatimites. Later on a disagreement arose between Lulu's son and Dhahir. One of the former's slaves conspired against his master, and gave Aleppo into the hands of the Fatimites, whose governor maintained himself there till 1023. In this year, however, Aleppo fell into the power of the Benu Kilab, who defended the town with great success against Romanus in 1030. Not till Dhahir's successor came to the throne in 1036 was Aleppo reconquered by the Fatimites, but only to fall, after a few years, again into the hands of a Kilabite, whom the caliph was obliged to acknowledge as governor until he of his own free will exchanged the city for several other towns in Syria; but even then the strife about the possession of Aleppo was not yet at an end.

Mustanssir ascended the throne at the age of four years. His mother, although black and once a slave, had great influence in the choice of the viziers and other officials, and even when the caliph became of age, he showed very few signs of independence. His reign, which lasted sixty years, offers a constant alternation of success and defeat. At one time his dominion was limited to the capital Cairo, at another time he was recognised as lord of Africa, Sicily, Arabia, Mesopotamia, and even of the Abbassid capital, Baghdad. A few days later his dominion was again on the point of being extinguished. The murder of a Turk by the negroes led to a war between the Turkish mercenaries and the blacks who formed the caliph's body-guard. The latter were joined by many of the other slaves, but the Turks were supported by the Ketama Berbers and some of the Bedouin tribes, and also the Hamdanite Nasir ed-Dowlah, who had long been in the Egyptian service. The blacks, although supported by the caliph's mother, were completely defeated, and the caliph was forced to acknowledge the authority of Nasir ed-Dowlah. He thereupon threatened to abdicate, but when he learned that his palace with all its treasures would then be given up to plunder, he refrained from fulfilling his threat. The power of the Hamdanites and the Turks increased with every victory over the negroes, who finally could no longer maintain themselves at all in Upper Egypt. The caliph was treated with contempt, and had to give up his numerous treasures, one by one, to satisfy the avarice of his troops. Even the graves of his ancestors were at last robbed of all they contained, and when, at last, everything had been ransacked, even his library, which was one of the largest and finest, was not spared. The best manuscripts were dispersed, some went to Africa, others were destroyed, many were damaged or purposely mutilated by the Sunnites, simply because they had been written by the Shiites; still others were burnt by the Turks as worthless material, and the leather bands which held them made into sandals.

Meanwhile war between Mustanssir and Nasir ed-Dowlah continued to be waged in Egypt and Syria, until at last the latter became master of Cairo and deprived the caliph once more completely of his independence.

MUSTANSSIR'S GATE AT CAIRO.

Soon after, a conspiracy with Ildeghiz, a Turkish general, at its head, was formed against Nasir ed-Dowlah, and he, together with his relations and followers, was brutally murdered. Ildeghiz behaved in the same way as his predecessor had done towards the caliph, and the latter appealed to Bedr el-Jemali for help. Bedr proceeded to Acre with his best Syrian troops, landed in the neighbourhood of Damietta and proceeded towards the capital, which he entered without difficulty (January, 1075). He was appointed general and first vizier, so that he now held both the highest military and civil authority.

In order to strengthen his position, he had all the commanders of the troops and the highest officials murdered at a ball. Under his rule, peace and order were at last restored to Egypt, and the income of the state was increased under his excellent government.

Bedr remained at his post till his death, and his son El-Afdhal was appointed by Mustanssir to succeed him. Upon the death of Mustanssir (1094), his successor El-Mustali Abu'l Kasim retained El-Afdhal in office. He was afterwards murdered under Emir (December, 1121) because, according to some, he was not a zealous enough Shiite, but, according to others, because the caliph wished to gain possession of the enormous treasures of the vizier and to be absolutely independent. Emir was also murdered (October 7, 1130), and was succeeded by his cousin, who ascended the throne under the name of Hafiz, and appointed a son of El-Afdhal as vizier, who, just as his father had done, soon became the real ruler, and did not even allow the caliph's name to be mentioned in the prayers; whereupon he also was murdered at the caliph's instigation. After other viziers had met with a similar fate, and amongst them a son of the caliph himself, at last Hafiz ruled alone. His son and successor, Dhafir (1149—1150), also frequently changed his viziers because they one and all wished to obtain too much influence. The last vizier, Abbas, murdered the caliph (March—April, 1154), and placed El-Faiz, the five-year-old son of the dead caliph, on the throne, but the child died in his eleventh year (July, 1160). Salih, then vizier, raised Adid, a descendant of Alhagiz, to the caliphate and gave him his daughter to wife, for which reason he was murdered at the desire of the harem. His son Adil maintained himself for a short time, and then El-Dhargham and Shawir fought for the post; as the former gained the victory, Shawir fled to Syria, called Nureddin to his aid, and their army, under Shirkuh and Saladin, put an end in 1171 to the rule of the Fatimites.

END OF VOL. XI.

INDEX

INDEX

INDEX